COMING OUT OF THE MAGNOLIA CLOSET

Coming Out
of the
Magnolia Closet

Same-Sex Couples in Mississippi

JOHN F. MARSZALEK III

UNIVERSITY PRESS OF MISSISSIPPI ∞ JACKSON

The University Press of Mississippi is the scholarly publishing agency of the Mississippi Institutions of Higher Learning: Alcorn State University, Delta State University, Jackson State University, Mississippi State University, Mississippi University for Women, Mississippi Valley State University, University of Mississippi, and University of Southern Mississippi.

www.upress.state.ms.us

Designed by Peter D. Halverson

The University Press of Mississippi is a member of the Association of University Presses.

Names and identifying details have been changed to protect the privacy of individuals.

First printing 2020

∞

Library of Congress Cataloging-in-Publication Data

LCCN: 2020931833

Hardback ISBN	978-1-4968-2911-5
Epub single ISBN	978-1-4968-2912-2
Epub institutional ISBN	978-1-4968-2913-9
PDF single ISBN	978-1-4968-2914-6
PDF institutional ISBN	978-1-4968-2910-8

British Library Cataloging-in-Publication Data available

For Larry
and
For all the same-sex couples in Mississippi who are changing
hearts and minds daily by simply being themselves

Contents

Acknowledgments

When I first considered interviewing same-sex couples in Missis-sippi, I planned it to be a short-term research project, leading to an article and possibly presentations at my professional conferences. After my initial meetings with couples, though, I realized that the stories contained in the hours and hours of transcripts were too rich to be contained in a journal article. What began as interviews with a few couples led to interviews with couples across Missis-sippi and over several years. What first began as my proposal to interview research subjects led to a desire to tell the stories of real people whose strength in the face of resistance, passion to make a better place for themselves and future same-sex couples, and love for each other, I admired. This book could not have been possible without their openness to talk to me and their willingness to share their stories.

Throughout the process of writing this book, many people pro-vided me with support and encouragement when I wondered if I could do it. My father, a prolific history writer, listened to my ideas, offered advice, and encouraged me during the ups and downs of the process. As a child growing up, I observed the passion he had for writing and making history come to life for his readers. I often drew on those memories when I wondered if I could endure another major revision of the book. My mother, who has edited my father's books for years, offered her support throughout the process and proofed an early draft of the book. Since I came out to them at nineteen, they have been allies of me and the LGBTQ community. They treat my husband, Larry, as if he were their fourth son.

The idea to weave my own story into the book originated from reading *Love and Loss in Life and Treatment* (2013) by my good friend, psychologist Linda Sherby, in which she weaved her own story of love and loss with those of the patients she treated in her psychoanalytic practice. She encouraged me to take the idea and run with it!

As I struggled to come up with a title for the book, I looked at my bookshelf and saw longtime family friend Clyde Williams's edited book of essays that he titled *From Behind the Magnolia Curtain: Voices of Mississippi.* The title of this book evolved from there.

Our friends Scott Strauss and Roy Adams, who have traveled with Larry and me on vacations, were the photographers at our wedding on Monhegan Island, Maine. As our wedding gift, they gave us a photograph album, from which came the wedding pictures in this book.

Many other friends and colleagues have offered their support and encouragement. Rhonda Neswald-Potter read an early draft and offered suggestions as I struggled to find the best format for the book. Stacee Reicherzer helped me find a transcriptionist and shared her own writing experiences with me. David Capuzzi, past president of the American Counseling Association and prolific author of counselor education textbooks, offered his advice on pursuing publication. My friend Shirley Godios asked me monthly during our telephone "coffee talks" how the book was coming along, enabling me to vent both my discouragement and excitement, depending on the month. My friend and novelist Deborah Johnson shared her own writing experiences with me and offered advice over many meals at J. Broussards in Columbus, Mississippi.

I want to thank the staff at University Press of Mississippi, especially director Craig Gill, for believing in this project and wanting to pursue publication with me.

Last but definitely not least, my husband, Larry, gave me the space to write, the loving support to see the project through, and a willingness for his story to be in the book.

REFERENCES

Sherby, L. B. (2013). *Love and loss in life and treatment.* New York: Routledge.

Williams, C. V. (1988). *From behind the magnolia curtain: Voices of Mississippi.* Jackson, MS: Mississippi Press Association/Mississippi Humanities Council.

COMING OUT OF THE MAGNOLIA CLOSET

Introduction

I'm driving down into south Mississippi to interview a gay couple. I exit off the interstate onto a two-lane road and into the woods. The trees come up to the very edge of the road and connect high in the sky, creating the effect of driving through a tunnel. Jeffrey and Leonard, two white men in their sixties, were described by another gay couple in the area as the "couple in the woods." I envision a quaint cabin and two bearded, lumberjack-looking men.

When I had spoken to them previously on the phone, Jeffrey and Leonard described several landmarks to guide me to the unmarked drive that leads to their house. I find a dirt road that appears to lead deeper into the woods, but in reality goes through a buffer of trees hiding an open area of green grass and a beautiful one-story house with an inviting front porch. The house looks like it came straight out of a country cottage magazine; it's not what I expected to find. Everything is perfectly landscaped, and a gravel path leads into a garden, out of which they both emerge. Jeffrey and Leonard are clean shaven and dressed neatly, in shorts and polo shirts. I rave about the paradise they have created, hidden away in the woods. They take me on a tour of their gardens before leading me into a back door of the house and into their kitchen where the smell of a turkey roasting in the oven greets me. They explain that they have Sunday dinner for any of their friends in the area who want to drop by. No RSVP is necessary. They are beginning to cook the afternoon before. They say that they never know who will show up and invite me to come any Sunday.

Sitting and talking to them at their kitchen table reminds me of sitting in my grandmother's kitchen—warm and comfortable. Jeffrey pours me a cup of coffee and their cat jumps up onto my lap as I press play on the audio recorder.

～

Overall, US society has become increasingly tolerant and, in some cases, accepting of lesbian and gay couples, and they are more visible in the United States than ever before. In 2012, for the first time, national polls showed that Americans support for same-sex marriage had surpassed 50 percent (McCarthy, 2014). In 2017, this surpassed 60 percent (McCarthy, 2017). Nevertheless, there is a disparity in the level of acceptance based on areas of the country and individual states.

Consider, for example, Mississippi and Vermont. In a Gallup poll (Newport, 2017) of residents' political ideologies, Mississippi rated as one of the most conservative states along with Wyoming and North Dakota. In this poll, 48.2 percent of Mississippians described themselves as conservative. There are no protections in Mississippi for lesbian and gay Mississippians unless they are provided under federal law. Mississippi has no employment or housing nondiscrimination laws based on sexual orientation, meaning that an employer can fire and a landlord can evict someone based simply on sexual orientation. When an amendment to the Mississippi constitution to ban same-sex marriage came to a vote in 2004, 86 percent of voters supported the amendment (CNN, 2004). Mississippi did not issue marriage licenses to same-sex couples until 2015 when forced to by the US Supreme Court (*Obergefell v. Hodges*, 2015).

Contrast this with Vermont, the most liberal state in the same Gallup poll (Newport, 2017). Vermont has issued same-sex marriage licenses since 2009, has prohibited discrimination based on sexual orientation and gender identity since 1991, and has had a hate crimes law based on sexual orientation since 2001. The population of Vermont is approximately 21 percent of Mississippi's total population (US Census, 2010), and the total area of Vermont is approximately

20 percent of the total area of Mississippi; yet, Vermont has at least double the resources for lesbians and gays. Many of these resources are located at a Lesbian, Gay, Bisexual, and Transgender (LGBT) community center, named "Outright Vermont" (2019) and housed in the city of Burlington. Outright Vermont, which was founded in 1989, offers youth programs, community events, education, and outreach across the state on topics such as anti-harassment, anti-bullying, and developing high school gay/straight alliances. In fact, there almost forty Vermont gay/straight alliance clubs at high schools in the state.

Although the first gay community center in the US was established in San Francisco in 1966 (D'Emilio, 1998), according to Centerlink (2019), a national organization of LGBTQI (lesbian, gay, bisexual, transgender, questioning, and intersex) community centers, Mississippi is one of only five states that does not have an LGBTQI physical community center listed in its directory. It does, though, have a virtual community center. The Mississippi Safe Schools Coalition (2019) lists twelve active high schools, six state universities, and one community college with gay/straight alliances. One of the high schools listed under active, Brandon High School, made national news in 2014 when its schoolboard voted to require students to get permission from parents to join any club. The superintendent stated he wanted to find ways to discourage "gay clubs" (Royals, 2015).

In 2014, the Human Rights Campaign (HRC, 2019), the largest national civil rights organization for LGBTQ Americans, opened an office in Mississippi as a part of its ProjectOne campaign to promote LGBTQ equality in southern states, calling the South the "new frontier." The response to HRC opening offices in the South was mixed, mostly ignored by Mississippi politicians except for the few towns that passed nondiscrimination laws based on sexual orientation and gender identity. In newspaper articles, some gay southerners were quoted as saying that they were not comfortable with "rocking the boat" with activism, stating that they believed they were quietly accepted as long as they were not too open about their sexual orientations (Somashekher,2014; Stolberg, 2014). One

Rob Hill, Mississippi HRC director, speaks at a rally in front of governor's mansion.
Courtesy of the Human Rights Campaign, Mississippi.

southern activist (Williams, 2014) in Tennessee wrote an open letter to the HRC stating that he was offended by the South being
called the "new frontier" when lesbian and gay southerners had
been working for years in their communities, "building bridges,
winning and losing campaigns, and making a difference for generations." In Mississippi, one older male couple told me they believed
they had been activists for years, by living as a same-sex couple in
their small town and showing people they were not the stereotyped
"gay people on tv" that small town southerners imagined them to
be. On the other hand, in 2018 when the students at Mississippi
State University (MSU) led an effort to have the first pride parade
in the college town of Starkville, HRC sent representatives to assist them, including sponsoring a party and distributing gay pride
paraphernalia. Students and local people like me appreciated their
supportive presence.

In May 2016, HRC sponsored a protest march and rally in front of the governor's mansion in Jackson to protest the passage of Mississippi House Bill 1523, the Protecting Freedom of Conscience from Government Discrimination Act (2016), allowing state officials to refuse to perform same-sex marriages and businesses to refuse to serve same-sex couples if they have religious objections to same-sex marriage. Although meaningless in the wake of the *Obergefell v. Hodges*, the US Supreme Court decision legalizing same-sex marriage, the bill also defines marriage as between one man and one woman. The state sodomy law, passed in 1839, continues to be on the books, although the US Supreme Court overturned such laws in 2003 (*Lawrence v. Texas*).

When I unexpectedly moved back to Mississippi over ten years ago, I had many questions: Why do lesbian and gay couples live in a state like Mississippi where only a minority of the people value their relationships? Why don't they move to a place like Vermont? How do they meet each other? What is it like for them to live in Mississippi, a state predominantly comprising small towns and rural communities? What type of reactions have lesbian and gay couples received from their families, communities, and churches? This book is my attempt to answer these questions based on my own experiences and my talks with lesbian and gay male couples across Mississippi.

TERMINOLOGY

As the reader may have noticed, thus far I have used the terms LGBTQ, LGBTQI, and gay and lesbian to refer to a community, depending on the term used by different organizations. For example, HRC uses LGBTQ, and Centerlink (2019) uses LGBTQI. Because the focus of this book is on same-sex couples, I refer to the narrators as lesbians and gay men. I also use "gay" to refer to both lesbians and gay men when I do not specify gender, such as when I refer to all of the "gay couples" that I interviewed. Using gay to refer to both lesbians and gay men is also consistent with the language used by most of the couples, including the female narrators who identified themselves as "gay."

A few of the female of narrators were previously married to men; however, they identified as "gay" and not as "bisexual." None of the narrators identified as bisexual, transgender, queer, or questioning, so I do not use the acronym LGBTQI to refer narrators. I also do not use the term "homosexual" to refer to a person or identity. This word has negative connotations, because prior to 1973 homosexuality was considered a diagnosable mental disorder by American Psychiatric Association (Drescher, 2015).

"Queer" is a broad term that has been adopted by many writers, scholars, and activists to cover any gender or sexual expression that is LGBTQI and/or not easily defined by strict identity-based categories, including those that vary from nonwhite, non-European cultures (Boyd & Ramírez, 2012). Howard (1999) defined queer as "all thoughts and expressions of sexuality and gender that are non-normative or oppositional" (p. xix), including those who use "queer" to describe their identity and those who do not (e.g., those people who have sex with same-sex partners but do not identify as gay). A few of my narrators used "queer" to refer to behavior or expressions but did not use the term to identify themselves. Other narrators were uncomfortable with the term, because it brought to mind negative slurs they had heard growing up. Consequently, I do not use the term "queer" to refer to the identity of the narrators. I do use it, though, when referring to an academic discipline (e.g., "queer studies" or "queer theory") or when citing other writers who use the term such as Gray's (2009) work on "queer youth" in rural American and Mason's (2015) "Oklahomo: Lessons in Unqueering America."

Our understanding of what constitutes homosexuality has changed over time (Halperin, 2002). In addition, as Stein (2012) explained, different activists at different periods in history have used different terms to refer to a "homophile, LGBT, or queer movement" (p. 5). To avoid confusion, I am going to follow Stein's lead and consistently use "lesbian and gay" when referring to the history of a movement unless I am quoting directly from a historian.

Evacuating to Mississippi

After living in cities with large lesbian and gay communities, I never expected that I would return to Mississippi, my childhood home. It happened in a moment. I was running through the French Quarter in New Orleans with an electronic keyboard under one arm and a clothes bag hanging on another. It was late evening on Saturday, August 27, 2005, and I had just finished playing my keyboard at a musical at Le Petit Theatre. Earlier, that afternoon, the mayor had called for a voluntary evacuation of the city. I wondered if I would be able to get out of the city before Hurricane Katrina hit. However, the theatre director wanted the actors and me to stay for the matinee show on Sunday. He argued that everyone always overreacts and then the hurricane turns away from New Orleans at the last minute. "Just look at Ivan," he said. The year before, Ivan, a Category 5 hurricane, appeared to be making a direct hit on New Orleans through the Gulf of Mexico. Louisiana residents in coastal areas were ordered to evacuate. New Orleans city officials called for voluntary evacuations. Along with more than a third of the population, I evacuated to North Louisiana with my now ex-partner, a friend, two dogs, and two cats. Trying to head north out of the city, we waited in traffic for hours. Around the time we finally reached our destination near Monroe, Louisiana, we heard on the radio that Ivan had weakened and turned to the east. As with so many close calls before, New Orleans was spared.

Regardless of such close calls that never came to fruition, I told the theatre director no. I didn't want to take any chances, imagining myself stuck in traffic on Interstate 10 as the hurricane churns up the Mississippi River. I knew that I would likely lose my opportunity to play at future shows, but I did not want to risk being stuck in a flooded city with no electricity or water. Besides, Xavier University, where I taught full-time, had closed in preparation of the hurricane and encouraged faculty and students to evacuate.

I ran down Royal Street past the antique shops, occasional drunks, and casual strollers, surprised that there were still people enjoying the French Quarter with a hurricane bearing down on the city. I crossed

Esplanade Avenue into the Faubourg Marigny, the next neighbor-hood down the Mississippi River bordering the French Quarter, and toward my house on Elysian Fields. I had already packed a bag. I loaded it, the keyboard, and my cat into the car. I saw the Superdome and city skyscrapers behind me as I drove past Xavier University on Interstate 10. Little did I know that except for pictures of a flooded campus on CNN, I would not see Xavier again until January 2006. I headed west toward Interstate 59 that would take me north out of Louisiana. I was evacuating to my parents' home in Starkville, Mississippi. I felt a strange sense of déjà vu, but in the opposite sense of the term. I had left my hometown after high school with the car full to go to the city, seeking a gay community. Now I was going in the opposite direction.

My move from a small town to the city was not unique. Histori-ans such as D'Emilio (1998) and Bérubé (1990) have described how lesbian women and gay men leaving their small towns to serve in World War II discovered that they were not alone. They met oth-ers like them in the Women's Army Corps and the men's branches (Bérubé). After the war, many moved to the cities, not wanting to return to their families where heterosexuality was the expectation, thus helping to form a gay "subculture" (D'Emilio, 1993, p. 471). A second wave of lesbians and gays moved to the cities during the 1970s and early 1980s in what Kath Weston (1998), anthropologist, called the "great gay migration" as the gay movement picked up steam. Today, many lesbians and gays living in small-town and rural America continue to move to the city when they come of age. Most of the gay people in Mississippi I knew in high school and col-lege moved to a large city when they were old enough to support themselves.

Queer studies and literature have traditionally focused on the cities, especially the cities on the east and west coasts (e.g., Gray, Johnson, & Gilley, 2016; Howard, 1997, 1999; Weston, 1998). This focus is not surprising, because the more visible communities are in the cities. However, Howard (1999), a historian, called this emphasis on the cities a "biocoastal bias" (p. 12); thus, scholars and writers ignored the gays and lesbians who did not move to the city, either choosing to remain in small towns and rural areas or not having a choice. Cities have often been portrayed as "urban meccas" for lesbians and gays, where they could come out of hiding and escape the repressiveness of rural life (Herring, 2010, p. 14). This urban/rural dichotomy in queer studies and literature mirrors the coming-out process of an individual: coming out of the closet means moving from an isolated place to a welcoming community (Halberstam, 2005; Howard, 1999; Weston, 1998). In other words, there is a belief that in order to openly identify as lesbian or gay, one must move to the city. Halberstam (2005), an English professor, coined the term "metronormativity" to describe this "conflation of 'urban' and 'visible' in many normalizing narratives of gay/lesbian subjectivities" (p. 36). Herring (2010), also an English professor, argued that metronormativity is a thread that runs through not only queer studies but queer culture, politics, literature, and even art. The gay community is too often portrayed as white, cosmopolitan, and of economic means. In order to be considered among the "in crowd," one must fit the mold of Ellen DeGeneres or Anderson Cooper, fashionable and sophisticated; what Herring termed "cosmo-urbanism" (p. 16). Gay people not fitting into this mold become invisible or less valued.

Like Herring (2010), writers from a variety of disciplines, have fought back against this narrative by discussing gay life outside the cities, including the history of life in rural America (Johnson, 2013) and in America today (Gray, Johnson, & Gilley, 2016). Some writers have focused on rural areas of specific regions or states such as Fellows's (1998) *Farm Boys: Lives of Gay Men from Rural Midwest*, Gray's (2009) *Out in the Country*, focusing on today's queer youth in Kentucky and Appalachia, Johnson's (2008) *Sweet Tea: Black Gay Men of the South*, and Thompson's (2010) *Un-natural State: Arkansas and the Queer South*.

Especially pertinent to this book is John Howard's (1999) *Men Like That: A Southern Queer History*, a study of male same-sex desire in Mississippi from 1945 to 1985. Howard (1999) argued that same-sex desire has always existed throughout history, including in Mississippi, although it was not necessarily connected to a gay identity. The state sodomy law was established as far back as 1839, indicating that Mississippians were aware of same-sex desires. As in other areas of the country after World War II, some lesbians and gays were quietly tolerated in Mississippi communities, depending on race, gender, and socioeconomic status. Gay white men of means, with roots in a community, were most likely to be quietly tolerated than others. Gay Mississippians who had transportation and had time off work, commuted from small towns and rural areas to Jackson, Memphis, and New Orleans to join the gay bar culture. A racially segregated gay bar culture in Jackson, the state capitol, existed during the 1940s and 1950s with bars later emerging in Biloxi, Meridian, and Hattiesburg. Whereas, in other parts of the country, lesbians and gays were actively persecuted during the McCarthy era, (i.e., linked to communists), "[Mississippians] were aware [of queer people] but chose to ignore. . . . For their part in the social compact, queer Mississippians maintained low profiles" (p. 142). This "social compact" in Mississippi ended during the civil-rights era as homosexuality became linked to civil-rights activists, both viewed as outsiders trying to change the "status quo." In 1965, police raided "tearooms," locations in public buildings that were frequented by "gay men seeking anonymous sexual encounters" (Thompson, 2010, p. 121), in Jackson and Hattiesburg and began to enforce the 1839 state sodomy law. It was not until the 1970s that gay activism began to emerge nationwide. In Mississippi gay activism began with the founding of the Mississippi Gay Alliance in 1973 by lesbian students and faculty at Mississippi State University in Starkville (Howard, 1999, p. 234).

Coincidently, my family moved to Starkville in 1973 from Pennsylvania, the summer before I began second grade, when my father accepted a faculty position at Mississippi State University (MSU). My parents and their families are from Michigan and New York, so Mississippi was a culture shock. Starkville being a college town made the adjustment less severe. College towns in Mississippi tend to be more liberal and diverse than surrounding counties; however, this is relative, because such places tend to be more conservative and less diverse than college towns in more liberal states. In the past two presidential elections for example, Oktibbeha County, in which Starkville and MSU lie, supported Obama and then Clinton, but each time only by a handful of votes. On the CNN electoral map, Oktibbeha County was a blue dot surrounded by red; however, it has been more a purple dot because of an ongoing battle between progressives, most of whom are associated with the university, and the "old guard."

In 2014, Starkville became the first municipality in Mississippi to pass an ordinance banning discrimination based on sexual orientation and gender identity; however, the Board of Aldermen repealed it in 2015 under pressure from some churches, overriding a mayoral veto of the repeal. More recently in 2017, Starkville elected its first female mayor, Lynn Spruill, who the Board of Aldermen had controversially fired in 2013 after she had served eight years as the city's chief administrative officer. Board members overrode a mayoral veto in a 5–2 vote and refused to answer questions from the public about why they wanted to terminate Spruill, whom they assumed to be lesbian. One board member, Ben Carver, who voted for termination said that "this is what the Lord wants me to do" and that he had "made his mind up years ago," after praying about it (Smith, 2013).

In the Starkville neighborhood where I grew up were families from Missouri, California, Wisconsin, Pennsylvania, and, of course, Mississippi. A Hungarian family moved in and taught my mother how to make chicken paprika with dumplings. To this day, it is one of my favorite dishes. Consequently, my younger brothers and I grew up with children from all over the country and the world. We even had an African American family living next door to us in our mostly white neighborhood, something that in the 1970s was likely not the case in most Mississippi towns. Nevertheless, we were still in Mississippi, and I discovered quickly as a child that I was a minority as a Catholic, speaking with a northern accent, and having a last name that was ethnic.

After high school I went away to college and lived in Buffalo, New York, where my family had spent time in the summers with my father's family. As a political science major, during my summer breaks I interned at the Pentagon in Washington, DC. After college, I stayed in Buffalo, working in a nursing home and teaching elementary school. Several years later at twenty-five, I returned home to attend graduate school at MSU. While in graduate school, I became involved in the university gay student group and developed a support group of gay and lesbian friends, straight allies, and supportive faculty members. I also met Michael who was my partner for twelve years. After graduate school, Michael and I moved to Fort Lauderdale and later to New Orleans.

Living in Fort Lauderdale and New Orleans, I maintained private practices in mental health counseling and served on the faculties of the mental health counseling programs at Barry University in Miami and Xavier University in New Orleans. I increasingly researched gay and lesbian identity-development issues in counseling to gain more knowledge in my field and, of course, to gain more knowledge about myself. I returned home frequently to visit my family but lost touch with many of my friends from graduate school who had moved out of the state. I wasn't sure how large a gay community, if any, still existed in my hometown or the surrounding area, and I did not know how to find out. After all, in the cities with large gay communities, people have the option to meet at the gay gym, the gay community center, the gay coffee shop, the gay bar, or even walking down the street in the gay neighborhood, itself. In small-town Mississippi, the only places that are gay are the homes of gay people living in the area, the internet, or a gay bar several hours away in Jackson, the capital city, or in one of the large cities in a bordering state.

I did know the faculty advisor for the gay student group on campus, and I emailed him and asked whether or not there was even a semblance of a gay community in the area. He forwarded my email to Fred, who he described as the "keeper of the gay list." Fred kept a list of email addresses of gay people who lived in the area (basically a group of people from several counties and a county in

Alabama on the state line) and sent out regular emails announcing weekly happy hours that took place at one of the restaurants/bars in town or at someone's house. Fred responded to my email almost immediately with a nice welcome and directions to the bar where happy hour would take place that week. It took place at a bar above a restaurant on Main Street in downtown Columbus, about twenty minutes from MSU.

Main Street in downtown Columbus is a wide street of two lanes and diagonal parking on either side of the street. Three of its blocks are lined on both sides by rows of two- or three-story brick buildings built at the turn of the century, typical of many small-town main streets in Mississippi. I arrived around six o'clock and noticed that there were few cars parked on the street in front of the restaurant. In fact, it seemed somewhat desolate. There did seem to be people in the restaurant, however, and I followed Fred's directions to an elevator in a lobby next to the restaurant that took me to the second floor of the old building. The elevator opened up right into the barroom, and I felt the eyes of all four people there watch me walk toward the bar where Fred and his partner Ralph were sitting. It was easy to pick them out, because they were the only ones there besides a bartender and a women drinking beer out of a bottle at the bar. Fred and Ralph appeared to be around sixty, and they were extremely welcoming. They were interested in my evacuation story and excited that I would be joining their happy hours, at least temporarily, until I figured out whether or not I would return to New Orleans. At some point one other gay man showed up, and he too was very friendly. I was struck by how down-to-earth the three were and that they didn't seem to care whether or not the bartender heard them talking about "gay things." In fact, Fred and Ralph seemed to know the bartender. I later learned that Fred and Ralph had lived in Columbus for over thirty years and knew almost everyone in town. They assured me that it was abnormal for there to be such a small group at happy hour, and they promised that if I kept coming I would notice that the crowds could range anywhere from a couple of people to forty. Of course, they said, if someone hosted the happy hour at his/her home, people would come in large numbers. I wondered, though, if I really wanted to stay in a place in which forty people was considered a large crowd when I was accustomed to hundreds of people at the gay bars in New Orleans. *The Big Easy* was in disarray, though, and I didn't know if I could go back there once the city opened up again. I owned a house with my now ex-partner, Michael, near the French Quarter, and I did not know if the house was livable. I was still on the faculty at Xavier University for whom I was continuing to teach online, because my students had evacuated all across the country. The university, itself, was literally under water. Consequently, I wasn't sure what the future would bring.

Over the next year, I traveled back and forth between New Orleans and Mississippi. I was fortunate that my house sat in one of the dry areas of the city and did not even have a broken window. Xavier's campus also eventually opened up again. Nevertheless, Xavier, in a financial crisis, laid off a third of its faculty. Although my position wasn't terminated, many of the tenured faculty lost their jobs, including a good friend and mentor. I wondered if my department of only three faculty would survive.

When I had first evacuated, a friend who worked at the Social Science Research Center at MSU had introduced me to the center's director who invited me and several other New Orleans evacuees, faculty from University of New Orleans and Loyola, to join the center. He provided us with office space, computers, and administrative support to work on our own research, teach online courses for our universities, and connect with other researchers there. Eventually I worked out an agreement between Xavier and the center to have a one-year joint appointment in which I taught an online course, returned to Xavier for monthly meetings, and worked on research grant projects at the center. My frequent trips between the two places reflected my own indecision on what I would do. I had one year to make a decision. I felt like part of me was in Mississippi and part of me was in New Orleans. I wasn't sure which place to choose. In fact, it seemed that when I was in one place I wanted to be in the other. While in Columbus, I missed the French Quarter, the little theatre where I played the keyboard from time to time, the gay bars, the coffee shops, restaurants, and the laissez faire attitude. When I was in Columbus, I had the feeling that I was too "out there" as an openly gay man. I missed that sense of being part of a place where it was certainly not shocking for someone to be gay.

On the other hand, when I was in New Orleans, I missed the peacefulness of the small town. At my house in New Orleans, sitting on the front steps on a nice evening I could watch the traffic go down Elysian Fields but often worried that someone walking down the street might try to rob me. I felt especially nervous walking the five blocks back from the French Quarter at night. I always stayed on crowded streets, but I worried sometimes when I walked down Dauphine by Washington Square at night and turned onto Elysian Fields. I remembered that a few times I ran from the corner of Elysian Fields and Dauphine to my house on Burgundy. I may have been overreacting, but there were always stories. The hardware store only a block or so from my house was held up during the day. When I first moved to New Orleans, a jogger was robbed and murdered early in the morning just blocks from my house. A friend of mine living nearby heard a noise one night in his apartment and discovered a man trying to crawl into his living room through a window. He literally pushed the man back outside the window, causing the intruder to fall flat on his back on the concrete sidewalk in the alley between two shotgun houses. In Columbus, I didn't feel that I was taking my life into my own hands when I sat on the porch or walked down to a friend's house in the evening. Of course, it wasn't or isn't that Columbus doesn't have its share of crime, but it was nowhere near the scale of violence in New Orleans at that time.

While I was in New Orleans, I also missed the tidiness of Columbus. To say that New Orleans is a dirty city is an understatement. There is a cacophony of smells ranging from vomit, urine, and spilled beer. In truth, however, the odor changes as you walk along. On one corner, you might smell coffee and beignets from Café Du Monde; on another crawfish boil and red beans and rice. But the other smells from the streets still hit you again as you walk,

especially on a warm summer evening. Walking outside the French
Quarter and around my house, I was constantly picking up trash.
People would finish a beer and simply drop the can on the ground
as they walked. The bottom of my shoes always felt like they were
covered with grime, and I never felt that my house was clean. This
was even more the case after the hurricane, when trash piled up as
people gutted houses and threw out refrigerators. The city always
seemed to have a grey cloud hanging over it, even when it was sunny.
And the hurricane certainly pulled off the veneer that hid the crime
and poverty from the world. Going down some streets off Claiborne
near Elysian Fields, one could imagine having been transported to
a third-world country; streets with no sidewalks, dirt front yards,
houses that looked unlivable with people sitting on decaying front
porches.

In his book *Another Country: Queer Anti-Urbanism,* Herring
(2010) stressed the importance of not doing the reverse of metronormativity, in other words, making rural areas the ideal. Looking
back to that time today, I realize my thinking at times reflected
metronormativity and at other times anti-urbanism. At the same
time, my thinking reflected a common theme of the gay couples I
interviewed. There is an underlying constant push and pull for many
Mississippi gay people, as the couples describe in the pages ahead.

After considering all the pros and cons, I decided to buy an old
home in Columbus with a wrap-around porch in a historic neighborhood of antebellum homes. I thought that if I was going to live
in Mississippi I was going to live in a neighborhood that reminded
me of some of the things I love about New Orleans: the history and
architecture. The house reminded me of some of the houses in the
Uptown area of New Orleans, the area up the river from the famous
Garden District. I could never have afforded this house in Uptown
New Orleans on a single, university faculty member's salary. I had
bought my home on Elysian Fields Avenue with my ex-partner several years before we ended our relationship. It was on the border of a
gentrified neighborhood and within blocks of blight and high crime.
The house needed a new roof and extensive renovations. When we

moved into the house, it was a double shotgun; in other words, there were two front doors that led into two separate apartments. After walking in the front door, a person had to walk through one room to get to the other. There were no hallways. A renter lived in one of the apartments; we lived in the other. After we learned that the renter was selling drugs out of the apartment, we did not renew his lease. We suffered financially as a result.

In Columbus, I could afford the house I bought and still have money left over. It cost about a third to a fourth of what I would have paid for a similar house in a nice neighborhood in New Orleans. Additionally, I knew at least three other gay men who lived in the neighborhood, and I coincidently bought my house from a lesbian woman. After dating an English professor at the local university for a while, I settled into single life determined to try it for a year: "it" being both living as a single gay man and living in Mississippi. It felt like being on a retreat from the chaos of New Orleans after Katrina. Meanwhile, I considered whether or not at the end of the year I would move to a large city again. I felt peaceful and calm in my new house. I loved sitting on the porch reading and landscaping the yard. I found the neighbors to be welcoming, and I was making a few gay friends. But I continued to have times when I missed the feeling of knowing that the gay bar was open if I wanted to be around other gay people. I searched job announcements for positions near large cities with strong gay communities and even went for an interview and turned down a position at a university near Chicago. The thought of being so far away from my family was uncomfortable, but I wondered if I would be forced to make a choice in the future between my family and meeting someone with whom I could spend my life.

Less than a year later, I met Larry at a party. Before long, my house became our house, and my thoughts of moving were put on hold. Another year went by, and we were renovating our old Columbus home. I felt more settled than I had felt in many years, but I still had lingering doubts about whether or not Mississippi was the place for me. Larry said he would move anywhere with me; in fact, he, too, wondered at times if it was worth staying when it did not seem like Mississippi wanted us, a gay couple. Our connection to friends and family, though, and the low cost of living meant that we vacillated between staying and leaving, just as I had before we met. We decided to put off a decision for a few more years until Larry was eligible for retirement.

MISSISSIPPI COUPLES

Queer oral histories originated out of the feminist movement of the 1970s with Elizabeth Lapovksy Kennedy and Madeline Davis's *Boots of Leather, Slippers of Gold: The History of a Lesbian Community* bridging women's studies with queer oral history in 1993 (Boyd & Ramírez, 2012). Around the same time, Allan Bérubé (1990) published *Coming Out under Fire: The History of Gay Men and Women in World War Two.* These classics and other oral histories have provided us with a deeper understanding of gay communities and activism (Rivers, 2012). Without them, the stories of gay people during these times and in these communities might have died with their narrators. Other queer histories and studies have helped us to see that queer people did and do exist, connect, and survive outside the cities and in rural areas (e.g., Howard, 1999; Fellows, 1998; Grey, 2009; Johnson, 2008).

Coming Out of the Magnolia Closet provides additional perspectives on gay life in the South that build on what we have learned from other queer studies in the rural South. First, other studies (e.g., Howard, 1999; Johnson, 2008) have been based on the interviews of individuals. The narrators' stories in this book are from my interviews of couples, sitting together and interacting with each other and me.

Second, I interviewed these couples before and after June 26, 2015, the date of the US Supreme Court's ruling on *Obergefell v. Hodges.* The couples' stories help us understand their varied reactions to legalized same-sex marriage, before and after *Obergefell v. Hodges.*

They show us how the reactions that couples have received from their families, communities, and churches have also varied and are not always easily defined.

Third, the couples' stories in this book help us to understand that, although there is progress, couples are still not accepted as equal to heterosexual couples; nor are they valued as Mississippians by their elected officials and many of the state's population as are other privileged citizens. On the evening of *Obergefell v. Hodges*, President Barrack Obama ordered that the White House be lit in rainbow colors (Obama White House, 2015). Lesbian and gay couples across the country, including in Mississippi, celebrated. As I celebrated with other lesbians and gays in my small town, it felt like, just for a moment, that we had reached the finish line. Unfortunately, as monumental as the events of that day, we all quickly remembered that we are far from a society in which all people, gay or straight, have equal rights, privileges, and opportunities. Gay couples are still attacked for simply holding hands in public across the country from New York to Washington, DC, to Texas (Shorey, 2019). There is no federal law prohibiting discrimination based on sexual orientation or gender identity. Gay couples continue to face issues across the country, especially in places like Mississippi where someone can fired from a job and refused service at a business simply for being in a same-sex relationship. This reality is even harsher for nonwhite gay couples and for those of low socioeconomic status.

Finally, the couples' stories help us understand how they develop gay communities and families within their towns and rural communities, continue to promote understanding and acceptance of their relationships simply by interacting with their neighbors, and find their way as same-sex couples in Mississippi, a place they call home.

Research Procedures

I spoke with fifty lesbian and gay couples across Mississippi. To meet these couples, I began by sending an email to the happy hour group in Columbus, asking people to refer same-sex couples who might be interested in talking about being gay or lesbian in Mississippi. I met several couples through such referrals. I also advertised on Facebook groups and websites for gay Mississippians which led to a few more couples. Some of the couples I interviewed then provided me with further referrals. Of the couples I met, thirty agreed to a formal, recorded interview. Other couples spoke to me informally, enabling me to learn about and share their experiences but not allowing me to quote them directly. For the couples who agreed to be formally interviewed, I recorded and transcribed our conversations with their permission. Fifteen of those conversations, which best represented the themes I heard from all of the lesbian and gay couples I met, are included in this book.

Prior to contacting potential participants, I obtained original approval from the Institutional Review Board (IRB) of the university where I was a full-time faculty member at the time in 2011 with annual continuing review until I completed the interviews in 2016. IRBs are committees at universities that review research proposals with human subjects to ensure that the research is ethical and adheres to federal regulations (American Psychological Association, 2019). Years before I began my research, the Oral History Association (Oral History Association, 2019) recommended that oral history be exempt from IRB reviews. When I first proposed my research, I was a faculty member in a clinical mental health counseling program housed in a college of social and behavioral sciences. As with other faculty researchers, I was expected to receive approval from the university's IRB prior to beginning my research. I did consult with the IRB prior to submitting an IRB research application to determine if interviewing lesbian and gay couples who consented required IRB approval. Although the IRB provided expedited review, I was required to submit an application in order to proceed with any interviews. Based on the IRB requirements, I adhered to the following research procedures:

Participants were volunteers, aged twenty-one and over, who self-identified as gay men and lesbians, who were currently in a relationship that has been ongoing for at least five years, and who lived in Mississippi. Potential participants were asked to contact me directly by phone or email. After contacting me, I mailed or emailed potential participants a consent form that explained my research, the interview process, and how I would protect their confidentiality. I asked them to review the consent form prior to a phone meeting with both participants (i.e., the couple). This phone meeting was an opportunity for me to answer any of their questions, ensure that the participants met the research criteria for participation, screen for any participants who were a member of a vulnerable group that could not provide consent (e.g., incarcerated, children, mentally disabled), and ensure that the participants understood the consent form. In addition to the other criteria, if a member of a couple appeared to be pressured to participate by the other member or any other person I would not have accepted the couple as research participants. Further, if I did not make this determination until the interview, itself, I would have ceased the interview and destroyed all data collected. There were no instances in which I believed any of the potential participants were from a vulnerable population or had been pressured to participate. I did determine that a few potential participants who contacted me were not eligible to participate in an interview. These potential participants had not been in a relationship for at least five years or did not live in Mississippi.

Participants who were eligible and who decided to participate in a recorded interview with me signed the consent form prior to the beginning of the interview. I conducted single interviews of approximately two hours with each couple and with both members of a couple present. Although this did not occur during an interview, in the event that one of the members of a couple refused to participate in the interview or asked to stop the interview at any time, I would have ceased the interview and all data collected from that couple would have been destroyed.

Audio tapes were transcribed by me and a professional transcriptionist who signed a confidentiality agreement, including the stipulation that she destroy any copies of the transcripts she had once submitting to me. I hold the only original copies of the transcripts which are stored in a secured file. Prior to including any portions of the transcript in this book, I deleted any identifying information about participants (other than general demographic information), including their names, names of people they discussed, places where they lived, employers, and any other key facts that they believed might identify them. I offered participants the option to provide me with a pseudonym, but most asked me to create one for them. Like Howard (1999), I encouraged participants to protect their anonymity, including asking them to let me know if there was anything they said during the interview that I should not include in the transcripts. Because participants' voices could identify their identities, once the transcripts were completed, I reviewed them for accuracy and deleted audio records per my agreement with them. Even if I had not been required to receive IRB approval, I still would have taken these steps to maintain participants' anonymity, because of the lack of protections in Mississippi for gays and lesbians.

THE NARRATORS

It is impossible to know if the couples I met were representative of all gay couples in Mississippi. A representative sample would involve interviewing a large sample from the total number of gay couples in Mississippi, assuming that the total number could even be determined. Based on the US Census Bureau's American Community Survey and the Census 2000, Gary Gates (2014) at the Williams Institute estimated that are almost 3,500 same-sex couples living in Mississippi. Of these couples, Gates reported that 58 percent of the couples were female and 68.7 percent were white, compared to 25.9 percent African American, 4.5 percent Latin American, and less than 1 percent Asian/Pacific Islander. Moreover, the majority of the couples (54 percent) were ages thirty to forty-nine compared to 29 percent aged fifty to sixty-four, 13 percent less than thirty years of age, and 4 percent over sixty-five years of age. Because it is difficult to know how many same-sex couples did not identify themselves as married or partnered, it is possible that the total number of same-sex couples is larger than reported.

The couples I interviewed have been in their relationships from seven to thirty years. I worked to ensure that the couples I spoke to were as representative as possible in several ways. First, I attempted to speak to diverse couples in terms of gender, race, age, socioeconomic status, and length of relationship. I spoke to equal number of male and female couples who ranged in age from twenty-five to sixty-five. They work in a variety of settings, including management, medicine, self-employment, professional, service, and blue collar. I did not meet any couples who would be considered impoverished or wealthy, but the couples represented both professional and working-class people. Most of the couples have always lived in Mississippi or lived in Mississippi most of their relationships; only a few have grown up or lived previously in a neighboring state.

Similar to Howard's (1999) difficulty recruiting black men to participate in his oral history, I had difficulty recruiting other nonwhite couples who were in a long-term relationship and were willing to sign a consent form to be taped. The Columbus social group, for example, rarely has a black person attend who is not a student from one of the local universities. I learned from a few couples that there once had been a regular group of gay black men who frequented a bar near Tupelo, but that establishment has been closed for several years. I also learned of parties for gay black men and women in Columbus and near the coast, but only after the fact. This does not, of course, mean that there are not black lesbian and gay men in committed relationships. I imagine, as Johnson (2008) has noted, the history of racism in the South, including in the gay community, would make it less likely that an African American same-sex couple would trust me, a white man. Nevertheless, of the couples who agreed to be formally interviewed, two are black (one male couple and one female couple) and two are interracial. The interracial couples include a male couple (a white man and a Hispanic man) and a female couple (a black women and a white woman).

I intentionally met couples living in a variety of settings across the state: rural, micropolitan (i.e., small town), and metropolitan. According to the United States Office of Management and Budget (2013), micropolitans are urban areas in the United States centered around a small town of 10,000 to 49,999 people. The definition is similar to the concept of a metropolitan area in which people live in the city or an area near the city with an urban core of at least 50,000. Anyone who did not live in a small town or in the micropolitan area of a small town I identified as rural. The reason I made the distinction between micropolitan and rural is because in Mississippi there are only five metropolitan areas (i.e. Gulport-Biloxi, Hattiesburg, Jackson, Pascagoula, and the section of the Memphis, Tennessee, metropolitan area that lies in Mississippi) encompassing about 44 percent of the state's population. Only seventeen of the state's eighty-two counties are metropolitan. About 34 percent of the state's population live in micropolitan areas; twenty-seven of the state's eighty-two counties are micropolitan.

Rural areas comprise thirty-eight of the state's counties and about 22 percent of the population. Consequently, gay men not living near a metropolitan area drive to the micropolitan areas to socialize and meet. In Columbus, for example, when someone hosts a party, people come, not only from Columbus, but also from surrounding counties. A few people even drive to Columbus from the nearby counties in Alabama. I focused on speaking to more couples from rural and micropolitan areas, because the majority of the states' counties are rural or micropolitan and because queer studies writings and research have traditionally paid less attention to lesbians and gays who live in nonmetropolitan areas. Of the couples I spoke to, about 30 percent live in rural areas, 50 percent live in micropolitan areas, and 20 percent live in metropolitan areas, although they do not view Jackson, the state capital, or other metropolitan areas such as Hattiesburg and the cities on the Gulf Coast as cosmopolitan. Additionally, I agree with Herring (2010), who pointed out that, although a city like Jackson is statistically considered metropolitan, as a whole, the people living in Jackson are probably more similar to the people in other parts of Mississippi than they are to people living in New York City or San Francisco. Nevertheless, I identify the type of area in which couples are living, even if metropolitan Mississippi tends to be more like micropolitan Mississippi than metropolitan New York.

I also interviewed couples living in each of the regions of the state, driving north and south, east and west, from one end of the state to the other, to see where Mississippi lesbian and gay couples call home. According to *Visit Mississippi*, Mississippi's tourism organization, the state can be roughly divided into five regions: Hills, Delta, Pines, Capital/River, and Coastal.

The Hills region stretches across the northern border from Southaven, included in the Memphis, Tennessee, metropolitan area, past Corinth to the Alabama line and south to Grenada and Tupelo, the largest micropolitan area of the state and known as the birthplace of Elvis Presley. The Hills are also home to Oxford, one of the state's three major college towns, and the University of Mississippi, aka Ole Miss.

The Delta region borders the Mississippi River from Tunica, known for its casinos, to just above Vicksburg and just below Yazoo City. The Delta includes Clarksdale, location of the Delta Blues Museum and touted as the birthplace of the blues. It also includes Delta State University in Cleveland and Mississippi Valley State University, a historically black university, in Itta Bena. Unfortunately, the Delta has one of the highest poverty rates in the United States, especially for African Americans.

Below the Delta, from the Mississippi River to the middle of the state and from Vicksburg and the Jackson metropolitan area to the Louisiana border is the Capital/River region. Jackson State University, another historically black university, is located here. East of the Delta and the Capital/River region from just below Tupelo to just below Meridian, the second largest micropolitan area in the state, is the Pines region. The Pines is home to Starkville, the college town of Mississippi State University, and Columbus, where I live.

Finally, east of the lower part of the Capital/River region and south of the Pines region to the Gulf of Mexico is the Coastal region.

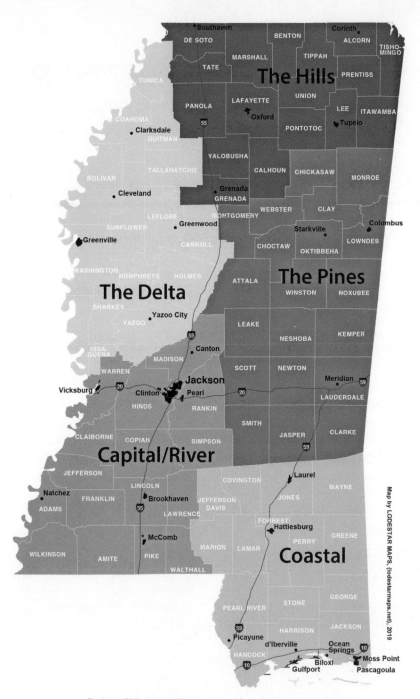

Regions of Mississippi. Map courtesy of Scott Noren, Lodestar Maps.

The coastal region includes the Hattiesburg, Biloxi/Gulfport, and Pascagoula metropolitan areas. Hattiesburg is home to the University of Southern Mississippi.

INTERVIEWS

I spoke to couples in coffee shops and restaurants, at parties, over the phone, and in video calls. Of the couples I interviewed formally, however, all but two of the couples invited me to their homes for the interviews. Meeting them in their residences allowed me see couples interact in the spaces they have created together. Couples also felt more comfortable talking about their relationships while sitting in their own homes. I was frequently struck by the warmth and love between them when they told stories about first meeting or coming out to family members as a couple. I was particularly surprised at how willing the couples were to answer my questions and how open they were with me. Part of that may have been because I am a trained mental health counselor and another part may have been because I am gay, myself. I think another important reason was that these couples really wanted to tell their stories to someone who wanted to hear them and would share them with others. Each interview lasted around two hours; but, almost all the couples wanted to keep talking after the formal interview, and we would often compare notes about my community and theirs.

As I promised to the couples, I protect their confidentiality by intentionally not providing anything but general information regarding their locations and any other unique characteristics. Only one couple asked that I use their real names, because they view sharing their story as an important part of their activism and outreach to the gay community. With the exception of a retired couple and two singly employed couples, most of the couples are dually employed. The couples work in a variety of settings, including management, medicine, self-employment, education, service industry, and other type of professional and working-class jobs. I do not reveal their specific jobs in order to protect their confidentiality. Identifying their jobs might reveal too much, especially because over half of them said that they had not come out (i.e., revealed that they are gay) at work. This is not surprising, since as I noted before, neither the federal government nor Mississippi have employment nondiscrimination laws based on sexual orientation.

For example, one of the men was just about to begin a new job when I interviewed him and his husband. When I asked him about his job, he said, "Unfortunately because they're owned by a very conservative family, I'm going to have to be careful about sharing anything about our relationship, but I needed a job." Other couples spoke of only being out to select coworkers. In other cases, as you'll read in the following chapters, some of the couples said they assumed that their coworkers knew that they are gay but that nobody ever discussed it.

Although I work to protect the couples' confidentiality, I have not changed their stories, other than to protect their identities. As much as possible, I let the couples express themselves in their own words. Although I do not include every moment of every interview, I do not edit their words, including not editing grammar or slang.

LOOKING AHEAD

Each of the chapters focuses on different aspects of the couples' experiences in and relationship with Mississippi. The first three chapters on community, religion, and family form Part One of this book, because they are related to each other. In small towns and rural areas, extended families live in one's communities and often go to the same church. The reactions that participants discuss regarding religion often cross over into family reactions; family reactions often cross over into community reactions. I have done my best to organize these chapters into these three themes; however, sometimes there is natural overlap.

Chapter One focuses on couples' positive and negative experiences in their Mississippi communities, especially their neighbors and coworkers. In this chapter, I use the term "community" to refer to the place couples call home in contrast to a discussion of a "gay community" in Chapter Four. Narrators who are black or in racially mixed relationships also discuss how their experiences as same-sex couples intersect with their experiences as racial minorities.

Chapter Two is about couples' positive and negative experiences with religion. Like family, religion is also a large part of the culture in Mississippi, including its resistance to same-sex marriage and relationships.

In Chapter Three, couples discuss their positive and negative experiences with their families. In Mississippi rural areas and small towns, one's family is often intertwined with one's community. Some couples live on the same land as family members, have a family member living with them, or have inherited a family home. Consequently understanding couples' relationships with their families is an important part of understanding the couples' relationships to Mississippi culture.

Throughout Part One I discuss that, although there has been progress, there is still evidence of a social compact of silence that Howard (1999) described in his study of male same-sex desire in Mississippi from 1945 to 1985, although the silence is expressed in both similar and different ways. Throughout the couples' stories a theme of tolerance but not acceptance is revealed; an unspoken admonition to live quietly, not act "too gay," and not demonstrate any displays of affection.

The chapters included in Part Two specifically look at the couples, themselves. Chapter Four focuses on how and where Mississippi couples meet, with couples sharing stories of their first encounters with each other and the evolution from being two single people to being a couple. I discuss how Mississippi gays and lesbians create gay spaces and community within their towns and rural communities. In Chapter Five couples discuss their views on legalized same-sex marriage, which are not as clear cut as one would imagine. Couples who have not married talk about whether they have plans to be married in the future or why they do not get married. Couples who have been married recount their experiences with their families and in their local communities related to obtaining a marriage certificate and presenting as a married couple.

Finally, in the conclusion, couples explain why they stay in Mississippi, answering a question about which many outside the state wonder and that I wondered, myself, when I returned to Mississippi. They also talk about whether or not they plan to stay in the future, revealing a love-hate relationship with a place they call home.

Because different couples focused on different areas to a greater extent than others, each chapter has different couples included. The first time a couple appears in the book, I introduce them to the reader, providing some background information for the reader. When the couple appears in subsequent chapters, I do not reintroduce them but refer the reader back to the chapter where they were first introduced.

Throughout the book, I share my own experiences as a gay man living in Mississippi in a same-sex relationship. Although I am the researcher who interviewed couples, I am also a participant who cannot help but be influenced by my own experiences as I observe and relate to the experiences of the couples. I do this by including some of my own experiences in each chapter, providing readers with an opportunity to consider how my own experiences may have shaped the questions I asked and the ways I related to the couples during the interviews.

I also provide background information and a brief review of literature as related to the subject of each chapter. Although I draw heavily from queer studies, including the writings on southern and rural queer studies, I take an interdisciplinary approach, also considering research and writings from history, sociology, psychology, and other areas when pertinent to the topic. I attempt to provide some context for the reader about how the Mississippi couples' relationships and experiences compare to those in other areas and times. Finally, the couples' stories, mainly in their own words, are the meat of each chapter.

In sum, what I hope that you, the reader, will experience as you read this book is a glimpse into the world of gay couples in Mississippi. How did we meet? What is it like to be gay in our communities? What type of reaction do we receive from our neighbors, families, and churches? Why do we live in Mississippi? Do we plan to stay or find a home elsewhere?

REFERENCES

American Psychological Association. (2019). Frequently asked questions about Intuitional Review Boards. Retrieved from https://www.apa.org/advocacy/research/defending research/review-boards

Bérubé, A. (1990). *Coming out under fire: The history of gay men and women in World War Two*. New York, NY: The Free Press.

Boyd, N. A., & Ramírez, H. N. R. (Eds.). (2012). *Bodies of evidence: The practice of queer oral history*. New York, NY: Oxford University Press.

Centerlink. (2019). Centerlink LGBT community center member directory. Retrieved from https://www.lgbtcenters.org/Centers/find-a-center.aspx

CNN. (2004). Election results: America votes 2004. Retrieved from http://www.cnn.com/ELECTION/2004/pages/results/ballot.measures/

D'Emilio, J. (1993). Capitalism and gay identity. In H. Abelove, M. A. Barale, & D. M. Halperin (Eds.), *The lesbian and gay reader* (pp. 467–76). New York: Routledge.

D'Emilio, J. (1998). *Sexual politics, sexual communities: The making of a homosexual minority in the United States, 1940–1970* (2nd ed.). Chicago: University of Chicago Press.

Drescher, J. (2015). Out of DSM: Depathologizing homosexuality. *Behavioral Sciences, 5*, 565–75. doi:10.3390/bs5040565

Fellows, W. (1998). *Farm boys: Lives of gay men from the rural Midwest*. Madison, WI: University of Wisconsin Press.

Gates, G. J. (2014). Same-sex couples in Mississippi: A demographic summary. Retrieved from the Williams Institute website: https://williamsinstitute.law.ucla.edu/demographics/mississippi-ss-couples-demo-dec-2014/

Gray, M. L. (2009). *Out in the country: Youth, media, and queer visibility in rural America*. New York, NY: New York University Press.

Gray, M. L., Johnson, C. R., & Gilley, B. J. (2016). *Queering the countryside: New frontiers in rural queer studies*. New York, NY: New York University Press.

Halberstam, J. (2005). *In a queer time and place: Transgender bodies, subcultural lives*. New York, NY: New York University Press.

Halperin, D. M. (2002). *How to do the history of homosexuality.* Chicago, IL: University of Chicago Press.

Herring, S. (2010). *Another country: Queer anti-urbanism.* New York, NY: New York University Press.

Howard, J. (Ed.) (1997). *Carryin' on in the lesbian and gay south.* New York, NY: New York University Press.

Howard, J. (1999). *Men like that: A southern queer history.* Chicago, IL: University of Chicago Press.

Human Rights Campaign Fund. (2019). HRC unveils unprecedented effort to bring equality to Mississippi. Retrieved from http://www.hrc.org/blog/hrc-unveils-unprecedented-effort-to-bring-equality-to-mississippi

Johnson, C. (2013). *Just queer folks: Gender and sexuality in rural America.* Philadelphia, PA: Temple University Press.

Johnson, E. P. (2008). *Sweet tea: Black gay men of the south.* Chapel Hill, NC: University of North Carolina Press.

Lapovsky Kennedy, E., & Davis, M. D. (1993). *Boots of leather: Slippers of gold: The history of a lesbian community.* New York, NY: Routledge.

Lawrence v. Texas, 539 U.S. 558 (2003).

McCarthy, J. (2014). Same-sex marriage support reaches new high at 55%. *Gallup.* Retrieved from http://www.gallup.com/poll/169640/sex-marriage-support-reaches-new-high.aspx

McCarthy, J. (2017). U.S. support for gay marriage edges to new high. *Gallup.* Retrieved from Gallup website: http://www.gallup.com/poll/210566/support-gay-marriage-edges-new-high.aspx

Mississippi Safe Schools Coalition. (2019). Directory of GSAs in Mississippi. Retrieved from http://www.mssafeschools.org/resources/directory/

Newport, F. (2017). Wyoming, North Dakota and Mississippi most conservative. *Gallup.* Retrieved from http://www.gallup.com/poll/203204/wyoming-north-dakota-mississippi-conservative.aspx?g_source=IDEOLOGY&g_medium=topic&g_campaign=tiles

Obama White House. (2015). *Time-lapse of The White House on June 26th 2015.* [Video]. Available from https://obamawhitehouse.archives.gov/photos-and-video/video/2015/11/03/time-lapse-white-house-june-26th-2015

Obergefell v. Hodges, 576 U.S. (2015).

Oral History Association. (2019). Information about IRBs. Retrieved from https://www.oralhistory.org/information-about-irbs/

Outright Vermont. (2017). Education & Outreach. Retrieved from http://www.outrightvt.org/.

Protecting Freedom of Conscience from Government Discrimination Act, Mississippi House Bill 1523 (2016).

Royals, K. (2015, Jan. 14). Possible gay club prompts change in Miss. School Policy. *USA Today*. Retrieved from https://www.usatoday.com/story/news /nation/2015/01/14/possible-gay-club-prompts-change-in-miss-school-policy /21778565/

Rivers, D. (2012). Queer family stories: Learning from oral histories with lesbian mothers and gay fathers from the pre-Stonewall era. In N. A. Boyd & H. N. R. Ramírez (Eds.), *Bodies of evidence: The practice of queer oral history* (pp. 57–72). New York, NY: Oxford University Press.

Shorey, M. (2019, Mar. 19). 15 things all straight people do that 2/3 of gay people are still afraid to do. *Buzzfeed*. Retrieved from https://www.buzzfeed.com/mjs538/ straight-people-do-this-but-23-of-gay-people-are

Smith, C. (2013, July 24). Board defies citizens, ousts Spruill. *Columbus Dispatch*. Retrieved from https://cdispatch.com/news/article.asp?aid=25777

Somashekher, S. (2014, Sept. 10). Gay rights group, after recent victories, turns to a new frontier: the South. *Washington Post*. Retrieved from https://www.wash ingtonpost.com/politics/gay-rights-group-after-recent-victories-turns-to-a -new-frontier-the-south/2014/09/10/22c72a68-3761-11e4-bdfb-de4104544a37 _story.html?noredirect=on&utm_term=.c1246f7dadc7

Stein, M. (2012). *Rethinking the gay and lesbian movement*. New York, NY: Routledge.

Stolberg, S. G. (2014, Oct. 7). Dealt a victory in court, advocates for gay rights focus on a new frontier. *New York Times*. Retrieved from https://www.nytimes .com/2014/10/08/us/politics/same-sex-marriage-gay-rights-supreme-court .html?_r=0

Thompson, B. (2010). *The un-natural state: Arkansas and the queer south*. Fayetteville, AR: University of Arkansas Press.

US Census. (2010). 2010 Census Data. Retrieved from https://www.census .gov/2010census/data/

US Office of Management and Budget. (2013). Revised delineations of metropolitan statistical areas, micropolitan statistical areas, and combined statistical areas, and guidance on uses of the delineations of these areas. (OMB Bulletin No. 13-01). Retrieved from http://www.whitehouse.gov/sites/default/files/omb/ bulletins/2013/b-13-01.pdf

Visit Mississippi. (2017). Mississippi regions. Retrieved from https://visitmissis sippi.org/contact-us/resources/

Weston, K. (1998). *Long slow burn: Sexuality and social science*. New York, NY: Routledge.

Williams, K. (2014, Sept. 17). The south is not a new frontier: An open letter to the Human Rights Campaign. *Huffington Post*. Retrieved from https://www .huffingtonpost.com/kip-williams/the-south-is-not-a-new-fr_b_5831554.html

PART ONE

CHAPTER ONE

Community

*After Larry and I had been together about a year, we bought match-
ing rings to symbolize our commitment to each other. We decided to
wear the rings on our right hands until we could be legally married.
When we finally were legally married, we switched the rings to our left
hands. One evening, a couple of months after our wedding, Larry and
I went to see a play at the local community theatre. During intermis-
sion, I went into the lobby. Standing there was an older couple that
had known me when I was in high school and when I was heavily
involved in the Catholic Church. I had not seen them in almost thirty
years. They began to ask me the normal questions about what I was
doing these days.*

*The wife noticed my wedding ring and said, "Oh, John, you're mar-
ried now. What is your wife's name?"*

*In the brief moment before I responded, I thought of all of the
following: "I've been wondering when I would get this question. . . .
Didn't they know I am gay? . . . I need to respond honestly, but this
is going to be very awkward. . . . Can I get out of this somehow? . . . I
hate situations like this!"*

*I finally responded, "Well, actually his name is Larry. We were just
married in Maine over the summer."*

*There was a brief pause that felt like several minutes. I watched the
wife's attempt to hide the shock in her face, although I noticed that
her mouth was beginning to open as if she wanted to say something
but nothing would come out. Her husband rescued her and asked a*

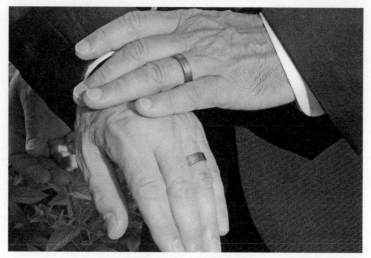

John and Larry's marriage rings.

few questions about whether they knew Larry or not. We stumbled through the niceties, and, anxious to get away from a tense encounter, I made an excuse to make a quick exit back to my seat where Larry was waiting for me.

When I first began recruiting couples to interview for this book, one gay man said to me, "You're not planning to write a book trashing Mississippi, are you?" When I responded that I just wanted to hear about their experiences, he and his partner agreed to meet with me. I received similar questions from other couples. It was not that they wanted me to ignore the discrimination and intolerance they faced as same-sex couples, but they wanted me to share their positive experiences, too. This is because in addition to identifying as gay, most of the couples also identified as members of their small towns and rural communities. The majority of the couples have lived in Mississippi most, if not all, of their lives. Most have roots in their communities, including families, close family friends, and often churches. Their communities, more than a physical location, are also a place they call home, among people with whom they identify as Mississippians.

It is hard to imagine, though, that gay Mississippians would have positive experiences. After all, a majority of LGBTQ people in the United States report that either they or other LGBTQ people they know have experienced offensive language, been harassed, or experienced violence because of their sexual orientation or gender identity. At least 20 percent or more of LGBTQ people say they have been discriminated against when applying for jobs or applying for promotion at their current jobs. Over a quarter of LGBTQ people report that they have not been treated fairly by the police or courts (NPR, 2017). Although some cities and state universities have nondiscrimination policies, as of 2019, Mississippi did not have nondiscrimination laws based on sexual orientation or gender identity for hate crimes, school bullying, housing and employment discrimination, public accommodations, or education (HRC, 2019). After four different transgender women were murdered in Mississippi over the past several years, some state legislators in 2019 pushed to expand Mississippi's hate crimes law to include gender identity and sexual orientation. The proposed legislation never moved out of committee (Harrison, 2019). Consequently, gay and transgender Mississippians have few protections unless already provided federally.

JOB DISCRIMINATION

Alicia and Rae

Alicia and Rae, two black women in their thirties, describe how Alicia lost her job when her boss learned that she and Rae were a couple. They have been together over seven years. They both grew up in Mississippi and have lived here all their lives. When they agreed to let me interview them, they did not feel comfortable having me come to their home, since their children would be there. They asked if they could come to my home and drove from their nearby town.

When they arrived, Larry answered the door and chatted with them a moment until I led them into the living room. Before we began the interview, they asked many questions about my relationship with Larry, including how we met, how long we had been together, and what it was like for us as a couple. I think that meeting in my home and talking about my relationship enabled them to trust me, because they both seemed more relaxed when I began the interview. Alicia and Rae have fun-loving personalities that make it easy to connect with them. Alicia is, according to Rae, "feminine" and talkative. Rae describes herself as "boyish." She is wearing blue jeans and a baseball cap.

"I got fired from being a manager after they found out that we got married," Alicia says.

"It was in the papers," Rae explains.

"They put us in the paper."

"When was this?" I ask.

"2013," Alicia replies. We got married in New Orleans, and we paid someone [who was a photographer at the local newspaper] to take the pictures. We didn't know he was gonna put 'em in the [local] paper and there we were, smack dab like a whole page."

"Yeah, we paid him to take pictures, and he was like, 'It was something different and it was a statement that needed to be made [in the local newspaper]'"

"So he didn't think it would be a problem, but it turns out it was," I say.

"It wasn't a problem for us," Alicia clarifies, "but it ended up being a problem for our jobs."

"So he asked you if he could put them in there?" I ask.

"No!" they both say in unison and laughing, before Rae clarifies for me:

"We didn't know they was in there until somebody called one of her managers."

"A manager called and said, 'I saw you in the newspaper!' I said, 'You saw me in the what?' She said, 'I seen y'all in the paper.' I called Rae. I said, 'Rae, you saw the paper?' She ain't worried, and I'm worried. I'm annoyed now. I'm like, 'Lord have mercy.'"

"And he [the photographer] was like, 'It was a statement that needed to be made, and it was a beautiful moment.' And really, if you didn't know me, you wouldn't know I was the one [in the picture]. You know I'm short haired [and in a suit]. If you didn't know that I was Rae then you wouldn't have known any different [from a straight married couple in the newspaper]. But he was like, 'It was a statement. I enjoyed every moment. It needed to be made.' I said, 'Well, I'm fine.'"

"'Cause he did it for the right reasons," Alicia explains. "It just so happened that I ended up losing my job behind it. But you know, it all worked out."

"And the thing with that is, if the higher up people at her job didn't know who I was, it could have just flowed on by. There's a lot that comes with being with me," Rae says chuckling. "Now the thing is, if I was a more feminine chick, they would've just think we were best friends. But I've been more masculine all my life; even when I was a kid."

"Even when you look back at her young pictures when she was a child, she look like a little boy. She look like she was in the wrong body."

"So Alicia, tell me what happened at your job after the manager saw your wedding picture in the paper" I say.

Alicia sighs before replying, "Before I got fired, they [Alicia's employer] called Rae's boss and got her suspended from her job. Rae would clock out, and she would come to the restaurant, and she would take her lunch break. The cameras [in the restaurant] are always rolling, so you always see anybody that comes in. They called her employer and said that she was there and she wasn't servicing the restaurant. Okay, she's on lunch break. Just as well as everybody else comes here and take they lunch break."

"Well they didn't know that her restaurant wasn't one of mine," Rae explains. "So they thought, 'Well, whatever they got going on and she's in the restaurant. There's no telling what they're doing with the product and the selling but that's not even one of my accounts. I have two accounts in town. That's it. But they didn't know, so they call my job, and I got suspended for a week because they have to do an investigation. They have to make sure that once they call they have to investigate to see well why are you in the restaurant? If you're in the restaurant were you on the clock?' I'm like, 'I didn't do anything wrong so give me my days off. I'm gonna relax.' I'm pissed. I'm angry. I'm upset because when her boss is in the restaurant, I'm coming and paying cash money. I'm using your ATM; I'm buying food. My money is just as green as anybody else. And, of course, my job had to do an investigation and once they learned the gist of everything and once I raised enough hell around there, they realized that there ain't nothing they wanna push. When I came back to work, I said, 'I won't even park my truck up there. I'm gonna take my truck home, and I'll come back in my car, and I'm gonna sit just the same in the place I was sitting. I'm not on work time, I'm not in they vehicle. I'm on my own time. Once they [Alicia's employers] realized they couldn't do anything to me, they fired her."

"One week later," Rae says. "They say they didn't have to give me a reason. Told me, 'Alicia we no longer need your services.' And I'm like, 'What?' And then after I find out that you fired me, you got the girl that you bring to take over my post sitting in her car waiting for me to leave the property."

"I'm sorry you've both been treated this way," I say.

"When it happened," Rae replies referring to Alicia's former employer trying to have Rae fired, "I had so much anger built up inside of me I didn't know what to do with it, because you're messing with my bread and my butter. And I knew I wasn't doing nothing wrong, but I mean with a lot of larger corporations [like the one I work for], they'll lose somebody before they lose a chain account. So I'm like I'm not doing anything wrong; I know I'm good, but it's a chain business. You'll lose one person that you're paying fifty/sixty thousand dollars as opposed to a chain restaurant, a chain business that you making all this money off of. But I let them know, 'If y'all come after me, you better believe I'm coming with everything in my power. I'm gonna sue the hell outta y'all.'"

HARASSMENT

Keith and Mark

I am interviewing Keith and Mark, both Caucasian men in their late forties, the day before their eleventh anniversary as a couple. They have lived in Mississippi for all eleven years and most of their lives, although both also lived out of the state for periods of time. Keith grew up in a small Mississippi village of less than two hundred. After growing up in north Mississippi, Keith moved to Birmingham, Alabama. He moved back to small-town Mississippi in 1999 after losing his job. He lived in a "little house" behind his parents' home in another small community. Mark moved back to Mississippi from New Orleans in 1996 because of a job. He had lived all over the country. They were both in their late thirties when they met.

Keith and Mark now live on the main street of a small town of fewer than five thousand people. They describe how people living near them treat them like any other neighbor; however, disturbingly, they also provide examples of the prejudice and harassment they have experienced.

"It will absolutely surprise you sometimes," Mark says. "When you least expect it, the people you don't even know and run into on the street, strike up a conversation with you. People know who we are, and we don't know who they are."

"How is that?" I ask.

"We're the gay couple that lives here on the main drag."

"Everybody knows that this is the gay house," Keith adds, "but our neighbors treat us just like they do any other neighbor. No different."

"We have laughed so many times over the years that we've lived here, that we wish we could put a big jumbotron out front so they could see just how boring we are." Mark laughs.

One of their neighbors knocked on their door one day after hearing rumors about their house at her beauty shop.

Keith tells the story.

"She said, 'I've got to see your pool.'"

"I said, 'Okay why?'

"And she said, 'Well, we heard that you had naked boy fountains peeing into the pool.'

"And that was the rumor in town that, you know, we built this and we had naked men statues fountaining into our pool and all that kind of stuff, you know. And that's what's been so funny is that people say that. I mean, so we always say, well yeah, we'll just put a jumbotron up and nobody will watch us because it'll be so boring."

They do occasionally spend time with their neighbors, although they have not had their neighbors over for the pool parties they host for gay friends who visit from other towns from time to time.

Keith points to a neighbor's house up a hill. "We'll go up the hill and sit in their backyard. They have a big backyard."

"When you're coming out of the driveway or you walking down the driveway they always stop and have conversations just like you would anyone else," Mark adds. "You wouldn't want to hang out together or anything. And we don't go to each other's houses and have dinner or anything like that but . . ."

Keith jumps in and clarifies the difference between neighbors and friends for them: "Just like you would with any other neighbor. They watch out for us, and we watch out for them. If we see their horses get out, we go call them or put them up, and they do the same for us."

"Occasionally, you hear the teenagers drive up and down the street screaming 'faggot.' One time I was walking the dog—when we lived in the other house—and a truck pulled up and screamed 'die faggot die.'" Mark says.

"But those were relatively isolated. We've had three or four incidences."

"Our other house was . . ."

"Paintballed on Halloween. So far it's been all kids' pranky-type stuff. It's never been more serious than that."

Alicia and Rae

Alicia and Rae both experienced job discrimination. Alicia was fired and Rae was suspended when their marriage was publicized in the local newspaper. Keith and Mark described both positive experiences with the neighbors but also verbal harassment and "pranky-type stuff." I was surprised about how matter-of-fact they were when they discussed their experiences. After stating that she was fired from her job, Alicia said, "But you know, it all worked out," seemingly minimizing her own anger that Rae expressed for both of them. I wondered if both couples had come to the conclusion that that's just the way it is, and that there is not much hope for it to change; an acceptance that they are living in a community with people who tolerate them, but also with people who distrust and may even hate them. Other couples also recounted times when they had been discriminated against, harassed, or rejected due to their sexual orientations. I share some of their stories in the next chapters in which couples described their experiences with religion and their families.

Any minority group, including gays and lesbians, faces oppression and discrimination: the overt examples are harassment and violence such as hate crimes or public figures making antigay remarks. What is not covered in the news and is not apparent to most people, though, is the constant subtle discrimination faced by gays and lesbians. In his book, *Microaggressions in Everyday Life: Race Gender, and Sexual Orientation*, psychologist Derald Wing Sue (2010) defines such microaggressions as "the brief and commonplace daily verbal, behavioral, and environmental indignities, whether intentional or unintentional, that communicate hostile, derogatory, or negative racial, gender, sexual-orientation, and religious slights and insults to the target person or group" (p. 5).

According to Sue (2010), microaggressions are often hard to prove, and the aggressor often has no understanding what has been said or done that is offensive. Consequently, minorities may be left feeling that they are imagining or are overreacting to a microaggression. A college student says to another that an outfit is "gay." Someone says that they don't care what goes on in the privacy of a gay couple's home, but they shouldn't be holding hands in public. A neighbor assumes that I am heterosexual or says, "I never would have guessed you were gay, because you watch sports." I see hundreds of advertisements for Valentine's Day that never show same-sex couples. A woman says to a clerk in a jewelry store that she is buying earrings for her wife, and the clerk gives her a dirty look.

Gays and lesbians never know when something will be said or done that demeans them. The constant barrage of verbal, nonverbal, and environmental slights can affect self-esteem and lead to internalized anger and frustration, especially when people accuse gays and lesbians of being oversensitive or overreacting to a microaggression (Sue, 2010). After a while, gays and lesbians anticipate such occurrences which makes it difficult to relax. They become hypervigilant and build defenses that shield them from the pain or the anticipatory anxiety of what will happen next. Walking around with these defenses up can be exhausting and depressing, like wearing a heavy, burdensome weight.

Rae is never told that she is suspended from her job because she a lesbian. However, if she did not look "boyish" and had been meeting a boyfriend after work hours would her managers have reacted differently? Would they have simply asked her not to go to the restaurant unless she was out of her work uniform or possibly even ignored it? Keith and Mark said that a rumor had circulated around town that they had "naked men statues fountaining into our pool." If they had been a heterosexual couple, would a neighbor come to their door to ask to see the "naked statues" by the pool? In addition to the discrimination and harassment they experienced, both couples are also describing microaggressions, because the aggressors in these examples would likely deny they were treating them differently from their heterosexual neighbors or employees. Do the couples unintentionally downplay the seriousness as a defense to protect themselves from emotional pain and from the anticipatory anxiety of what will happen next?

RACE

In addition to the stress of being a sexual minority, three of the couples, two African American couples and one interracial couple, discussed the stress of being both a racial minority and a sexual minority. I focus on the experience of the gay narrators who identify as black or African American for several reasons. First, all of the narrators who identified as a racial minority were black. One narrator identified as being of Hispanic origin, but he did not respond in depth to my inquiries regarding his experience as a Hispanic gay man. Second, according to the US Census Bureau (2018), African Americans are the largest minority racial and ethnic minority group, comprising about 38 percent of Mississippi's almost three million residents and by some estimates 25.9 percent of same-sex couples (Gates, 2014).

Third, Mississippi has a long history of racial discrimination and violence toward African Americans. In its report on lynching in America, the Equal Justice Initiative (EJI, 2017) reported that "racial terror lynching" of African Americans occurred in Mississippi more than in any other state during the period from 1877 to 1960. EJI stated that "racial terror lynching was a tool used to enforce Jim Crow laws and racial segregation—a tactic for maintaining racial control by victimizing the entire African American community, not merely punishment of an alleged perpetrator for a crime" (Key finding section, para. 3). In addition, Finnegan (1997) argued that lynching was used to maintain "white supremacy" and to maintain the "social, economic, and political constraints that white racism demanded" (p. 215). After the US Supreme Court in 1954 declared segregation of public schools to be unconstitutional (*Brown v. Board of Education*), white businessmen formed the Citizens' Council, with chapters throughout the state, to oppose the civil rights movement in Mississippi by spreading propaganda and retaliating economically against anyone who supported black civil rights. In 1956, the state legislature formed the Mississippi State Sovereignty Commission to "monitor and disrupt civil rights activities across the state" (American Radio Works, 2019, Sovereignty Commission section, para. 1).

In 1961, James Meredith, a black war veteran, was denied admission to Ole Miss (the University of Mississippi) in Oxford. With the help of the NAACP, he successfully fought for admission all the way to the US Supreme Court. Governor Ross Barnett, for whom a reservoir is still named outside of Jackson, threatened to fight against the Supreme Court order to admit Meredith in September 1962. A riot broke out at Ole Miss when federal marshals escorted Meredith onto campus. The violence, which was viewed on national television, led many moderate Mississippi whites to abandon the Citizens' Council; however, while the civil rights movement won victories nationally in the 1964 Civil Rights Act and the 1965 Voting Rights Act, the Ku Klux Klan engaged in racial terrorism against African Americans and white supporters of the civil rights movement through 1968 (American Radio Works, 2019).

When I began second grade in Mississippi in 1973, I attended a desegregated high school, although classes were grouped by test scores, meaning that there were classes with almost all black students and my class had only a few black students in an almost all-white class. Across town, other white students attended the "Academy," one of many private schools formed in small towns across Mississippi in the 1960s and 1970s so that white parents could avoid sending their children to a desegregated school. According to the National Center for Education Statistics, in 2017, of the 615 students at Starkville Academy, 607 were white and 8 were black.

RACE RELATIONS

The black narrators were some of the younger participants, all having been born in the 1980s. Although they did not grow up during the civil rights movement, their parents and grandparents lived during a time of racial terrorism in Mississippi. They have heard the painful stories of their family members. During their lifetimes, there has been progress, although it often feels like "one step forward and two steps behind," as one narrator said. There is still insensitivity and a lack of understanding from many in the state, including some white politicians. For example, Mississippi is the only state to continue to have a state flag with the Confederate Dixie symbol on it, even though the Dixie flag was used by segregationists and is still used by white supremacist groups today. In 2001, a vote to change the state flag failed by a large margin. In 2015 after the massacre of nine black parishioners of a church in Charleston, South Carolina, by a white supremacist who posted a picture of himself online with a Dixie flag, efforts to change the state flag failed in the Mississippi legislature. On the other hand, all of the eight state public universities and many cities throughout the state no longer fly the state flag in protest (Pettus, 2017). In 2017, the Mississippi Civil Rights Museum, funded by the state legislature opened in Jackson. The museum's galleries "show the systematic oppression of black Mississippians and their fight for equality that transformed the state and nation (para 2). A year later, during the 2018 campaign, Mississippi Senator Cindy Hyde-Smith, a white woman, who was running against Representative Mike Espy, a black man, said at a rally about one of her supporters: "If he invited me to a public hanging, I'd be on the front row." Supported by Mississippi Governor Phil Bryant, Hyde-Smith did not appear to understand why her remarks were so offensive in the context of the state's history, saying, "I referred to accepting an invitation to a speaking engagement. In referencing the one who invited me, I used an exaggerated expression of regard, and any attempt to turn this into a negative connotation is ridiculous" (Elliott, 2018).

Alicia and Rae

Alicia and Rae described how they believe they are treated differently by the police because they are black.

Alicia explains what happened when they pulled up to a highway patrol roadblock outside of town on the highway. She believed it was "because of the car that we drive. We got rims. They [the police] assume that it's a drug dealer car. When they pulled us over, he [the policeman] said, 'Where's the dope at?' He pulled Rae out of the car. She was in the back sleeping. You know, I like jewelry. Rae don't like jewelry, but I got Rae carats. When she dress, she dress, and she got carats on her hands.

He [the policeman] said, 'Oh you must got a good job.'

Rae said, 'Yeah, I got a good job, and I'm blessed that I don't have to harass nobody for a check.'"

"They wanna know where the dope is," Rae says incredulously. "I'm so far from being a drug dealer.

"I said, 'Sir, do you think that I would have drove to you if I knew I had drugs in my car?'"

INTERACTION OF RACE
AND SEXUAL ORIENTATION

Sexual minorities who have other minority statuses (e.g., race, ethnicity, gender) may be considered "double" or even "triple minorities." They can face prejudice and stigmatization based on their sexual orientation, race, or both. Rae told me that she believes she has been passed up for promotions, because of her minority status. She explained:

"A lady [at my job] said, 'You need to be training the others, 'cause you work circles around them men you work with.' I said, 'Well, I have to. You know, I can't just go out here and just do whatever. I have to exceed the expectations because number one, I'm a female; number two, I'm black; and number three, oh my gosh, I'm gay.'"

Rae's experiences fit with those of other LGBTQ "people of color" nationwide, who are twice as likely as white LGBTQ people to report discrimination by police and in applying for jobs (NPR, 2017).

Noah and Terrance

Noah and Terrance are both twenty-six years old and both identify as African American men. They have been together almost six years and are engaged to be married. Noah has lived in Mississippi since he was five years old, his family moving here from a neighboring state. Terrance was born in Mississippi, although he moved away with his mother and stepfather as a child, before coming back as an adult to live near his father. Noah and Terrance live in a small house they have rented near the center of their town. Noah and Terrance are enthusiastic and engaging, especially Noah who is the conversationalist of the relationship. I find his energy to be infectious as I ask them how they met. After offering me a cup of coffee in the kitchen, we move into a sitting area where they speak about their experience with racism and the pressure they feel to live two lives.

"What's it like being black and gay in Mississippi," I ask.

"They're one and the same," Noah clarifies. "The reason I say they're one and the same is because they're just a part of who we are. If you look at personality traits or just outside appearances, we're all human. And then they're separated by color; they're by gender, by race, by tattoos or not, by social class, and there's a stereotype to go with all of those. Like, Terrance and I speak very well so we already have that 'You talk white' thing going. And then we have that gay thing as well, which also translates to that talk-white-thing most days as well."

"From whom?" I ask.

"From both sides. From black people and from white people. Some of Terrance's cousins were like, 'Why you talking so white?' [The other day] I had customers in a five-minute span, two different tables. At one table it was a white grandma, a white woman, and her daughter. At the second table I had a white grandma, maybe a middle-aged momma, and then two like-my-age kids. The first table was like:

"'You speak so quickly and white.'

"And I go, 'I'm sorry?'

"And she goes, 'You speak white.'

"And I'm like, 'What does that mean?'

"'You know, like proper. Like I do. You speak white.'

"And I was like, 'Um. I don't think you can actually speak a certain color.'

"So the second table—two tables down—heard the conversation. I'm visibly mad. So the next table goes:

"'You know, I don't think you talk white, I think you talk blue.'

"And everyone's laughing so I went, 'Yeah.'

"And then the grandma goes, 'Um, there's a *Black Black* and a *White Black*. And you're a *White Black*.'

"So by this time I go, 'Lady, do you have any idea how racist that is?' Then I took their plates, and I just walked away. I bolted out of the door. And I go back and get their check out for them, and the two kids my age told their grandma:

"'Hey, why did you say that to him? Like, he's just had to deal with this. Like, you probably should apologize.' So at least she apologizes.

"She goes, 'Oh, I'm sorry for saying *Black Black* and *White Black*. I meant there's *Black Trash* and *White Trash*.'

"So those are like some things that we still deal with today. Mississippi is one of the worst states, because they're so behind; and, so you see more of that in Mississippi in like small conversations with people."

Noah also spoke about his experience as a gay man in the black community.

"There's homophobia in the black gay community itself," Noah says.

"[There's the attitude that] if I can live this lifestyle [on the down low] so can you. Keep your mouth shut. You need to get married and you can do whatever you do on the side."

"Living two lives basically," I observe.

Terrance nods his head, as Noah continues.

"There's a lot of guys that I know that are *dl*," Noah says, referring to "down low," or men in opposite sex relationships, who also have sex with men on the side. "They would not even look at me; not even talk to me, because we were friends when I was in the closet. We were cool; we hung out. But now that I'm out and proud, I would never lie and tell their business because it's not my business, it's theirs. They are lowdown. I don't have to live with that. You know if I did anything I would pull them aside and encourage them to be themselves. And it is tough with me because I just don't understand how being black you grow up and you learn about civil rights, you learn about what people went through just based on the color of their skin. This is told to us as young kids, because we still experience, you know, mass incarceration of blacks in the war on drugs in cities and discrimination today. And these people of color who are gay have the issue with open, proud people. I just don't understand it, and burns me up. It burns me, because I'm a very passionate person."

Jeffrey and Leonard

Jeffrey and Leonard (introduced in the introduction as the "couple in the woods") have lived in Mississippi for over twenty years. Jeffrey grew up in Mississippi and Leonard in Louisiana. They first met at a Christmas party in the 1970s in California. When Jeffrey inherited his mother's home in rural Mississippi, they moved back. They described their experience with racism both among gay people in their area and a family member.

"There are a lot of just incredibly conservative gay couples in Mississippi, who are really on the same line as some of the heterosexual people, who might frighten you because they're *so* conservative in terms of race and politics. Sometimes I have trouble understanding where they're coming from, because I don't understand how you can live our life . . ."

"How can you exchange one prejudice for another?" Leonard interjects.

"So you have run into gay couples who were prejudiced," I ask.

"Oh yeah," Jeffrey responds, "incredibly so . . . rabidly so . . . You know, you just go 'WOW,' did we have any of the same experiences?"

"I don't want my proximity to them to be mistaken as commiserating," Leonard adds.

"And we've never had a black person come to any of the get-togethers around here. Now when I was young I knew black gay couples, and I had black gay friends; but I only had one black boyfriend."

"How is it that you both do not share the prejudices that you've said some others around you have?" I ask.

"I guess because I grew up next door to a black family and played with their little girl," Leonard replies. "She's a childhood friend and her mother was a nurse, who was just a really caring and hardworking person."

"Did Catholicism have much effect on that with you, with your family?" Jeffrey asks Leonard. "Because it did in my situation."

"Yeah, because I was such a Catholic. I was an altar boy, grammar school career . . ."

"I know it definitely did for me. My dad used to say he was a racist as a young man. When he was forty, he was in a terrible car accident and had a terrible brain injury. After that he was not racist at all and became a proponent of civil rights. We had a cross burned out at the end of the driveway in the 1960s."

"So the cure for racism: you knock 'em in the head?" Leonard says as Jeffrey and I laugh.

"Well, I'm sure it is the part of his brain that was affected, but I was maybe six when he had the accident. Anyway, I only knew him pretty much as the person after the accident. He was pro–civil rights, but it all revolved around the Catholic Church and President Kennedy. He just really felt that you had to treat people with respect. I think that really had a big effect on me and my sister, especially. We were the youngest in the family. Then there's my brother who's racist.

He'll use the 'n' word just to tweak you; just to get your reaction. And you'll just say, 'yeah, yeah, yeah, take your hate somewhere else.'"

Just as Jeffrey and Leonard observed, during my time in Mississippi, I have also noticed that black gays and lesbians are not as visible in the larger community as are white gays and lesbians. For example, we rarely, if ever, have a black gay man or lesbian show up to one of the get-togethers in Columbus. Over in Starkville, black professors, professionals, and students often attend the Mississippi State University/Starkville gay professionals group; however, I have never seen a black or interracial gay couple at a get-together. Alicia and Rae have had similar observations:

"It's very segregated [here]," Alicia says. "And I thought when I came [out to events to meet other gays and lesbians with Rae that] everybody just all get together and she was like, 'No, not really. You might see one or two but you don't really see any white people.' Everybody kinda segregated. I'm so glad that my grandmamma raised me [to believe] that a person's a person. I don't care what you do. I didn't have [to say], 'Hey momma, I'm gay,' because we didn't see it. And I don't care whether you're a boy or girl, man, black, Chinese, whatever, you know; we just take you in. It doesn't matter.

The segregation by race at gay social events is actually not surprising when one considers the history of race relations in Mississippi. Although there has been progress, especially in the college towns, we are far from a culture in which everyone is treated equally, regardless of race. Black lesbians and gays may experience pressure within the black community to be heterosexual, but they may also be unsure whether or not they will be accepted into a gay community that is, or appears to be, majority white (Lewin, 2018). In other words black lesbians and gays often experience heterosexism in the black community, and they are often subjected to racism in the white LGBTQ community (Balsam et al, 2014), a product of the racism within the overall white communities (Johnson, 2008). Consequently, they may feel that they have to make a choice between two communities: the

LGBT community and the African American community (Lewin, 2018). Conflicting allegiances can make it difficult to integrate the different identities, thus, for many, the difference between being black and gay versus black or gay.

It is important, however, to recognize that regardless of the race or ethnicity, most lesbians and gays are subjected to heterosexism and homophobia in their communities. Johnson (2008), professor of African American studies and performance studies, noted that there is a popular myth that the black community is less accepting of lesbians and gays than the white community. The narrators in his oral history of black gay men in the South, provided examples that "many black communities around the South, and especially those in rural towns, accommodated sexual dissidence in ways unimaginable" (p. 6). Likewise, the black narrators I met told me stories of both support and rejection from their families and the black community, just as the white narrators did of their families and communities. In fact, Jerry and Karl, a young, white couple introduced later in the chapter spoke of the support they had received from their African American friends:

"You know," Karl says, "the friends that I have who are African American tend to be more open because they know what it's like to be discriminated against. It's just that theirs is because of their color; where ours may be sexual orientation. I don't think that we as gays are going through the same things they went through, but it is still a degree because you're saying that you have a group of people who are less than."

Tolerance

Although most couples described both positive and negative experiences living in their communities, the majority of the couples did not describe communities that necessarily accepted them as a couple but described communities that *tolerated* them as a gay couple. In gay and lesbian identity development models (e.g., Cass, 1979; Marszalek, Cashwell, Dunn, & Heard, 2004; Marszalek & Pope, 2008), models that explain the developmental process of people becoming aware that they might be lesbian or gay, tolerating the idea that they are lesbian/gay, and moving to a place of full acceptance of a lesbian/gay identity, there is a difference between tolerance and acceptance. Tolerance is acknowledging that one is different from the majority, but not accepting it, in fact, often viewing oneself as "less than." Acceptance, on the hand, is acknowledging that one is different from the majority and also recognizing that one's differences do not make one any less worthwhile.

According to these identity development models, one must first become aware that one is different from others. Lesbian and gay adolescents, for example, may move from a place of denial to a place in which they realize that they are different in some way from other adolescents, but they are not sure how. Cass (1979), a clinical psychologist, described this process as one in which people move from a stage of confusion about their sexual orientation to a stage of comparison, in which they begin to realize that they are different, in some way, from others. When they reach a stage of tolerance, they acknowledge the idea that they *might* be lesbian or gay. I believe this process of moving from confusion to comparison to tolerance to acceptance also applies to society, including Mississippi towns. Referring to 1950s Mississippi, Howard (1999) wrote:

> Around deviant sexuality, a quiet accommodation was the norm. Whether they believed homosexuality to be an immutable state of being for certain individuals ... or a set of behaviors deemed sinful but forgivable, most ordinary Mississippians overlooked expressions of queer sexuality all around them. Of sexual deviance, they were not "ignorant" in the traditional sense of the word. They were aware, but rather "chose to ignore." ... For their part in the social compact, queer Mississippians maintained low profiles. (p. 142)

Twenty-first-century Mississippi is obviously different from 1950s Mississippi. First, the state has been forced to change as the nation has changed. The US Supreme Court overturned the state sodomy law in 2003 (*Lawrence v. Texas*), meaning that it is no longer illegal for same-sex couples to have sex, and in 2015, ruled that same-sex couples have a federal right to marry (*Obergefell v. Hodges*). Nevertheless, as I described in more detail in the introduction, Mississippi is one of the most conservative states, has few resources for LGBT people, and has a law in effect, HB 1523 (Protecting Freedom of Conscience from Government Discrimination Act, 2016), allowing state officials to refuse to perform same-sex marriages and businesses to refuse to serve same-sex couples if they have religious objections to same-sex marriage. Although Mississippi is required by the US Supreme Court to legally recognize same-sex marriage, HB 1523 defines marriage as between one man and one woman. Same-sex couples live among family and neighbors who voted for the state legislators who passed this bill and a governor who signed the bill into law. Unless they live in the state capital or one of few towns that has a nondiscrimination ordinance banning discrimination based on sexual orientation, they have no legal protection from being terminated at their jobs for simply being open about their relationships.

Second, it is virtually impossible for today's Mississippians to not, at least, be aware of the fact that there are people who not only have homosexual sex but also identify as gay. There are gay characters and celebrities in movies and in television shows. Other states have elected openly gay people to the US Congress. Even in small-town Mississippi, gay issues make the local news. In January 2015, for example, Brandon High School made the news when the schoolboard changed its policy on student groups to make it more difficult for students to create a gay-straight alliance group (Royals, 2015). In 2015 the Starkville Board of Aldermen voted to repeal a domestic partnership and nondiscrimination policy based on sexual orientation (Ganucheau, 2015).

Despite the progress in federal laws and visibility, the narrators I interviewed provided evidence of the "social compact" described by Howard (1999) still, in many cases, being intact. I believe this unspoken societal compact of today is a variation of the following, depending on the community and individuals involved: We [the community] will tolerate you [lesbian and gay people] if don't act too *queer* and if you don't ask us to talk about *it*. "Queer" means everything from public displays of affection between a same-sex couple to someone who is considered too flamboyant to someone who does not meet the societal gender expression norms (e.g., a masculine woman or a feminine man). "It" means any type of discussion on same-sex issues, including but not limited to marriage, civil rights, HIV/AIDS and other health issues, and sex. Breaking this compact can lead to discrimination, harassment, and/or rejection.

Of course, in stating this compact, along with the repercussions of breaking the compact, I am making a broad generalization. In the upcoming chapters on family and religion there are examples of family, community, and church members providing loving support to same-sex couples. However, the theme of this "social compact," this "conspiracy of silence" arose over and over in the narrators' stories.

SOCIAL COMPACT

Jeffrey and Leonard

As with many other couples I interviewed, Jeffrey and Leonard, (introduced in the introduction as the "couple in the woods") do not describe living in a place that is necessary hostile to gays and lesbians; in fact, they speak of a small town nearby that elected a gay mayor and that has two lesbians running a popular diner. They spoke of the dinners they have at their home for other gay people living in the area and a neighbor who came to them when she learned her son was gay.

"Well," Leonard begins, "I think it's kind of thinly veiled here, but there is a tolerance. When we were first here, our mayor was gay, and it kind of fertilized the pasture."

"It was *so* gay mecca for a long time that it was a little frightening," Jeffrey adds.

"We were talking about this last night." Leonard says. "For about two months now, it's the first time in literally years that there was not someone reenacting historical events and things in drag in a photograph in our newspaper . . ."

"We had this one very lovely character; *he's* a character. I knew him all my young life growing up, but he came out in later life. He dressed as a female in Civil War costumes, Halloween, whatever. We also have a popular restaurant run by a gay couple—two women. They're fun. It was just very out there, you know. A lot of little parties all the time. The community really got together. They tried to start like a little supper club which, you know, just didn't work out but . . ."

" . . . they saw gay people having a good time, so they kind of climbed on board," Leonard says completing his sentence.

"And the community really accepted a lot of it. Now it seems to be cooling a little bit."

"What's been the cause of that?" I ask.

"Don't know . . ."

"Well the political tide changed," Leonard suggests.

"Yeah, the mayor resigned."

"And some of the ancillary people, like the beautification committee, changed personalities."

"I think Katrina really sparked a lot of it," Jeffrey says, referencing the gay evacuees from New Orleans during and after Hurricane Katrina who stayed in the area.

"The bringing up the awareness [that there are gay people around]."

"So you're saying that you had several gay people who were involved with the city government and different committees in town?"

"Oh, yeah," they say in unison.

"I think one of you said as we were walking into your house that I should do a study on this town?"

"Yeah," Jeffrey says, "my sister was saying that to us. I was surprised when she said that; but I've often wondered over the years, because there were so *many* people from here who turned out to be gay that we grew up with. It's just crazy!"

"So these aren't people that necessarily just moved here. You're talking about people who grew up in this area and stayed."

"Yes. Well, not all stayed, but there are a *lot* of gay folks from this area."

"Did you ever see that movie *It's in the Water*?" I ask referring to the 1997 satire about a Texas town panicking when a resident says that the water made him gay.

"Well that's our joke here. There's something in the water, 'cause people will come here—friends of ours who come to visit—and when they start meeting all the other gay folks that we know around here, they're like, 'God, it's just something in the water around here!'"

"I think overall," Jeffrey continues, the straight community has been *very* accepting over the last number of years, but I always view it with a little caution because I know the people here. We know that there can be some interesting backlashes. Some you never understand."

"What kind of things have you heard about," I ask.

"I've heard of kind of shunning people."

"Their own family members?"

"Yes, and the term that I used was *shunning,* which is getting back to, you know, the *Mayflower.*"

"Puritanical?"

"Yeah, but you know it's a heavily Southern Baptist area. If gay people get too involved in politics around here, there's usually something that's gonna happen. There's gonna be someone to speak out eventually, you know. It just depends on the situation if it's tolerated, or they find out pretty quickly that it's not gonna be tolerated."

"What was the reaction to the gay mayor?"

"Overall, quite good in the town. Now in the periphery out where we live, you would hear comments and things."

"He brought a huge physical appearance impact on the town," Leonard adds. "You may have noticed all of the landscaping in town? That wasn't there before he came."

"He landscaped the whole town," Jeffrey says chuckling.

"He bought up a lot of real estate and . . ."

" . . . he garnered a lot of respect, because he saved the town. The town was truly, truly dying."

Sophie and Faith

Sophie and Faith, two Caucasian women in their early sixties, first became a couple over fifteen years ago. They live on an expansive property with several ponds, a barn, and trails in the woods ten miles south of the nearest town. On the day I met them, they have invited two other lesbian couples and me to lunch. I exit off the four-lane highway onto a two-lane state road. There are houses and trailers sprinkled on hilltops on either side of the road leading away from town. I'm watching for the red mailbox they said I would see on the right-hand side of the road after passing a farm. I turn on a gravel path just past the mailbox, wind through woods, past a barn, a pond, and up a hill. I notice out of the corner of my eye that a dog is running alongside my car, accompanying me to their home. I slow to a crawl afraid that I will hit it. At the top of the hill, I see six women sitting on a deck attached to, what looks like, a ranch-style house with vinyl siding. I park my car in front of another small barn and walk up to the women. They all stand as I walk up the steps to the deck, introducing themselves to me. Sophie suggests we go inside and have lunch before I interview them. We enjoy, what turns out to be a full dinner of chicken spaghetti, salad, rolls, and iced tea. A large pound cake, fresh out of the oven, is sitting on the counter for dessert. The women tell me that are like family to each other and have regular Sunday afternoon dinners. After lunch, the other women go back outside to enjoy the beautiful spring weather on the deck, while I talk to Sophie and Faith alone.

Sophie and Faith describe how they choose to live in two separate worlds: one where they only socialize with other same-sex couples and one where they keep their relationship private. They describe a culture in which people are "two-faced," seemingly accepting you as gay in person but actually speaking disparagingly about you to others in the community.

"We don't really do things with like straight people or couples," Faith begins.

"That's probably because of me, because I just . . . ," Sophie pauses and gathers her thoughts. "The weekend is our weekend, and I just want us to be the way we are."

"Yeah, I don't have that need to run around with straight people. Some people have a need to because they couldn't feel accepted, or they need to be accepted by straight people. I have never had that problem. I personally don't have that need."

"I guess I just . . . I just want to be who I am, but I can't do it in front of straight people, because I guess I'm fearful that they'll all of a sudden just cut you off."

"I think my job is my big hold back."

"I'm pretty sure they all know," Sophie says referring to her employers. "They have got to know, but it's not something I wanna talk about with 'em. I don't care for 'em to want to talk to me about it."

"So it seems to be comfortable if they know, but it's almost like: 'We're not gonna talk about it, you're not gonna talk about it, and that's comfortable for all of us,'" I speculate.

"Right," Sophie replies nodding her head. "And I'm okay with that."

"And, you know, that's okay with me," Faith agrees.

"And it seems like if I were to switch jobs, then you've got to hear the questions. And I'm at a point in my life I don't want to answer questions."

"Did you go through that before, people asking a lot of questions?" I ask.

"Yes. And you know, you have to lie. There are times I've had to lie about different questions. Back when we were in our twenties and thirties, it was different then. [People would ask], 'Are you dating anybody now?' Of course, they're talking about straight ones. So you lie about it," Sophie says chuckling before asking Faith, "Did you have questions like that?"

"Oh yeah, when I was getting flowers from women, and you were one of 'em. I had to lie about that or grab the card before anybody saw it."

"I mean, it's uncomfortable sometimes, because they don't understand. We're in Mississippi; they'd get rid of ya just as quick as they can hire ya. It's sad."

"It is. It's easier for most of our friends, because they're all retired. It makes a big difference."

"Maybe we'll be that way when we retire. I don't know."

"Yeah, I don't know," Faith repeats.

I ask them about the ways they believe the community would not support them if they were open about their relationship.

"I think they're two-faced." Sophie says as Faith nods. "I mean, they say they support gay marriage or being gay, but at the same, they don't. And I think they're just two-faced, especially your wealthy and the socialites. And I don't think that I'm being paranoid, but just the other day when we were in the store and that lady—I didn't know who it was that you spoke with," Sophie says to Faith. "I could tell that she knew that we were together. I could tell by the way she was looking at me."

"She was sizing you up," Faith says.

"She was sizing me up, and it was just uncomfortable. It's just like, 'Why don't you just come out and ask?' I mean I probably look but . . ."

"No, they've probably always known that I was gay and never seen who I was with, because she worked [with me]."

"But I mean, I was very uncomfortable, because she just kept staring at me."

"That was odd; you're right about that," Faith agrees.

"So I think that's pretty much, they're just two-faced."

"Well, right. That's my opinion: that there's a lot people who think that they support us and they're for us but they don't. It's like Sophie said, they're two-faced."

"But you know how they think, 'Well, okay, Sophie's a good person.' She can't be that way,"

"I don't trust 'em. They're players, and they'll play you for what they can get out of you. And then at their tea party, they're talking about you being a lesbian or gay. Because I hear 'em, you know, just sitting up there talking about people you know. I know that they're looking down; they're making fun and talking about 'em; when they showed up they were polite and like, 'Oh, you're accepted.' You know what I'm talking about. And I know how they are. I ain't doing it." Faith says adamantly.

"And I guess that's maybe why we pretty much just stay away."

Marty and Sam

Sam and Marty were both born in and have always lived in Mississippi. In their late fifties, they have been together over half their lives—thirty years. Sam and Marty live in a place they described as "the middle of nowhere." To get to their house, I exit off the highway onto a narrow two-lane road that leads into a small town of around four thousand people. Although I had driven the highway many times over the years on the way to the coast, I had never strayed further from it than stopping at a gas station within sight of the exit. With the bustle of the highway and the liveliness of the coast, it's easy to forget that there are quaint little communities along the way unless you actually drive beyond the fast food restaurants and gas stations adorning the highway like tacky jewelry on a long, lanky body. I drive over a small hill just beyond the exit, and it's almost like the highway doesn't exist. I continue through countryside past an occasional trailer before a green marker at the top of a hill welcomes me to the small town. Sam and Marty live in an unincorporated community a few miles from the town, a cluster of houses around a four-way stop in the road that leads into downtown. I interviewed them before *Obergefell v. Hodges*.

Marty and Sam offer an example of the unspoken contract that Howard (1999) in *Men Like That* described with queer people and the community. They feel uncomfortable with being too "out there." Similar to Sophie and Faith, they also describe a fake acceptance, in which *tolerance* means accepting you to your face but rejecting you behind your back.

"In what ways would you say you've received support for your relationship in the community?" I ask them.

"We've been together so long," Marty responds, "that . . . even straight people who normally might find it bothersome . . . we didn't flaunt it, and I think they thought, 'Oh well, they may be gay but at least they're making that house look better than it did'; and, so they give you more leeway. I think maybe it educated some people along the way that [say], 'Well, they're not really flamboyant. They stay to themselves pretty much. They work on the house and maybe they're not as bad as they're portrayed all the time'"

"We don't have the flag outside, you know," Sam says referring to a rainbow flag. "I mean, we have all different types of friends. We have every economic group, every political group. It just really doesn't matter. What we do in the bedroom or what we do in this house is nobody's business."

"I'm sure there's some people that smile in our face, but probably talk about us behind our back. But at my age I could care less. I mean even if they do at this point, you reach a point in life where we don't have to be worried about if we're gonna lose our jobs or be comfortable enough financially. It's like, 'Okay if you don't like me it's not the end of the world.'"

"We do know some people that will, you know, smile in our face, and we do know that they talk about us. But, I could care less," Sam says echoing Marty.

"How do you know?" I ask.

"Because it comes back to us," Sam responds.

"Especially if you're in a small community," Marty adds.

"We're talking about Sue."

"What kind of stuff has she said?"

"An instance was last year," Marty responds. "I did an art festival here. I just was doing it to have another activity in the town, and to show the historical part of it."

"They had parades and all that stuff," Sam adds.

Marty continues, "I was president of the Chamber of Commerce, so everybody in town basically knows me. Anyway, she decided to sort of help encourage a rumor around town that this parade was going to be like in New Orleans, and there were going to be naked men shaking their dicks at people; and I was bringing drag queens in and all this. I'm going, 'I don't mind what you say about me, but I do mind when you're hurting something, you know. That upsets me.' And that's the only time really that, what Sam used to call my *queerness,* came out. 'Cause I sent a word back to her, that if it didn't stop, I was going to personally pay somebody to come open a florist to run her out of business. She's a florist, So, I was gonna be her major competitor just for the spite of it!"

"You told somebody you knew that would get it back to her?" I ask.

"Yeah, and it did. It got back to her. And it stopped. If I had to bankrupt myself I would sell roses for a penny a piece. And it was like, 'Leave me alone! I don't mind you picking on me, but don't pick on something I'm trying to do.' I had invested a lot of money to do this, and it was a big deal for the town. Had it not worked out or people became really scared, I would have lost many thousands of dollars."

"In the end, did it work out okay?" I ask.

"Yeah. Turned out really good, but people . . . you know . . . a few asked me about [the rumors], and I said, 'Oh come on, you know me; I would never do anything to hurt young children or throw something in people's face. You know I wouldn't do that. I don't know why you even thought to listen to something like that.'"

Doug and Harry

Doug and Harry, two white men in their seventies, have been together over forty years and live in one of Mississippi's college towns. College towns tend to be more progressive compared to other areas of the state, although, as I mentioned in the introduction, they would likely be considered slightly to the right of moderate in an area of the northeast such as New York. It's been a while since I have visited this town, so I take some time to explore the area and the university before heading to their house on the outskirts of town. I remember from our earlier phone conversation that Harry is retired professor from the nearby university, and Doug works part-time at a department store. They have been in Mississippi since they first met in their mid-twenties.

Doug and Harry describe tolerance as being a two-way street: not only do people tolerate them as a gay couple, but they also tolerate people who do not fully accept them. I ask them about their experience as a couple in their town.

"We've never been firebombed or had a cross burned in our yard," Doug responds sarcastically.

"And you say that, and it's interesting, because about twenty years ago when we were looking for a house, I remember telling the realtor, 'Ben, you know we are a gay couple, and I really don't feel comfortable being at the end of a road somewhere that is a little too obscure and a little too out-of-sight.' I think you have to be smart enough to keep your eyes open and be aware where you are. He was shocked by that. He had never even thought of that. But

I think you have to think in those terms and that visibility can be good in terms of security."

"Would you feel that way now if we were just moving here?" Doug asks Harry.

"If we were just moving here, I don't know. I think times have changed dramatically over the years and whether we are a little more naïve; I mean, naïve in the fact that you feel comfortable in the space you're in; and, therefore you're not aware. But, it's interesting that you do feel accepted and that some of the feedback you get is interesting."

"Doug talked earlier about having a social circle that you feel welcome in. So you two have a lot of heterosexual friends in the community."

"Compared to the number of gays?" Harry responds. "Yeah, but we are smart enough to know that some of our friends tolerate us."

"You mean some of your straight friends tolerate you."

"Right, I mean they're real nice to us, but we know that they ... you know ..."

"You mean tolerate in terms of being gay."

The both nod as Harry says, "It's like our regular Friday night cocktail group which is all straight except for us. There are two or three of the spouses in that group that are just real 'Bubba Rednecks'; however, over the years some of the ones that we really didn't know have just evolved into really sweet, nice, close friends. There are others that you just.... Well, you like their wife, but you just know that if they could have a good reason not to come that night they would. And, sometimes they don't ... and that's okay."

"And they know their wives are in good hands, you know?" Doug adds.

"Does that make you uncomfortable?" I ask. "Like, if you're having a party at your house, and you have some people there that you know *tolerate* you?"

"No ... no ...," Harry replies, "it doesn't bother me at all. My philosophy is that if they put themselves out to come to our house, than it's their problem, not mine."

"We tolerate people, too." Doug says.

"So knowing that some people do not fully accept you does not affect the support you feel from your social circle?"

"Oh heavens.... No." Doug replies.

"I don't really feel that way," Harry says. "I don't really feel that that has been an issue, and I think the reason it has not been an issue is that we put ourselves out front in terms of service to the community and didn't wait to be asked to do things. I mean, I could understand how that could be the case. Somebody could move to town and feel like I don't know any gay people; I can't really get involved and whatever. But my philosophy's always been that you're gay all the time, but part of what makes you gay from the outsider's point of view is what you do with sex. And, sex is such a small, minute part of a twenty-four-hour day/seven-day week. So get over it!"

Jerry and Karl

Jerry and Karl are both thirty-two years old and both identify as Caucasian men. They have been together eight years and have always lived in Mississippi as a couple. They both grew up in south Mississippi and have family living in the area.

When I park in the driveway of their home, I notice that they have collegiate sports lawn flags for the Ole Miss Rebels and the Southern Mississippi Golden Eagles next to the sidewalk that leads from the driveway to the front door. I jokingly ask them if a Mississippi State Bulldog is welcome in this house. They laugh and immediately launch into a story about how most of their friends are fans for other schools and about how they cheer for each other's teams except when they play each other. In a small state like Mississippi with three large universities sporting Division I football teams, it's inevitable that fans of the three schools will marry, become friends, and be neighbors.

We sit at their dining table where they have laid out pictures from their wedding. A dog that appears to be about the size of a

Jerry and Karl's marriage ceremony in an Episcopal church in Vermont.

small pony comes over and introduces himself to me with a lick of my hand. I have a nice view of their well-maintained backyard and deck through a large sliding glass door.

Jerry and Karl believe that people respect them in their community, because they aren't the "typical gay person." In other words, they believe they do not fit the image held by many small-town and rural Mississippians of the stereotypical gay person who lives in a large metropolitan area, is promiscuous, flamboyant, and "in your face." Their description of fitting in and also pushing the envelope when challenged is yet another example of the unspoken social contract of tolerance of those who do not "rock the boat" too much.

"I think we've been respected more," Karl explains, "because people don't see us as Karl and Jerry, the gays. I'll give you a prime example. Our neighbors across the street are in their seventies. They both are Sunday school teachers at the most conservative Baptist church in town but he even told me one time, 'I used to would have said you were going to hell but after knowing you, I can't say that.' You know, I think even people in our church have said that. Because I'm not knocking the people that do it, but we don't parade in. We didn't come into the church waving a rainbow flag, you know. We don't come in with glitter. I think people see us as just a committed couple. Some people would say, 'Well that's because you've lived your life in a closet.' No, even when I was by myself, it hadn't been shoved down people's throat. Even the things that Jerry and I do as a hobby are not what your typical gay person would enjoy; you know, any kind of sporting event. And I think people have respected us because it's not been pushed in their face."

"But we're not in the closet either," Jerry adds.

"I mean look at my car tag," Karl says with a laugh.

I remember seeing the bumper sticker on one of the cars in the driveway: a sold blue square with a yellow equal sign. I know that it represents the Human Rights Campaign (HRC), the well-known lesbian, gay, bisexual, and transgender political lobby and advocacy group.

I reply, "Human Rights Campaign. I saw that. That's how I knew I was at the right house," I say mischievously.

Jerry and Karl laugh.

"I told Karl that's how you would know! But, yeah, people seem to treat us pretty normally. When we moved in, we heard that the girl who we bought the house from told a couple of neighbors, 'Oh this sweet little gay couple is moving in.'"

"Sweet little gay couple," I repeat.

"Yeah, so they knew before we even came, but I don't think anybody even says, 'Well, that's where the gay couple lives'"

Bob and Matthew

Bob and Matthew, two Caucasian men, live in a neighborhood in Jackson tucked away from the sprawl along the interstate. They are one of the younger couples I speak with, having met in their twenties some nine years ago. They both greet me at the front door of their split-level house built in the 1970s. Walking into their house is like stepping back forty or so years in time. All of the furniture and décor is mid-century modern, as if stepping onto the set of the old television show *I Love Lucy*. Bob and Matthew enthusiastically show me around the house, telling stories of where they found various pieces of art and furniture, before telling me how they are careful who they are "out" to, because they are not sure how someone may react.

"In the circles that Matthew and I both work in," Bob says, "we have our coworkers and the people that we deal with who are pretty much higher-income, upper-middle-class, good Junior Leaguers. And you never quite know what's acceptable, what's not acceptable, what's gonna make someone else uncomfortable, because they're so concerned about what's proper; what a proper southern gentleman is and does and says. We both run into it at work, and we both run into it socially and it's awkward sometimes."

"When you say you run into it, you're talking about not knowing if it's going to be acceptable for you to be gay?" I ask.

"Right," Bob responds. "Like, I don't discuss being gay at work. My coworkers know and everybody's fine with it amongst my coworkers, but I don't discuss it with our clients. It's just not talked about, because I don't know what the perception is. I get myself into this bubble—where I'm like, 'Oh, everybody loves gay people, everybody's fine, we're just people like everybody else'—and then every once in a while we get that culture shock of someone or something that just brings you back."

"Can you give me an example?" I ask.

"Yeah," Matthew responds, "we were just coming back from a trip, and we were going to eat pizza that night in Belhaven. We had been in Washington, DC, where men were holding hands with each other, and it was a lot more open. We saw gay couples out together everywhere."

"We were there for a gay wedding," Bob adds.

"Yeah, we were there for a gay wedding, and we were feeling very good. We had been on cloud nine with all the gay experiences; then we come back and we're sitting there and this redneck, college student made a comment about a 'queer movie' or something."

"Was he directing his comments at you?"

"No," they both say in unison.

"We overheard a conversation," Bob says.

"And then he got into talking about sex, and that he would bash the head of a woman or of a man if he found out she was a man."

"He was talking about a transgender person." Bob adds.

" ... transgender ... He said, 'I would just bash the hell out of that person, you know?' And they were college kids, and I was thinking, 'We have just gone back, again ... '"

"Another kind of closer to home example," Bob says. "We have one of our really good friends that we hang out at her house all the time, and she has lots of gay friends. Well, her sister lives a block away from her house and her sister's married but she has this guy on the side ..."

"A fuck buddy." Matthew says.

"Yeah ... for lack of a better word, I guess. Anyway, the sister and her husband have an open relationship, so it's a strange dynamic. It's very foreign to us, but when we drove up one day the 'fuck buddy' referred to Matthew's Nissan Cube as our 'Fagmobile.'"

"Talking about us ... !" Matthew says angrily. "Your earlier question was how do we feel normal compared to other couples. Well, they are a heterosexual couple, and she has him on the side. She has two kids. One kid is bald-headed, because she eats her hair constantly."

"It's an anxiety disorder." Bob says.

"And so, this is a heterosexual couple who are just totally messed up ..."

"They have swinger parties at their house ..."

" ... parties and all types of things so, our relationship seems ten million times normal compared to theirs, you know. It's just a bad situation. 'Fagmobile,'" Matthew repeats angrily. "He won't stay close to us. He's always getting up and turning his butt the other direction when he walks out and makes comments."

"He's turning his butt the other direction?" I ask with a perplexed look on my face.

"No, he's trying to go away so we're not looking at it."

"Oh give me a break," I say incredulously.

"I know . . ."

"It's just things like that that make you more aware that sometimes I just live in this little bubble where I just have it in my head that everything's fine. So, I have to kind of filter myself sometimes, because I don't know. . . . Not that I'm completely concerned with making someone else uncomfortable, but just the fact that I don't want to create drama," Bob says.

"And I don't think I have rainbows shooting out of my ass, because I'm not . . . I'm very masculine, you know." Matthew exclaims. "You know, I was in a store with one of my friends, a girl friend, and this guy behind us kept watching me; kept looking at her. We were just talking and stuff, and then I heard him make a comment and he said, 'Oh, that's his fag hag right there. I just figured it out.'"

"I was like what the hell?" Matthew continues. "She was from Michigan. She had never been friends with a gay person before. So here she comes down to Mississippi and one of her first experiences being friends with me was being called a 'fag hag.'"

"People can be so cruel," I say understandingly.

"I know. She said, 'Yep I am!' with pride."

Drew and Neal

Drew and Neal live in a gated community in the suburbs of Jackson. Jackson is probably the only city in the state that is large enough to have suburbs. As in many other US cities, over the years the population of the suburbs has increased while the population of Jackson, the core of the metropolitan area, has declined. As I drive past the same chain restaurants and stores I remember seeing in the suburbs of New Orleans, I think to myself that this community could be anywhere in the United States.

Drew and Neal, two white men, are in their late forties and have lived in Mississippi all their lives, although they moved to the suburbs after they met. They have been together as a couple over twenty years. They tell me about how a neighbor retaliated against them when Neal was elected president of the neighborhood property association before they were legally married. Similar to what other couples have described, they believe they have been accepted by most neighbors, though, because they are not "flamboyant."

"I ran for and was elected president for two terms," Neal explains. "Being the kind of outgoing, gregarious person that I was, everybody knew me, and they trusted our motives and our sense of esprit décor. And then immediately, a backbiting came in the form of this homeowner who started slurring me. She was *not* chosen to be president, and in vitriol for not being voted in as president, she began to slander me as a 'faggot' and 'keep him away from your children,' and 'he's not even owner of that house.' She'd gone to the county property office and found that Drew's name was on it [the deed], and she was saying, 'He's not even a homeowner. He can't be on the board.'"

"And the homeowner issue was communicated to the neighbors through a letter that she reproduced and sent to all of them," Drew adds. "She sent it to us too."

"As if . . . as if, 'you are on notice.'"

"That must have been a shock," I say.

"No, it wasn't a *shock*," Neal responds. "It was *ugly*. But, nowhere in the documents—because I had read all of the covenants and bylaws—nowhere in there does it say that you have to be a homeowner to be voted in and represented. So, she was just being ugly and petty and, you know, I was elected again as president the next year, because we were doing a great job."

"That must have been satisfying," I say.

"This was really upsetting Neal," Drew says. "Now I would rather have my eyes gouged out than to sit through a homeowners' association meeting! I absolutely hate that stuff and want nothing to do with it ever, but Neal was doing a great job at it. So, we just simply, re-deeded the house in both names and that solved the issue; and it allowed him to kind of take the high road and say, 'You know, as a matter of fact, I am the owner of the house, so back off.'"

"I went to her house," Neal explains. "I said, 'We will expect you to go check the records and bring a copy of it if you choose to challenge me.'"

"You knocked on her door?"

"Yeah."

"How did she react?"

"Ugly. Like, 'You may have me this time but ...'"

"Well, what's funny about it is that she's still pretty snotty to Neal, but she is friendly toward me in the neighborhood. If I'd see her walking the dogs or something, I'll nod 'hello,' but that's about it."

"Okay," I say switching gears, "Any positive support for you two in your community?"

"I think lack of negative is the best positive," Neal replies. "I think that we've lived in the neighborhood longer than everybody but two people who still live there. And people have chosen to move into our community and be nice, and that's wonderful; to be part of the patriarchs of our neighborhood, and to be thought of as nice neighbors, and to have people call and say, 'I've cooked a big mess of red beans and rice. Would you like some?' I think our community in our neighborhood has been the best support."

"The neighborhood is primarily single people and older people. The older people tend to be widowed or widowers and...."

"I'm seen as the neighborhood handyman."

"Neal is the guy that all the little old ladies call to come help them change a light bulb or fix a lock or something like that. And, you know, it's that sort of thing. We want to be a good impression for them, and I think we do provide a good role model. If straight people, who are a little skittish about homosexuality, who don't know any gay people, or have never been around them ... I think they have in their head the idea that every gay person is a flaming drag queen, and we're pretty far away from that image, I think.

"We don't fly the rainbow flag, and we don't have pink no-show socks," Neal says. "You know, we don't wear the 'uniform.' I mean, that's not really our generation to do that, and I think it's comforting for someone to realize that you don't have to be that caricature to be a gay person. And, you know, we're not offensive in that alien sort of a way . . . that some people think, 'Oh, I thought that's what gay people were.'"

"Yeah, I think it's interesting that when I was in college most of the gay people I knew were pretty flamboyant, pretty loud. And, that was fine, but I couldn't really identify with that. And, it was only after being out of college for a year or two and living in Jackson, and my first boss here was gay, and he was a good role model for me. He was just this hard-working guy who had been successful in his career, and was, no doubt about it, very gay. But, he wasn't that flamboyant image that I didn't feel comfortable with. He was just very average, and when I met Neal what immediately drew me to Neal—other than a physical attraction—was that he was very intelligent; and he seemed to be that normal person who was just . . . You know, he worked, he went to school, he did these things, and I think that's just who he is."

Neal reaches out and grabs Drew's hand before saying, "I can do this, and he doesn't recoil. This is . . . we are not this kind of people."

"What does that mean?" I ask.

"Physically demonstrative, you know, outside the home. I'm doing this just to model it. But, there are some couples that one of the partners would like pull back, but we're not that way; although I mean I had to make myself use that as a model. It showed me that Drew was completely comfortable with that because he would trust . . ."

"Pulling back in public, you're saying . . ."

"Yeah, and that's something that I find very comfortable and comforting about Drew: he trusts that I'm not going to do something that would make him uncomfortable, although I pushed a limit in that I normally wouldn't do that. I trusted how he was going to respond, and I think it's that level of intimacy that gives comfort."

"So, there's a comfort in the relationship that you can just be yourself. Is that what you're saying?"

"Yes."

"So you each have much different stories in terms of coming-out experiences," I note. "I wondered if, as a couple, if you think that you're more out as a function of being part of a couple than you would be if you were single?"

"As a couple," Drew says, "because we've lived so long in our neighborhood together, it's probably easier for somebody to identify us as being gay; whereas, if either of us were living there alone, we wouldn't necessarily . . . they wouldn't necessarily have any reason to believe that. You know, when we talk about being out, I don't think that there's really much that either of us do in the way we live our lives or the way we act or dress. I'm certainly not political in any way. Neal is more than I am, but I don't know that anyone would necessarily know that we're gay without us telling them."

"How do you introduce yourselves as a couple?"

"This is Drew," Neal says laughing.

"Honestly, I don't know that I've ever . . ." Drew pauses before remembering, "for a period of time I was working for a company that was very open to that sort of thing. They had domestic partner benefits with our insurance and that sort of, so in those situations . . ."

"It was a paperwork openness . . . it was not . . ."

"Yeah, but for instance, if we were at a work function, a party or something like that, I would introduce you as my partner, Neal."

"But—like in the neighborhood—it usually is more of a natural thing; people just kind of come to realize. We don't go and say, 'Hi, we're the gay couple in the neighborhood.' It's just, 'I'm Neal; I'm Drew.' And they eventually realize, 'Oh they live there together . . . oh they must be gay.'"

"Which doesn't sound that much different to what a straight couple would do," I say.

"Exactly," Neal says.

Anna and Delia

Anna and Delia, thirty-three and thirty-two years old respectively, moved to a small town in the Mississippi Delta three years ago to work on a grant project assisting children living in poverty. They have a unique view of Mississippi, because although they live here, they also view it from the outside, knowing that they will not be here forever. They met in California over ten years ago and around the time they were completing their graduate school degrees. They were married in Massachusetts in 2011. Anna emigrated from Western Europe to attend college in the United States and identifies racially as white. Delia grew up in the United States and identifies as biracial. They are raising two children together.

Anna and Delia previously lived in cities with large, vibrant LG-BTQ communities. Before they moved to Mississippi they spoke with another lesbian couple at a nearby university about what it was like to be a lesbian in Mississippi. They were surprised when the couple told them it was okay as long as you are not "too out." Delia, in particular, was uncomfortable with the unspoken social compact of tolerance.

"Tell me about your experience living in your community as a couple," I ask.

"In general," Anna begins, "it was a little bit hard to meet people, even though people are very, very friendly. It seemed like I was going around trying to see where are the other people with little children? I guess couldn't find them. But in terms of a couple, it's like one of the pieces of advice we got before we moved here. People said, 'Just don't like shove it in people's faces.' I think maybe I stuck to it a little bit more than Delia.

"I'm not saying you shoved it in people's faces," Anna says to Delia, "but for me it's like if I don't know somebody, it's not the first thing I'm going to tell somebody; even though it very quickly then becomes impossible to not [tell] because people are like, 'Oh, where are you from and what brought you here?' I either say something evasive, or I immediately kind of come out [and say], 'The reason I'm here is because of my wife.' Delia I think is a lot more upfront."

"I have a different perspective," Delia says, "because I grew up in an interracial family—my dad's black, my mom's white—in the rural Midwest, where my dad was the only black person people had ever met. But my parents' motto was to just be who you are. I don't think this was conscious of them. I sometimes think to their detriment, because someone might say something that was like unintentionally racist, and they would just like kind of let it slide. But it was just kind of like you be who you are, and you just live your life and model that an interracial couple can be totally normal; and that's just what it is. People will just accept you, and that's kind of my motto. Like, we're not rainbow-flag-flying people."

"We're queer; we're here; get used to it," Anna says, leading the three of us to laugh.

"Confrontation isn't my approach," Delia says more seriously after we have finished laughing. "I'm very open. Within the first conversation that I have with someone, I lay it out. I mention my wife, because when you're living in an area where there may be some homophobia, I just throw that out there so that you know. Because there's no point in hiding it, you're going to find it out regardless, and then it's gonna be weird. I think when people have bad reactions, it just comes from discomfort, awkwardness that: 'I thought you were married to a man. I said all these things and made all these assumptions, and you didn't correct me. And now I found out, and now it's just incredibly awkward. And I don't want to deal with that awkwardness, so I'm just like backing out of the interaction.'

"I think the other thing," Delia continues, "is that we're very open; me specifically. Like there's not a stupid question. You can ask anything you want, and I'll—I mean probably not a sex question—but I'll answer."

"Well, people ask a lot of questions about the kids and where did the kids come from, and they sometimes would get very detailed," Anna adds.

"When I started working here," Delia says, "there was this Pentecostal woman. She's like forty-five [years old]. She's like one of my friends here in the Delta. She's Pentecostal, doesn't believe in same-sex marriage, etc., etc. And when I said I had a wife she's like, 'Wait ... you're a gay?' And she has like all these questions and some of those questions no one had answered for her. So she's like, 'Okay, so who proposed, and like you changed your last name, and how did you know?' and like all these questions. Most times I think you get logistical questions that people . . ."

"Delia's grandma was like, 'Who's gonna wear the ring?'" Anna interjects.

"For someone who's openly gay and who's living here, I think one of the things about us that makes us more approachable is that for a very untraditional lifestyle, we are a very traditional box. [When we moved here] I was working, Anna was at home. We had kids. We were young. We were married. It was just like a framework."

"Very normal," Anna adds.

"A normal framework, but the only difference was like one of us didn't have a penis. But otherwise, it was like pretty much a box: You're a young married couple with kids and you have a professional job that people understand which is in a framework that people could like fit into their frame of reference."

"So would you say that you broke the stereotypes that people believed about lesbian couples?" I ask.

"Yes," Delia responds. "Some of it. I think yes and no. I think that more stereotypes are associated typically with men and homosexuality. I think there's a lot more stigma around that. But I also think that there's no other 'out' people here really that we know. It's also easy to dismiss us as the exception rather than the rule; like they're the *cool gays*."

"In one way," Anna says, "it was kind of easy for people to understand our family, but in other ways they were just very confused about what we were saying, like 'Oh, this is my wife.' Like our neighbors for weeks they kept asking: 'So, is she your sister?' We'd say, 'We're married, we're a couple, we have children.' They'd be like, 'Is she your sister? But is she your mother? Married to who? Where is the kids' dad?' [We'd say,] 'Um, we sleep in the same bed.' It took a little while and eventually then they were like, 'Oh yeah, okay, they're married.'

"But I think our experience has just been that we haven't gotten any negative reactions. I mean there are some people who said like,

'Oh, well I don't believe in gay marriage, but I'm still gonna treat you nice."

"They actually said to your face, 'I don't believe in gay marriage?'" I ask incredulously.

"Oh yeah, yeah," they say at the same time.

"My Pentecostal friend," Delia adds. "I mean, she'll make side comments. I just remember her talking about [the television show] *Scandal* and there's a gay character in *Scandal*. She made some kind of like side-eye nasty, nasty comments about it; like somehow it was funny because she doesn't support marriage, and she also commented about my letter which I posted on Facebook before it got published in the newspaper. She's like, 'I knew you were talking about me!' I had said in there, 'I have friends who don't agree with my marriage, but we're still friends.' But anyway, she was watching *Scandal,* and she was making some side comments about the gay character there and giving some side-eyes. I was like, 'C'mon Jessica.' And it was interesting, because in her mind she had compartmentalized it into something separate. It was like gay men, and it was like something different. So, yeah, we have people who don't believe in things like marriage."

"I've not had anyone actively say anything to me," Anna says. "The worst reaction I've gotten was like someone not continuing the conversation; very subtle like where it didn't even bother me. Like I'm talking to another mom and then the conversation maybe ends a little sooner than it would have otherwise ended, but no one has said anything offensive to me."

"Anna, I wanted to go back to what you said a little earlier," I say. "You said that when you two first moved here, some people told you just don't throw it in their faces."

"We had some questions like what would it actually be like to live here as a same-sex couple? Are we gonna get harassed? There are a lot of negative stereotypes about Mississippi. It might not be safe for us to live here. It might not be, I don't know, emotionally safe for us to live here. So I asked the question to some of the people at the university that we talked to [before we moved here]. They were like, 'Just be subtle about it, don't be like too . . .'"

"I think that is wrong," Delia interjects.

"She doesn't believe in that approach," Anna clarifies.

"I don't believe in that. Well, the difference is that she is an educator, and she's like, 'Oh, it's like fluffy little puppy. It'll come out naturally.' Like sometimes with some of the classes she will tell people that she wants to build that rapport, and also I think you think of yourself [professionally] where personal information is not necessary. Then I'll show up and people will be like, 'Who is that?' It'll be like, 'That's my wife.' And it'll be like a month in the classroom, and they'll be like, 'Huh?' So my perspective is, I think that approach is not great because what I see with a lot of Mississippi gay people is: you keep your head low and you're so happy. I understand where that comes from. You've been treated so badly. Where I'm coming from—San Francisco, Boston, New York—we have the pantheon of like gay rights. So we come into the situation kind of like feeling like we don't have anything that we need to be quiet about. I think that that frames the way that people respond to you. Like, I don't really listen to him anymore, but do you know Dan Savage? Like *Savage Love*."

I nod my head affirmatively, remembering that Dan Savage is a gay activist who has a weekly newspaper column and podcast.

"He's always saying that coming out is like: if you treat it like cancer, people are gonna react like cancer. And, I don't recall any bad reactions. The only reaction was: I have like two memories of a side look, but those were people who I didn't really know or see again. The only thing that happens that bothers me sometimes is people will refer to [Anna as] 'partner or your friend.' It's like, '*I am legally married*,'" Delia says emphatically.

"When I was pregnant," Anna says, "and we were just at the prenatal appointment."

"How they were drilling us . . ."

"[One of the staff said,] 'She calls her *her wife*.'"

"And I got that paperwork, and it had wife in quotation marks. I got so mad. I was gonna write them this really nasty letter, but then they forgot to charge us for our appointment."

"Yeah, they forgot to bill us," Anna repeats.

"That kind of stuff makes me really upset, because it's like we're legally married. We are literally legally married, so it's not a quasi-relationship."

∼

In describing the experiences of LGBT youth in rural America, Gray (2009), professor of communication and culture, wrote that they must balance "the logistical needs to fit in and conform to the familiarity that structures rural life" (p. 168) with a need to be visible and experience LGBT culture. Similarly, my participants described a push and pull between fitting into their rural and small-town communities, while expressing their lesbian and gay identities through connection with others. The dilemma that many of the couples express is being true to themselves in the face of unspoken (and sometimes spoken) messages from their communities that they should not "rock the boat." This is the social compact of silence that I described in the beginning of this section: *We [the community] will tolerate you [lesbian and gay people] if don't act too queer and if you don't ask us to talk about it.*

For their part, many of the couples described how they cooperated by not acting too queer, both as a way to fit into their communities but also because they do not want others in their community to be uncomfortable. One couple said it was a choice between making others uncomfortable or being uncomfortable themselves. Several couples said that they don't "fly a rainbow flag" on their homes and that they don't "throw something in people's face," in other words not calling attention to their sexual orientation. Similarly, Jerry and Karl described themselves as not being "your typical gay person," and believing that "people have respected us because it has not been pushed in their face." Drew and Neal said that believed people were more comfortable with them, because they did not fit the "gay caricature" that is "offensive in that alien sort of way." Sometimes, though, it can be difficult to know what's going to make someone uncomfortable, as Bob and Matthew expressed: " . . . you never quite know what's acceptable, what's not acceptable, what's gonna make someone else uncomfortable, because they're so concerned about what's proper; what a proper southern gentleman is and does and says. We both run into it at work, and we both run into it socially and it's awkward sometimes."

On one hand, from the outside it can appear that repressing one's "queerness" in public could be related to internalized homophobia; in other words, the negative, homophobic, and heterosexist messages that LGBT people receive from families, churches, and society, as a whole, from a young age. These messages can lead to self-hatred and a desire to fit society's definition of "normal." On the other hand, not allowing one's "queerness," as Sam termed it, to come out can be what Howard (1999) described as a "resistance strategy, a means to protect oneself from discrimination, verbal or physical assault, and/or rejection but also to enable the creation of psychic space for individual contemplation and affirmation—and, on occasion, action" (p. 32). Sophie and Faith provide an example of this resistance when they say they avoid the awkwardness of interacting with heterosexuals by living in separate worlds in which they only socialize with their gay friends. In this way, they say they can be themselves on the weekends, without the pressure of feeling the need to hide behind a pretense of heteronormativity. Similarly, Doug and Harry say that they know that some heterosexual men "tolerate" them but that they tolerate them, too; in other words, both Doug and Harry and the heterosexual husbands of their female friends use silence as a means of resistance: enabling Doug and Harry to maintain friendships and the heterosexual men to resist accepting them as gay men.

As I noted earlier in this chapter, the tolerance that narrators says they receive for not being too queer, is not the same as acceptance. In fact, several of the narrators such as Sophie and Faith present tolerance as being "two-faced," stating that community members say or indicate that they accept them but then talk disparagingly about them behind their backs. Just as couples talked about not being overly queer as to make others uncomfortable, they describe heterosexual community members not being open about their true feelings about homosexuality and same-sex relationships in order to avoid an uncomfortable social interaction. A few couples expressed that the tolerance projected by community members can feel comfortable until they realize that it's fake. For instance, Bob said, "I get myself into this bubble—where I'm like, 'Oh, everybody loves gay people, everybody's fine, we're just people like everybody else'—and then every once in a while we get that culture shock of someone or something that just brings you back."

This reoccurring theme of couples describing their heterosexual neighbors as being tolerant but "two-faced" plays into the stereotype of southerners being passive-aggressively polite. Comedians from the south such as Ellen DeGeneres have joked about southerners using the term, 'Bless your heart" to express concern for someone when they are really insulting them. On the CBS television *Late Late Show* in 2018, host James Corden asked DeGeneres what it meant when a southern women said, "Darlin', bless your heart," to him after he had difficulty parking his car. DeGeneres explained to him that it was really an "insult," as if the woman were saying to Corden, "You poor, stupid person!" The audience on the *Late Late Show* laughed loudly at DeGeneres's response; it's humorous, because it touches on the passive-aggressive politeness stereotype.

White (2012), a professor of psychology, suggested that southerners are polite because of a "culture of honor" (Nisbett and Cohen, 1996). In their book, *Culture of Honor: The Psychology of Violence in the South*, social psychologists Nisbett and Cohen argued a "culture of honor" in the South is responsible for higher rates of violence compared to other regions. They suggested that the origins for this culture trace back to the original Scotch-Irish settlers and a herding economy with little government oversight where a settler would be required to protect himself and his family from theft. This requirement to protect oneself included protecting one's reputation. For men, not responding to insults would make them look weak. Based on their research of participants' reactions to insults, they further hypothesized that southerners did not necessarily prefer violence but were more likely to resort to violence if threatened. Further, as White (2012) explained, politeness serves as a means to avoid insulting others and the threat of violence

Larry told me that before he came out to his family, he learned that his three brothers had speculated about his sexuality. During one of their conversations, as one of his brothers said he believed Larry was gay, his wife began to cry and yelled at her husband, "Don't you say that about him!" In other words, calling him "gay" is an insult and should not be expressed out loud. Other couples expressed similar feelings. For example, Sophie said, "But you know how they [community members] think, 'Well, okay, Sophie's a good person.' She can't be that way." Marty said, "They're not as bad as they're portrayed all the time [on television]." Neal said that he believed people were more comfortable with them, because he and Drew were not the "caricature" gay person.

The social compact still evident in Mississippi today serves as a "don't ask, don't tell" policy, what Mason (2015), a professor of gender and women's studies, described as "unqueering." It is the tolerance-but-not-acceptance environment of people and behavior that are not too queer. Many of the lesbian and gay couples oblige in order to assimilate into their communities as Marty described: "What we do in the bedroom or what we do in this house is no-body's business." What that statement does not take into account is that any relationship is more than sex. Not acknowledging one's relationship or having one's relationship acknowledged means not being fully accepted by a community as couple. To what extent, I wonder, are lesbian and gay Mississippians' own acceptance of themselves affected by a lack of full acceptance from their families and communities; or are they simply doing what they have to do to survive in a place they call home?

∽

After Larry and I were legally married and settled back into our lives in Mississippi, I realized I felt happier than I had ever remembered feeling. I did not miss the high cost of living and the traffic in a big city. I found that I enjoyed the friendliness and laid-back mentality of a small town. However, nagging thoughts would continue to creep into my head: "What am I doing here in Mississippi? If only we could move this house to a place with more gay people. Do I want to live in a place where being gay is so shocking to so many of the people?" I remembered a black student once telling me what it was like for her when she was one of only a few black people living in a town in Iowa, and I felt like I could relate.

One of the couples I interviewed, in reference to their social life, said, "We weave ourselves into straight society here." I wondered if that was what Larry and I have done. We live in a traditional, older neighborhood on a narrow street with sidewalks and houses close enough together that you can see whether or not neighbors are sitting on their porches. We interact with our neighbors when we work in our yards, visit on our porches, and occasionally have meals together. We watch out for their houses when they are away, and they do the same for us. We're treated as a couple, I suppose, because that's how we introduce ourselves. The difference from living in a large city with a vibrant gay community is that we do have to weave ourselves into straight society. We are a minority and cannot blend into a gay neighborhood as was possible for me when I lived in Fort Lauderdale or New Orleans. There are both pros and cons to this. Being a minority can feel lonely and isolating at times. On the other hand, we are part of the community. Could we live someplace else? Would we miss the warmth of a small town where you constantly run into people you know?

References

American Radio Works. (2019). *State of siege: Mississippi whites and the civil rights movement.* Retrieved from http://americanradioworks.publicradio.org/features /mississippi/index.html

Balsam, K.F., Molina, Y., Beadnell, B., Simoni, J., & Walter, K. (2014). Measuring multiple minority stress: The LGBT people of color microaggressions scale. *Cultural Diversity and Ethnic Minority Psychology, 17*, 163–74. doi:10.1037/a0023244

Brown v. Board of Education, 347 U.S. 483 (1954).

Cass, V. C. (1979). Homosexual identity formation. *Journal of Homosexuality, 3*, 219–35. doi:10.1300/J082v04n03_01

CBS. (2018). The Late Late Show. Retrieved from https://www.youtube.com/watch?v=EyrnqjV61ZY&feature=youtu.be

Elliott, D. (2018). GOP senator's "public hanging" comment roils Mississippi runoff election. *National Public Radio*. Retrieved from https://www.npr.org/2018/11/12/667050590/gop-senators-public-hanging-comment-roils-mississippi-runoff-election.

Equal Justice Initiative. (2017). Lynching in America: Confronting the legacy of racial terror (3rd Ed.). Retrieved from https://lynchinginamerica.eji.org/report/.

Finnegan, T. (1997). Lynching and political power in Mississippi and South Carolina. In W. F. Brundage (Ed.), *Under sentence of death: Lynching in the south* (pp. 189–218). Chapel Hill, NC: University of North Carolina Press.

Ganucheau, A. (2015, Jan. 21). Starkville aldermen vote to rescind equality resolution. *Clarion-Ledger*. Retrieved from https://www.clarionledger.com/story/news/2015/01/21/starkville-aldermen-rescind/22100881/

Gates, G. J. (2014). Same-sex couples in Mississippi: A demographic summary. Retrieved from the Williams Institute website: https://williamsinstitute.law.ucla.edu/demographics/mississippi-ss-couples-demo-dec-2014/

Gray, M. L. (2009). *Out in the country: Youth, media, and queer visibility in rural America*. New York, NY: New York University Press.

Harrison. B. (2019, Feb. 5). Sexual orientation, gender identity, disability, could be covered by Mississippi hate crime law. *Mississippi Today*. Retrieved from https://mississippitoday.org/2019/02/05/sexual-orientation-gender-identity-disability-could-be-covered-by-mississippi-hate-crime-law/

Howard, J. (1999). *Men like that: A southern queer history*. Chicago, IL: University of Chicago Press.

Human Rights Campaign. (2019). State maps of laws and policies. Retrieved from https://www.hrc.org/state-maps/hate-crimes

Johnson, E. P. (2008). *Sweet tea: Black gay men of the south*. Chapel Hill, NC: University of North Carolina Press.

Lawrence v. Texas, 539 U.S. 558 (2003).

Lewin, E. (2018). *Filled with the spirit: Sexuality, gender, and radical inclusivity in a black Pentecostal church coalition*. Chicago, IL: University of Chicago Press.

Marszalek, J. F., III, Cashwell, C. S., Dunn, M. S., & Heard, K. (2004). Comparing gay identity development theory to cognitive development: An empirical study. *Journal of Homosexuality, 48*(1), 103–23.

Marszalek, J. F., III, & Pope, M. (2008). Gay male identity development. In Kurt L. Kraus (Ed.), *Lifespan development theories in action: A case study approach for counseling professions* (pp. 294–327). Boston, MA: Lahaska Press.

Mason, C. (2015). *Oklahomo: Lessons in unqueering America.* Albany, NY: State University of New York Press.

National Center for Education Statistics. (2019). Private school universe survey. Retrieved from https://nces.ed.gov/surveys/pss/

National Public Radio. (2017). Discrimination in America: Experiences and views of LGBTQ Americans. Retrieved from https://www.npr.org/documents/2017/nov/npr-discrimination-lgbtq-final.pdf

Nisbett, R. E., & Cohen, D. (1996). *New directions in social psychology: Culture of honor: The psychology of violence in the South.* Boulder, CO: Westview Press.

Obergefell v. Hodges, 576 U.S. (2015).

Mississippi Civil Rights Museum. (2019). *About the museum.* Retrieved from https://mcrm.mdah.ms.gov/story/about-the-museum

Pettus, E. W. (2017, Feb. 21). No penalty for Mississippi universities for furling state flag. *Clarion-Ledger.* Retrieved from https://www.clarionledger.com/story/news/politics/2017/02/21/no-penalty-for-mississippi-universities-furling-state-flag/98227056/

Protecting Freedom of Conscience from Government Discrimination Act, Mississippi House Bill 1523 (2016).

Royals, K. (2015, Jan. 14). Possible gay club prompts change in Miss. School Policy. *USA Today.* Retrieved from https://www.usatoday.com/story/news/nation/2015/01/14/possible-gay-club-prompts-change-in-miss-school-policy/21778565/

Sue, D. W. (2010). *Microaggressions in everyday life: Race, gender, and sexual orientation.* Hoboken, NJ: John Wiley & Sons.

US Census Bureau. (2018). Quick facts: Mississippi. Retrieved from https://www.census.gov/quickfacts/MS

White, L. T. (2012, Apr. 24). Southern comfort: Why Southerners are so polite. *Psychology Today.* Retrieved from https://www.psychologytoday.com/us/blog/culture-conscious/201204/southern-comfort

CHAPTER TWO

Religion

When Larry and I decided to get married on Monhegan Island, Maine, neither one of us wanted a religious ceremony. We intentionally chose an officiant who was not affiliated with a church; in fact, Maria is a notary public. In Maine, a notary public can sign a marriage license. We originally planned to have the ceremony on one of the cliffs overlooking the ocean, but we were surprised by the number of family members and friends who planned to come to our wedding. Some of the people might not have been able to walk the trails all the way to the cliffs. Besides, we wondered, what would we do if it rained? The Monhegan Island Community Church is one of the few places on the island to be able to host an indoor wedding.

The church was perfect. It is a quaint, gray frame wooden building in the center of the village. A steeple rises three stories to the right of the front door. If it were not for the steeple, the building would look like an old schoolhouse. Built in the 1800s, the church was never electrified. The only lighting is provided by candles and gasolier lanterns hanging over the aisle lined by two rows of wooden pews. It smells like old wood and candles, a comforting smell from my days as an altar boy at St. Joseph's Catholic Church in Starkville, Mississippi. We realized that this church was the finishing touch. Although we did not want a religious wedding, we wanted it to be spiritual.

Kathy was the contact for the church. I spoke to her on the phone in January. She was one of the few residents who remained on the island during the winter. I wondered how she would react when I told her we are a same-sex couple. She was enthusiastic and said that we would be the first gay couple to get married on the island. She paused, though, and said that there was one little catch. In order to reserve the church we must agree to allow the minister to be present during the ceremony. She told me that the reason for the rule is to ensure that no damage is done to the historic church. She suggested that we meet with him prior to the wedding.

We were hesitant to meet with the minister. We've both had bad experiences with religion, although we had differing experiences with religion growing up. Larry grew up in a family that occasionally went to church but not regularly. When Larry came out, he had family members who had become religious as adults encourage him to turn to a fundamentalist religion rather than "choose a homosexual lifestyle." One family member told him that he was "worried for your soul." He asked Larry to come to a service where the minister preached about the "sins of homosexuality." Larry walked out of the service.

I grew up going to a progressive Catholic Church where our priest came to our house regularly for dinner. I never heard a word in church about homosexuality, although I learned in college that the larger church viewed homosexuality as "inherently disordered." My brothers and I were altar boys, and I was the church organist in high school. I felt a sense of peace and comfort in church, with people that felt like family to me. To this day when I run into people in town that went to St. Joseph's, I feel a kinship with them. I even contemplated becoming a priest after I graduated from college, as I struggled with reconciling my religious and sexual orientation identities. As I grew older, I realized that I could not attend a church that viewed me as "disordered." I found other ways to nurture my spiritual identity.

When I was first coming out at nineteen years of age, I spoke to a priest at Spring Hill College, the Jesuit college I was attending in Alabama. I wasn't sure how to deal with the realization that I was gay and that the church viewed same-sex behavior as sinful. I admired Fr. William and had a good relationship with him. He seemed to be more progressive than some of the priests I had heard about from other students. However, when I spoke to him about my confusion, he gave me the standard Catholic line.

"It's okay, John, if you are gay. But you must not act on your desires. Do not go to gay bars or get involved with any gay groups. You will be tempted to act out on your homosexuality. You will find that it is a slippery slope. Now let's pray together."

His words added to my own internalized homophobia. I felt like there was something wrong with me. It took several years for me to feel and to know that I was not the one who had something wrong with me. I don't want our wedding to be ruined, because the sight of a minister in the back of the church might trigger our anger. We would not be able to meet with the minister until the day before the wedding. Kathy assured us, though, that he is very "open-minded." I hoped that she was right.

～

In order to understand the culture of the south and its communities, one must consider the influence of religion. Religion affects the politics, social life, and even physical space of southern communities. In some places, people joke that there is a bar on every corner. In Mississippi, it often feels like there is a church on every corner. In most small towns, the church steeple is the largest "skyscraper" downtown. People identify each other, not only by race and work but by religion.

When I first moved back to Mississippi, one of my neighbors introduced herself to me and asked, "Have you found a church home?" She showed concern on her face when I replied that I did not go to church. Larry and I are one of the few families in our neighborhood on Sunday morning that are not seen leaving our home dressed up and on our way to church. After all, we are living in the capital of the Bible belt. Mississippi is the most religious state in the United States, with 59 percent of residents stating they are very religious and that they go to church regularly (Newport, 2017).

For many Mississippians church is more than a place to go on Sundays; it is a community within their community. In addition to identifying as gay, most of the couples also identified as members of their small towns and rural communities. In their communities,

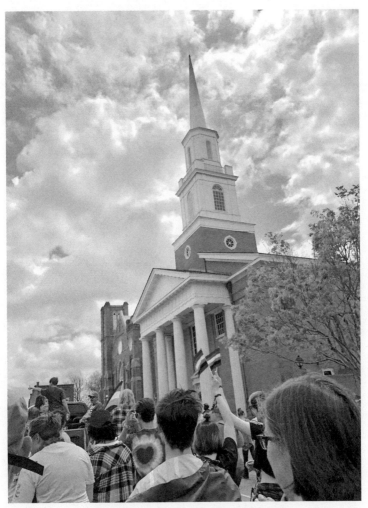

Pride Parade passes First Baptist Church in Starkville.

for most of their lives, they went to the same church with the same people, including their families, neighbors, and friends. Like their heterosexual counterparts, they are at least partly identified by others by the church they attend (or attended). Accordingly, as Lewin (2018) maintained, in addition to focusing on the sexual orientation and gender identities of LGBT people, we should take into account other aspects of their identities, such as religious/spiritual. As the couples in this book tell their stories, they speak to their experience as lesbian women and gay men, but also as Mississippians, as members of their small communities and towns, as members of their families, and for many, as members of their churches.

Most churches, though, have not been hospitable to gay Mississippians. Howard (1999) wrote that prior to the 1970s, although not approved of, homosexuality was not something widely discussed in Mississippi churches. Churches' reactions changed in the 1970s and 1980s as the gay rights movement gained steam nationwide. The public denunciations of homosexuality by churches, especially Southern Baptist churches, became more pronounced when the Universal Fellowship of Metropolitan Community Churches (MCC) formed a congregation in Jackson in 1983. MCC, a Christian non-denominational church, was founded by Troy Perry, a gay man and former Pentecostal minister, in California in 1968 to provide a "primary, positive ministry to gays, lesbians, bisexuals, and transgender persons" (MCC, 2019, Introduction section, para 1). Perry made national news, including *Life* magazine in 1971, for officiating marriage ceremonies for same-sex couples as a MCC minister (MCC, 2019).

The Mississippi Moral Majority sent mailers across the state warning Mississippians of the danger of a "homosexual church" turning Jackson into "another San Francisco or Houston" (Howard, 1999, p. 246). The state's largest newspapers in Jackson, covered the debate between religious leaders who denounced MCC and the Mississippi Gay Alliance who supported it. Ironically, Howard said that the focus on the Mississippi gay community in the press made closeted, religious gays and lesbians aware that they were not alone.

Today, according to a Pew Research Center (2014) poll, 83 percent of Mississippians identify as Christian with 41 percent identifying as Evangelical Protestant. Further, 72 percent of Evangelical Protestants believe that "homosexuality should be discouraged," and 75 percent oppose same-sex marriage, compared to 59 percent and 67 percent respectively for all Mississippi Christians. The religious beliefs of Mississippians seep into politics, as the state resists full acceptance of LGBT civil rights. Many politicians and religious leaders continue to fight to prevent lesbians and gays from receiving the same rights and respect as heterosexuals, believing that granting equal rights is an attack on their religious beliefs and values.

Governor Phil Bryant expressed this view in defense of House Bill 1523 (Protecting Freedom of Conscience from Government Discrimination Act, 2016), allowing state officials to refuse to perform same-sex marriages and businesses to refuse to serve same-sex couples if they have religious objections to same-sex marriage: "The people of Mississippi have the right to ensure that all of our citizens are free to peacefully live and work without fear of being punished for their sincerely held religious beliefs" (Campbell, 2017, para 4). House Bill 1523 was originally filed by House Speaker Philip Gunn, a trustee at the Southern Baptist Theological Seminary (Allen, 2016) and a former elder at Morrison Heights Baptist Church in Clinton, Mississippi, whose pastor spoke out publically against the "new cultural reality" of the US Supreme Court's legalization of same-sex marriage in 2015 (Dreher, 2015, para 3).

Consequently, as gay couples attempt to fit into their communities, they are living among people who do not value their relationships, likely believe that they are immoral, and do not believe that their relationships are worthy of legal protection. For those who grew up in a church that taught that homosexuality is a sin, many were faced with a choice between coming out and leaving their church versus remaining closeted and staying in their church; a choice between being true to oneself and being a part of a community.

RECONCILING SEXUAL ORIENTATION AND RELIGIOUS/SPIRITUAL IDENTITIES

As I discussed in Chapter One, coming out, both to oneself and to others, is a developmental process that happens over time. There have been many gay and lesbian identity development models (e.g. Cass, 1979; Marszalek, Cashwell, Dunn, & Heard, 2004; Marszalek

& Pope, 2008) that explain the developmental process of people becoming aware that they might be gay, tolerating the idea that they are gay, and moving to a place of full acceptance of a gay identity. In addition to accepting one's sexual orientation identity, an important developmental task is reconciling different aspects of one's identity. This reconciliation can be a difficult task when youth realize they are gay while hearing messages in church, either directly or subtly, that "homosexuals are evil."

Difficulty in reconciling sexual orientation and religious identities, especially for those who heard antigay messages, can lead to shame, guilt, internalized homophobia, and other mental health concerns such as depression and risk for suicide (Page, Lindahl, & Malik, 2013; Ream & Savin-Williams, 2005; Sherry, Adelman, Whilde, & Quick, 2010). According to the American Association of Suicidology (2019), LGBT people are more likely to attempt suicide than non-LGBT people due to risk factors, including, among other factors, minority stress, bullying in the schools, and lack of support for coming out from families, peers, school, and religion.

Noah and Terrance

Noah (introduced in Chapter One), engaged to be married to Terrance, told me on the phone (when I scheduled the interview with them) that he became so depressed during his struggle to reconcile his faith with his sexual orientation identity that he contemplated suicide.

"I found a way to overcome that [depression]. And I can speak about it now, because I'm not in that place in my heart anymore.... Even though I'm still a Christian," Noah explains, "I did abort Christianity for a while. Because being from the south and growing up in the church [where] they don't ever speak of anything positively, I grew up always thinking that homosexuality was a sin and that I was going to hell for loving the same sex. And so it was tough for me to come to terms with that and be okay with me being gay. Before I came out to my family, I was out to my friends, at work sometimes, too. So it was tough for me to, you know, cope with that. So when I was ready to come out, I was ready to come out as a gay Christian."

"How did you come to terms with it?'

"I did a lot of research. I started researching the term 'abomination' in Leviticus. I looked up a lot about Sodom and Gomorrah in Genesis; Paul in Romans writing about the sexual act between men and boys; not the sexual act between two consenting adults who love each other. So when you look at the Bible, and a lot of people don't do this, and that's a really big issue when it comes to Christianity and having a mind of your own because God gives us our mind. . . . It was a really tough time for me. I was a very big believer in Christ, but I couldn't believe in something that wants me to go to hell. So I needed to find out why I felt that way. Am I right to feel this way? Should I be feeling this way? I needed to find the truth basically, and you cannot argue faith with facts. Or science, you can't argue science and history with faith. It just doesn't work that way."

Lesbians and gays who have reconciled their sexual orientation and religious identities within themselves and who attend churches that are antigay or are not gay affirming may focus on different aspects of their overall identity in different circumstances. When they are in church, for example, they may focus on their religious identities, not their sexual orientation identities (Lewin, 2018). They may continue going to churches that preach that homosexuality is a sin, because these churches are their communities (Johnson, 2008). One lesbian couple told me that they continue to attend the same churches they attended before coming out, each going their separate ways on Sunday. Although they sometimes hear their ministers make disparaging remarks about homosexuality, they ignore the remarks. They said they continue to attend their churches, because their families identify with these churches, they feel a sense of community there, and they know that there are other closeted lesbians and gays in the church who also ignore the antigay messages.

Lesbians and gays living in rural areas who would like to find a church that is openly gay affirming will likely have to travel to a city with a MCC or Unitarian Universalist Church (UUC) (Woodell, Kazyak, & Compton, 2015). In Mississippi, there are MCCs in Hattiesburg and Jackson and UCCs in Jackson, Tupelo, and Oxford. Several of my couples also described the Episcopal Church as gay affirming and the only church in their towns they could attend openly as a couple and feel accepted.

Several counselor education colleagues and I conducted a study on the experiences of twenty-five lesbian women and gay men who grew up in religious communities across the Unites States (Crockett, Cashwell, Marszalek, & Willis, 2017). Many of the respondents discussed how difficult it was for them to come out as gay, because of the conflict they experienced between whom they knew themselves to be versus the negative, homophobic messages they had internalized from years of attending a church with antigay beliefs. For these respondents, the majority of them either changed religions or left organized religion altogether, finding other ways to nurture the spiritual sides of themselves. On the other hand, respondents who grew up in religious communities that were gay affirming did not have the same conflicts in reconciling their religious/spiritual and sexual orientation identities.

Similarly, Woodell, Kazyak, and Compton (2015), sociologists, interviewed twenty-four Christian lesbians, gay men, and bisexual women living in rural areas of seven southern states, including Mississippi, to study how they reconciled their religious and sexual orientation identities. These participants reconciled identities by focusing on a personal relationship with God or finding an accepting church. For their participants an accepting church might be a church that is not necessarily gay affirming but that does not talk explicitly of homosexuality (i.e., hell and brimstone speeches), similar to Faith and Sophie (introduced in Chapter One), who are members of a church where the minister does not speak explicitly about homosexuality but is also not gay affirming.

Faith and Sophie

"We go to a Baptist church which sometimes is . . ." Faith begins.

" . . . stiff for me," Sophie interjects amused. "But this is Faith's church. I was raised Presbyterian, and I wouldn't mind going to the Episcopal Church; but, I believe—and you can tell me if I'm wrong—[it] would bring you more out."

"Yeah, they're pretty out, and she's not ready to do that. Most of the people go to the Episcopal Church are people I work with. They tend to bring you out."

"So you both go to the Baptist church together?" I ask.

"Mm-hm," they say in unison.

"We went today," Sophie says.

"And what is that like?" I ask.

"I mean, we're still in the closet," Sophie responds. "It's tough."

"Ours is different," Faith says though. "Ours has a lot of poor people go to it. It's a "come-as-you-are."

"Flip-flops and shorts on Sunday or whatever."

"And he ministers to the mentally ill, and there's a group home that he picks up for church."

"Church van brings 'em."

"It's a mixture. It's black and white, which you don't see in a lot of [churches]."

"And I think that I feel a little comfortable in it, because, you're helping people that need help. And like my mother used to say, 'If they're looking at what you're wearing to church, they're going for the wrong reasons,'" Sophie finishes as the three of us laugh.

"There's a lot of people from the drug house," Faith says.

"It's not in a good part of town," Sophie explains.

"So when you go into the church together, how do they see you?" I ask.

"We don't know," Faith says. "Our little friends, Bobby and Sandra that sit behind us, who are wonderful, good people, never ask no questions."

They tell me that when they couldn't find one of their dogs, Bobby and Sandra came out to their farm to help them search. Since that time, Faith and Sophie assume that they know they are a couple, but Bobby and Sandra have never asked; nor have Faith and Sophie told them.

"Now, Miss Williams, she just kind of looks at us, you know and . . ."

"She's the preacher's mother," Sophie finishes.

"She knows we are [gay]."

"Well, yeah. I mean, I'm sure everybody in the church knows."

"Well, matter of fact, we know they do," Faith says, "because Rita [a friend] was in the doctor's office one day,"

" . . . with one of the little old ladies," Sophie continues as they tell the story together.

" . . . and a woman who went to our church"

" . . . was asking where she [Rita] went to church."

"And she [Rita] said the Episcopal Church. She [little old lady] said, 'Well, I go to this church [Sophie and Faith's church]. We have a gay there.' She said, 'The homosexuals sit on the left side'; she was talking about the men. 'And the lesbians sit on right side'; and that's me and Sophie." We laughed about that!

"So it didn't make you uncomfortable hearing that," I ask.

They both shake their heads and say "no" at the same time.

"So it's kind of like don't ask, don't tell?" I ask.

"It is," Faith replies. "It's don't ask, don't tell. You know we've contemplated leaving several times. And I don't like the Episcopal Church. Sophie is different."

"Sometimes when I'm in church, I just have to keep my mouth shut when I'm a little irritated about something he's preaching on."

"What kind of stuff does he preach on that bothers you?" I ask.

"Well, I mean it won't be anything really rough," Sophie says. "I can't think of anything offhand, but sometimes I'm like, 'I don't agree with that.'"

"No. He's never harped on homosexuality," Faith agrees. "It's just not really homosexual, just some things you don't agree with."

LOOKING FOR A NEW CHURCH COMMUNITY

At some point in their lives, most of the Mississippi couples I interviewed left a church that was antigay or was not explicitly gay
affirming. Many couples no longer attend church because of their
negative experiences. Some of these couples told me that they consider themselves to be spiritual but not religious, like Larry and me.
In some instances, only one member of a couple attends church such
as one male couple who told me that one of the men stays home on
Sundays while the other is heavily involved in his Episcopal Church,
including attending a yearly retreat for gay Episcopalians in another
state. Other couples like Noah and Terrance still identify with their
original religion, but have not found a compatible church. Alicia and
Rae (introduced in Chapter One) recently left their churches and
are looking for a gay-affirming church, so that their children do not
hear negative messages about their mothers as Alicia describes: "Our
churches aren't [accepting of lesbian and gay couples]. My church
ain't; her church, I won't even go to that church. I was sending my
kids to that church with her mom, and my little boy come back and
say, 'All the preacher's talking about is, if you are a boy you are supposed to be with a woman.' And so I won't even go to her church.
She no longer goes to her church. So we're in the process of trying
to find an accepting church home that we can go as a family."

The next couples, since leaving their original churches, have
found gay-supportive churches such as MCC or the Episcopal
Church. One lesbian couple even founded their own MCC, after
leaving a church that taught that homosexuality is a disease like
alcoholism. Frequently, and whether or not they attended, couples
like Faith and Sophie described the Episcopal Church as a place in
their communities that they felt welcome.

The United States Episcopal Church, of the worldwide Anglican Communion, has a longer history of acceptance of their LGBT
parishioners compared to other mainstream religions. Integrity, a
national organization to promote "full inclusion" in the Episcopal
Church for lesbian, gay, bisexual, and transgender Episcopalians

and their allies, was founded in 1974 (Integrity, 2018). Two years later, the General Convention of the Episcopal Church "declared that homosexual persons are children of God who have full and equal claim with all persons upon the love, acceptance, and pastoral concern and care of the Church" (Episcopal Church, 2019, para 1). Since that time, Gene Robinson became the first openly gay bishop in 2003, the church blessed same-sex relationships and authorized the ordination of transgender priests in 2012, and it approved same-sex marriage ceremonies in 2015. The movement toward acceptance in the Episcopal Church was not without controversy, with some conservative congregations splitting from it and forming their own Anglican Church of North America in 2009 (CNN, 2018).

Mary and Nancy

Mary and Nancy, two white women in their sixties, are retired grade school teachers who have been together since 1979. They live in the country outside a micropolitan area and next to another lesbian couple with whom they are close friends. The two couples share two ponds and a chicken coop on the land around their houses. Mary and Nancy originally went to a Baptist church were they heard negative comments about lesbians and gays. Like many of the other couples, they describe the Episcopal Church as the most gay-affirming church in their small community. Mary and Nancy started the first Integrity group at their church almost thirty years ago.

"How was the reaction to it at the church?" I ask.

"Oh, it was interesting." Nancy continues. "It was—actually looking back on it—it was fun to watch how it evolved, because it started with: a friend of mine called me and said, 'I've learned about this Integrity group. What do you think?' I was like, 'Well, I think it's great, you know. Let's see what will fly.' So we went to the pastor at that time, and he was very supportive and said, 'You know, let's meet with the community.' So we did. We met with a community of those within the church: the gay community, the lesbian community. We met on a Sunday afternoon at the priest's house. I can remember, we were like, 'Do we want to do this?' And one of the young men who has passed now said, 'You know, I have been humiliated and beat up all of my life, and I go to church to be supported; and I just do not want to be beat up within my own church.' And so, it was a very scary thing at that point because that was . . ."

"1989 or '90," Mary finishes.

"Yeah, and so we said, 'Let's all go home while we think about it for a week.' And, we came back the next Sunday and sat down and everybody's like, 'Let's do it!'" Nancy finishes laughing.

"What changed, like for the guy who was so worried?" I ask.

"I think it had to do with the safety that he felt within the community, within the big community itself. The support was so big. I mean our church, even at that time, was known as the gay-friendly church. So, I think that's what it was, and he wanted to make a difference for future generations. He knew that."

"You ever run into any problems? Any kind of difficulties?" I ask.

"The only problem I had," Mary replies, "was when Ellen [DeGeneres] came out, and everything started being so outspoken about gays. We were Baptist at that point in our lives."

"Both of you were Baptist?"

"Yeah, and Nancy was a Sunday school teacher and very active. We went to every service. We were very faithful. But we'd get into the Sunday school class, and they'd be sitting there talking about gays and saying they were child molesters and all this stuff. I took it about as long as I could for me. I stayed probably—I knew how much she loved it—probably stayed longer than . . . than . . . [I should have]. It was getting really hard."

"You wanted to react," I note.

"Yeah, but someone told me that maybe we should try the Episcopal Church, So I went over to speak to the priest. When I went up there, I told her, 'Well, I need to tell you I'm gay and my partner and I have been together for sixteen years. I don't know if we're at the right place or not.' And she just picked me up and hugged me and said, 'Don't you know being with someone that you love for sixteen years could be nothing but a blessing from God?' And when she said that my entire life . . . because God supported me . . . I was able to have everything. . . ." Mary chokes up as she tries to complete the last sentence.

"It makes you emotional just talking about it," I say. "It's a beautiful story."

"It is beautiful," Nancy says. "And at that point, with us being in the Baptist Church, for me, it was very important to be there, because I felt like I was there for a reason. I felt like I was there for a reason to help them learn and for me to learn from them. And I felt like I was supposed to be there and then when we got to that point, and Mary was so upset and having a really hard time, it was as if God was saying, 'You've done what you were to do.' You know, 'You've done there, you've been there, you've done all that you're gonna do, because you're not gonna change their mind.'"

"They loved her," Mary says.

"They loved us. So it was like we were there for a reason."

"It was part of our journey."

"And then we left and went to the Episcopal Church. It felt like that was a very important place to be. No matter how hard it was. It was meant to be."

"The [Baptist] pastor passed away just in the last year or so," Mary says. "And of course we went out to his funeral and everything. And, of course, everybody was very loving and hugging. And his son told me before we walked out of the church, he said, 'Mary, I've never talked to you or Nancy about anything. Y'all know we love you.' And he said, 'I just wanted to tell you that my father loved y'all very much.' I always felt like he loved us, but he couldn't, you know, get away from what he was taught."

"That must have been really painful for you back then, but then something beautiful came of it," I say.

"Exactly," Mary replies.

Jerry and Karl

In addition to being legally married, Jerry and Karl (introduced in Chapter One) wanted to be married in a church. They consider themselves to be very spiritual and are actively involved in their Episcopal church. Karl called the Episcopal Diocese of Vermont in search of a minister who would marry them and received a list of retired priests who were performing same-sex marriages.

"I was looking at this list, and I was like who do I call first?" Karl explains. "And the person that I called. . . ."

Karl pauses and has a serious look on his face.

"It was no doubt THIS is who it was supposed to be. And she has been like this mother/grandmother, you know. Jerry got wigged out with me 'cause I even called her one night crying. I said, 'I can't do this, religiously, I can't go there.' And it was here that she said, your marriage and salvation are two totally different things. And you know, you're not saved by who you marry. She's just been wonderful. And now we're Facebook friends and still talk to her."

I wonder about Karl's conflict about the wedding, and he tells me that back in 2004 he had actually voted to support the Mississippi constitutional amendment banning same-sex marriage in the state.

"I think, at the time I was still going to that Assembly of God church, and I was still being preached about homosexuality and hell every Sunday. But, there's [sic] things in the Bible that you just have to take and look at them in your personal life. The story of Jonathan and David; I'd never heard that. But you're not gonna hear it in a Baptist or Assembly of God church."

"Could you tell me the story?" I ask.

"Okay, David was who killed Goliath in the Bible. And Jonathan was his best friend. He says in the scripture, 'I love you. My love for you is greater than that of a woman.' And you know, the Baptists or whoever say, 'Oh well, they were just good friends.' The bishop of the Episcopal church basically said that leaves no doubt of what they were."

"I grew up Baptist, and he grew up Assembly of God," Jerry adds.

"It's a branch off of Pentecostal." Karl explains. "The sermon that really made me leave the Assembly of God Church was when the pastor said, and I quote . . . 'Homosexuality is the worst sin there is.'"

"And he's sitting there. Maybe twenty-five people, and every one of them are his family members or their friends; all senior citizen couples. And here's Karl, the only young guy sitting there. So I mean, it was obvious who it was directed to."

"And Jerry's mother—it's took my mother a little bit longer to come around—but Jerry's mother is by far the biggest defender who will argue down on this issue that it's not a choice. I mean, we're talking Baptist Sunday school teacher."

Karl's voice becomes more somber.

"I even had an Assembly of God preacher to tell me this one time that he had a son that died of AIDS [who was presumably gay]. He said, and I can remember going to his house and crying one day and he said, 'You live the life to the cards you're dealt.' I tried to change for so long, and it's what it is."

I ask him if he feels differently today.

"Oh yeah. You know every now and then, especially with where we live, there will be somebody that will say something; whether it be on Facebook or whatever and not necessarily meant toward me or to hurt anybody. Where I used to would get defensive, I almost feel sorry for YOU, because you just don't know the truth. I mean, do I still get fighting mad? Yeah. And you know, I think especially with where we live, it's fine to be able to quote the scripture. I think a lot of people around here do that. But what it written to address was what was going on underneath it. And like the bishop of our national church has said, 'Is homosexuality in the Bible? Yes. Is it referring to how we know homosexuality today? Absolutely not.' And that's my little sermon on it."

"Tell me about your church in Mississippi," I say.

"Our church here has been way beyond accepting, and it's amazing how open they are," Karl responds.

"Karl will sit there on a Sunday morning in church and have his arm around me," Jerry adds.

"I think as my priest here said, there may be people that are not gonna meet you 50/50, but they will still love you and support you. And even though we've only been in this Episcopal church two and a half years, I think from everything we've heard, it was never an issue at this church because they refuse to let it be. I think, especially in the beginning, at our church, people there really thought, 'Are they gay or are they brothers or are they friends?' Our church is very gay populated as most Episcopal churches are. Even the little old people in that church are truly wonderful. We have this little lady in our church; and we're coming back from taking Communion, and she flags me down. I guess there was a lot of the gays that were out that day; *out* meaning not at church. They were absent that Sunday. She tracks me down and says, 'Where's the rest of ya'll at?' And I said, "'Well, Miss B., I guess Jerry and I are just representing for everybody here today!'"

They laugh again, and I find myself admiring their ability to find humor in their experiences.

"But we have a lot of gay people in the church," Jerry says more seriously. "I mean, even our organist. And if he left the whole church would just mourn his absence."

"We have a very young priest, and I don't know what his stance is," Karl says. "The Episcopal diocese in Vermont requires even same-sex marriages do premarital counseling. But we did not seek it through our priest because this is his first church. He's young. And more than that, we did not want to put him in a position that it might could cause him a backlash where people don't pay their pledge or whatever."

"We didn't want to put him in a weird spot," Jerry agrees.

Brandiilyne and Susan

Susan is fifty-two, and Brandiilyne is forty-two. They identify as white women and have been a couple about five years. They have lived in Mississippi all of their lives. Brandiilyne laughs a little before

Brandiilyne Dear leads outdoor MCC service.

beginning to tell their story of how they met and eventually started their own church, because their story is not common nor is it a fairy tale.

They founded Joshua Generation MCC (JGMCC) in Hattiesburg in 2014, where Brandiilyne is the pastor. JGMCC is affiliated with the MCC, the same MCC that first came to Jackson in 1983 to the consternation of the Mississippi Moral Majority (Howard, 1999). Worldwide, MCC boasts almost 300 congregations and 43,000 members. JGMCC is "a radically inclusive ministry that accepts everyone . . . regardless of age, race, sexual orientation, gender identity, or social status" (JGMCC, 2019, para 1). I interview them on Skype, because they are too busy leading their congregation to find a time to meet on a weekend. As we talk, they are sitting in what they describe as the "sanctuary" of their church.

"Well, I was a pastor, and I had a ministry for drug addicts and alcoholics. I had just opened a recovery center for women. And this center held ten women. It was a six-month program. They came in for six months, and then we'd get more as we went. We'd just opened it, and I told my secretary one day, 'I need to find a gym that will donate gym memberships for the girls, so we can take 'em to the gym, and they can work out as part of the holistic approach to getting them clean and all that.' She said, 'Oh, come with me,' and she took me to Susan's gym. Mind you, I'm married. I'd been married for the last eight years. My husband and I were practically roommates. We had no . . . [physical connection] or nothing like that. So anyway, I get there. I walk in and Susan sits back in her chair like this."

Brandiilyne demonstrates how Susan sat back in her chair, moving away from her with her arms crossed. She continues her story: "She looks at me, you know, kind of angrily as I'm asking for six thousand dollars' worth of gym memberships. She knew who I was because in my ministry we tried to 'pray the gay away.' In the denomination that I was in, which is a nondenominational denomination, homosexuality is an evil spirit and you gotta help people get delivered from addiction, from alcohol, from drugs, homosexuality, or whatever it was. So, a former member of my ministry was a member of her gym. She knew who I was, and so when I walked in and asked for donations, she was not happy about it. She was kind of intimidating. I thought she was cute, but she was still kind of intimidating. She said, 'I'm just gonna have to put a pen to it and get back to you.' I said, 'Well, I'll tell you what, I'm gonna go ahead and join the gym and, you know, here's my money, sign me up, what do I do?' And so, that kind of started me [down the road of realizing I was attracted to her]. I was completely flirting with her and had this crush. I was putting my makeup on, and going to the gym, and being all cute on the treadmill—or trying to be cute on a treadmill. I really wasn't. And she was going through a really bad breakup at the time. She had been in an eight-year relationship. Her and her partner were breaking up. So, of course, I go into pastor mode. I try to minister to her or whatever, and we became really good friends.

And it kind of started there. I told her how I felt about her, and she told me 'hell no!'"

Brandiilyne chuckles before continuing: "I wasn't expecting that response. She said, 'Hell no! You're my pastor. You're married. I'm not gonna let you ruin your life. This will ruin your life.' And, so we decided to be friends, and a week later I was moving in with her.

'Because she got kicked out of *everything*," Susan says laughing.

"Yeah. I didn't have anywhere else to go.'

"She got churched!"

"Yeah."

"How did you reconcile that within yourself in terms of going to a church that advocated 'praying the gay away' and then falling in love with Susan?" I ask Brandiilyne.

"Well, God really started dealing with me about my sexuality about two years before I even met Susan. And God was really showing me a picture of what I'm doing now and pulling me out and, you know, inspiring me to start a ministry. I wasn't sure how I was gonna do it because I couldn't reconcile [it with] what I was being taught and what I believed. And so I wrestled with it for a long, long time, and [then] I met her. I walked into my pastor's office, and I told my pastor, 'I'm leaving the ministry; leaving Luke [her husband].' I said, 'I'm done. I'm not doing this anymore.' I couldn't live a lie anymore. I decided it was more important for me morally to live honestly than it was to live a lie and be a hypocrite. It was better for me to walk away completely than to stay in this life. My pastor told me, 'No, you're just having a midlife crisis.' I was thirty-seven at the time. And I'm like, 'This is not my midlife crisis. I'm gonna have my midlife crisis at sixty-five, and that's just the way it's gonna be.' And he told me I couldn't quit; that he was gonna put me on a sabbatical. So he and his wife took me to their house to stay with them until I came to my senses. And that week I had some classes in Jackson that I had to go to with two people on my ministry team, and on the way home I told them about Susan. And I got in my car, and instead of going back to my pastor's house like I was supposed to, I went to Susan's house instead. That was on

Brandiilyne Dear baptizes congregants.

a Saturday, and they outed me to my pastor; then on Sunday my pastor resigned me from the pulpit."

"Publicly," Susan says, repeating it with emphasis in her voice.

"It was horrible. It was a horrible time. They called my name from the pulpit. They outed me to my entire community, my entire family. It was bad."

"Were you sitting in the church when this happened?" I ask.

"No, I was not there that day. Thank God. As a matter of fact, everyone was in church. And my house, my parsonage was across the street; so I walked out of my front door into my office each day. And while everybody was in church, I was in my house trying to get as many of my belongings as I could while everybody was in church. It was really bad. It was tough. I almost turned from God completely, because I couldn't separate Christianity and what the church did to me from Christ; so I had a hard time with that for about three years. It was tough. They tried to put us out of business."

"They did," Susan reiterates.

"My pastor said from the pulpit, 'You need to be loyal to God with your money.' That meant not coming to the gym."

"We had a lot of members from the church that came to my gym. It never really rebounded."

"Most people knew who I was because I was in the newspaper a lot because of my ministry. So everybody knew who I was. They knew my face, and of course everybody knew what was going on at this point; so anytime we would walk into a restaurant or anything people would stop. It was *so* awkward and *so* uncomfortable. We just kept walking and walked past people, and finally I just stopped noticing."

"Did you have friends you could lean on?" I ask.

"I did," Susan responds.

"Yeah, Susan did, and so I kind of latched on to her friends. They became my friends. I didn't have anybody. I didn't have anybody spiritual to talk to, so I was having a real identity crisis. I wouldn't change any of it. I believe that all of it happened for a reason. It helps me to understand what other LGBT people have been through in their spirituality. If I had not experienced that I don't think that I would minister in such a way that I do now."

Many people assume that lesbians and gays are not religious/spiritual; that being gay is incompatible with religion/spirituality. The Mississippi couples tell a different story. In their stories, many of them describe a yearning to be a part of a religious community, along with the hardship and sometimes fear of losing their religious communities. Mary and Nancy spoke of a gay man who feared losing the support he felt from their church if they faced backlash for starting in Integrity group. Karl needed reassurance from an Episcopal minister that it was okay for him to marry Jerry. Many struggled to find a way to stay in their original churches, but eventually had to make the difficult choice to leave. As with the participants in other studies of how gay people reconcile their sexual orientation and religious/spiritual identities (Crockett, Cashwell, Marszalek, & Willis, 2017; Woodell, Kazyak, & Compton) some couples are still searching for a new church home, others have found spirituality outside of religion, and others have found a new gay-affirming church community.

The couples tell both heartbreaking and heartwarming stories. As the couples described their journeys to reconcile their sexual orientation and religious/spiritual identities, many couples spoke of the people who did not support them or tried to stand in their way, either directly, as Brandiilyne described, or indirectly through messages from the pulpit, as Karl heard.

Their resilience in the face of these messages is remarkable. Noah overcame his despair and even suicidal thoughts, to reconcile his gay identity with his Christian beliefs. After being shunned and removed from her position in her church for expressing her love for Susan, Brandiilyne found a new calling in life, starting a MCC so that she could minister to other LGBT people. Many couples, like Mary/Nancy and Jerry/Karl, changed Christian denominations after not being able to reconcile the beliefs of their church communities with their gay identities.

Couples also spoke of the people who supported them along the way. Both Mary and Karl spoke of the Episcopal ministers who affirmed that is was okay to be both gay and Christian, a message they had not heard in the past. Mary's new minister said to her: "Don't you know being with someone that you love for sixteen years could be nothing but a blessing from God?"

Surprisingly, a few described ministers from antigay churches that seemed to be conflicted, themselves, when they tried to reconcile the church teaching on homosexuality with the people they knew. Mary and Nancy spoke of her former Baptist pastor: "I always felt like he loved us, but he couldn't, you know, get away from what he was taught." When Karl became distraught when he first realized that he was gay, he spoke to a minister at the same church where he had heard explicitly that homosexuality was sinful. The minister told him that he had a son that died of AIDS [who was presumably gay] and said, "You live the life to the cards you're dealt."

Finally some couples provided further examples of the social compact of silence that I discussed in Chapter One: *We [the*

*community] will tolerate you [lesbian and gay people] if don't act too
queer and if you don't ask us to talk about it.* Karl and Jerry do not ask
their local minister to provide the required premarital counseling
for the Episcopal Church, because they want to protect him from a
"weird spot" and "backlash" from the congregation.

Faith and Sophie mentioned friends who always sit behind them
in church and who have been out to their farm; however, Bobby
and Sandra have never asked about Faith and Sophie's relationship
status; likewise, Faith and Sophie have never told them. Previously,
in Chapter One, Faith and Sophie talked about their distrust of
heterosexual community members who they described as "two-
faced." It may not feel safe for them to trust another couple in their
church, even if they are "good people," especially because they are
not sure if they would be fully accepted and because neither one of
them is "out" at work. Because nobody asks questions and because
the church does not explicitly comment on homosexuality, they
find it acceptable; in addition, they continue to attend their church,
because as Sophie says, "This is Faith's Church." In other words, it's
part of Faith's identity and community. Nevertheless, the fear of being outed is one of the reasons that they have not left their church
and attended the Episcopal Church, although Sophie would like to
try it out. Because they consider it to be gay affirming and know that
there are parishioners who are openly gay, they fear that word would
get back to coworkers who also attend the Episcopal Church. On the
other hand, both in their discussion of their community and here
in their discussion of their church, they assume that other people
know that they are a couple. Nonetheless, it feels safer if they do not
"rock the boat," because that might change speculation and gossip
to reality, thus, challenging the status quo.

~

*After dinner on the evening before our wedding, Larry and I meet with
Howard, the visiting minister who will be at the Monhegan Island
Community Church for the month. We had spoken to him on the
phone, but had never met him in person. We had invited his wife and*

him to join our family and friends at the rehearsal dinner. He and his wife are warm and down-to-earth. My family and friends instantly fall in love with them.

We meet in a common room on the first floor of the hotel. The room is filled with books and nautical maps. We can hear the waves lapping against the shore below. He asks us why we are getting married. We talk about our relationship, how we feel like we were meant to be together, that we want to make a commitment in front of the people we love. We tell him we are not religious but are spiritual. We didn't ask a minister to perform the service, because of our previous experiences with religion. But we would appreciate it if he would say a blessing at the end. Howard is understanding, stating that it saddens him that we have had negative experiences with religion. He asks to pray with us. He says a prayer blessing us and our families and being thankful that he is able to share in a special moment in our lives. I feel held by the moment and feel an old wound beginning to heal inside.

REFERENCES

Allen, B. (2016, Mar. 31). Bill termed anti-gay authored by Baptist lawmaker. *Baptist News Global.* Retrieved from https://baptistnews.com/article/bill-termed-anti -gay-authored-by-baptist-lawmaker/#.XH7BQYhKjIW

American Association of Suicidology. (2019). Lesbian, gay, bisexual and transgendered resource sheet. Retrieved from https://www.suicidology.org/resources/lgbt

Campbell, L. (2017, Oct. 1). "Religious freedom law," House Bill 1523, will take effect Oct. 6; appeal planned. *Mississippi Today.* Retrieved from https://mississippitoday .org/2017/10/01/house-bill-1523-will-take-effect-oct-6/

Cass, V. C. (1979). Homosexual identity formation. *Journal of Homosexuality, 3,* 219–35. doi:10.1300/J082v04n03_01

CNN. (2018). Episcopal Church fast facts. https://www.cnn.com/2013/10/28/world/ episcopal-church-fast-facts/index.html

Crockett, J. E., Cashwell, C. S., Marszalek, J. F., & Willis, B. T. (2018). A phenomenological inquiry of same-sex attraction and religious upbringing. *Counseling and Values, 63,* 91–109. doi:10.1002/cvj.12075

Dreher, A. (2015, July 20). "Biblical marriage" rally draws supporters to Jackson. *Jackson Free Press.* http://www.jacksonfreepress.com/news/2015/jul/20/biblical-marriage -rally-draws-supporters-jackson/

Episcopal Church. (2019). LGBTQ in the church. Retrieved from https://www.episcopalchurch.org/lgbtq-church

Howard, J. (1999). *Men like that: A southern queer history.* Chicago, IL: University of Chicago Press.

Integrity. (2019). About Integrity. Retrieved from http://www.integrityusa.org/about-integrity

Johnson, E. P. (2008). *Sweet tea: Black gay men of the south.* Chapel Hill, NC: University of North Carolina Press.

Joshua Generation Metropolitan Community Church. (2019). A word about JGMCC. Retrieved from http://www.joshuageneration.rocks/about-us.html

Lewin, E. (2018). *Filled with the spirit: Sexuality, gender, and radical inclusivity in a black Pentecostal church coalition.* Chicago, IL: University of Chicago Press.

Marszalek, J. F., III, Cashwell, C. S., Dunn, M. S., & Heard, K. (2004) Comparing gay identity development theory to cognitive development: An empirical study. *Journal of Homosexuality, 48*(1), 103–23.

Marszalek, J. F., III, & Pope, M. (2008). Gay Male Identity Development. In Kurt L. Kraus (Ed.), *Lifespan development theories in action: A case study approach for counseling professions* (pp. 294–327). Boston, MA: Lahaska Press.

Metropolitan Community Church. (2019). History of MCC. Retrieved from https://www.mccchurch.org/overview/history-of-mcc/

Newport, F. (2017, Feb. 8). Mississippi retains standing as most religious state. *Gallup.* Retrieved from http://news.gallup.com/poll/203747/mississippi-retains-standing-religious-state.aspx

Page, M. J., Lindahl, K. M., & Malik, N. M. (2013). The role of religion and stress in sexual identity and mental health among LGB youth. *Journal of Research on Adolescence. 23*(4), 665–77. doi:10.1111/jora.12025

Pew Research Center. (2014). Religious composition of adults in Mississippi. Retrieved from http://www.pewforum.org/religious-landscape-study/state/mississippi/

Protecting Freedom of Conscience from Government Discrimination Act, Mississippi House Bill 1523 (2016).

Ream, G. L., & Savin-Williams, R. C. (2005). Reconciling Christianity and positive non-heterosexual identity in adolescence, with implications for psychological well-being. *Journal of Gay and Lesbian Issues in Education, 2,* 19–36. doi:10.1300/j367

Sherry, A., Adelman, A., Whilde, M. R., & Quick, D. (2010). Competing selves: Negotiating the intersection of spiritual and sexual identities. *Professional Psychology: Research and Practice, 41,* 112–19. doi:10.1037/a0017471

Woodell, B., Kazyak, E., & Compton, D. (2015). Reconciling LGB and Christian identities in the rural south. *Social Sciences, 4,* 859–78. doi:10.3390/socsci4030859

Chapter Three

Families

It's July 6, 2013, the day after our wedding. Larry and I walk down to the dock on Monhegan Island to take the ferry back to the mainland. Howard, the visiting minister at the Monhegan Community Church, and his wife meet us there and hand us flowers. They say that it is tradition to throw flowers off the boat when you leave the island. If the flowers float back to shore, it means you will return. Howard's wife adds, "Make sure you go to the back of the boat when you throw the flowers and watch the dock. Something amazing will happen."

The ferry pulls away and we watch children run to the edge of the dock preparing for the boat to leave. During the summer on Monhegan, it's commonplace for children to jump in the water as the boat is leaving, probably an excuse to jump in the water. The day before, we saw a young boy go to the top of the hill above the dock, ride his bike at maximum speed to the bottom of the hill, down the dock, and into the water. For a brief moment, the bike and boy were suspended in the air before hitting the water. Then, with the help of some friends, he pulled the bike out of the water and prepared to do it again.

As Larry and I are about to throw our flowers in the water, we see Howard and his wife waving at us. Howard yells at the top of his voice, "This is for John and Larry." Then he jumps into the cold water. The people on the ferry around us applaud. We throw our flowers into the water, watching them move toward Howard who is treading water and waving to us. He becomes a distant speck in the distance as the ferry moves further away from the island, past the seals sunning themselves on a rock and out into the open water.

Larry and I return to Mississippi after the wedding wondering if we will feel different. We do. It's difficult to put into words, but we feel even more connected to each other, feel accepted by many of our family and friends as a married couple, and know that, at least in many states, we are recognized as legally married. Part of me does not want to return. I wonder if it will be difficult to return to Mississippi after the acceptance and love we experienced in Maine. Another part of me reminds myself that we are returning to our home and that there is no perfect place.

Nevertheless, I have some lingering hard feelings over never hearing a "peep" about our wedding from several of Larry's family members and receiving a text a few days after the wedding while we were still on vacation in Maine: "I know we don't necessarily agree on your lifestyle with John, but I wanted you to know that I am happy that you are happy and nothing will ever change my love for you and John. Congratulations to you both!"

I'm not sure how to take this. I am both understanding and furious. She says she loves both of us and that she is happy for us. But she doesn't agree with our lifestyle? What does that mean? I find myself gravitating toward the fury while reminding myself this is from a college student who has likely heard her parents talk. Like her parents and many others in our community and nation, she is conflicted. She is trying to balance what she has heard from her parents' conservative church versus her experiences with Larry and me. She once told me that Larry and I were her favorite uncles, because we are "fun."

At the same time, Larry and I, as do many gay people, become tired of constantly having to educate others about our relationship and being gay. We had detected disapproval or, at the least, lack of excitement over our marriage from several of Larry's family. A month or so before the wedding, we were with this niece's parents at another family wedding. Larry asked his brother and wife how they felt about us getting married, because they had not spoken of it other than to say that they could not attend. They said that "we don't have a problem with it" and quickly changed the subject.

∼

Looking down on the Island Inn and houses above the dock on Monhegan Island.

In the previous chapters, couples have spoken about their experiences as gay couples but also as members of their communities and, for many, as members of their churches. In small towns and rural communities, people are also identified by the family from which they were raised. Recently, a women approached me in the grocery store and said, "You're a Marszalek, aren't you?" When I told her I was, she asked which of the three brothers I am. Once she figured out who I was in the birth order of my brothers and me, she told me which of her sons and daughters had been in school around the same time as me. She then asked about my parents and told me how she knows them. After around ten minutes of asking about my family and telling me about her family, we parted ways in the coffee aisle. This is a regular occurrence for me and Larry.

Families are often intertwined with community and church life, as families show up at the same church and community functions, even after children have grown and begun their own households. Even if they do not show up to the same functions, many families gather regularly for dinners and outings. Consequently, for Mississippi gay couples living near family, even if they have not come out to their families, their families will likely know that they are living with someone of the same sex or, at the very least, that they are not in a relationship with an opposite-sex partner.

As one would expect, as the couples have shared their stories throughout this book, they have spoken about their coming-out experiences to others and the degree to which they are open about their relationships. As I discussed in Chapter One, coming out can be both a "one-time event" such as coming out to a family member, and an ongoing, even daily process, as couples interact with different people in their communities (Oswald, 2002, p. 377). As couples discussed coming out to family members, many tended to talk about the "one-time event": the large, life-changing moment when they revealed their true sexual orientation identities to a family member. On the other hand, some couples described something akin to having an elephant in the room that everyone knows is there but does not acknowledge directly; a place between staying in the closet and coming out; a middle ground in which a gay family member is known to be living with someone of the same sex, but their relationship is not named unless as pedestrian descriptors like "friends" or "roommates." Bob and Matthew (introduced in Chapter One) described this dynamic in their relationship with each of their parents:

"They [Bob's parents] know that Matthew and I are a couple, but they don't really grasp the situation; like they don't understand it. So, when they're here or when we go to visit them, we sleep in separate bedrooms. And so it's very . . . ," Bob pauses to find the right word, ". . . unusual; like they know, but they don't acknowledge it."

"I'm the roommate," Matthew says sarcastically.

"They think of you as friends?" I ask.

"The guy that rents from Bob."

Bob nods, "Yeah, Mom has referred to him as that before, but not in the last couple of years but . . ."

"That's how my mom refers to you," Matthew says chuckling.

"Now Mom just refers to you as my *friend* Matthew," Bob says using his fingers to make quotation marks in the air. My mom's a preacher's daughter. So not only were they strict Southern Baptist, but she came from a Southern Baptist preacher's house. She had a very strict upbringing and then she brought us up that way. So we still don't talk about it. We don't—I don't want to say don't acknowledge it, but it's just easier not to deal with. Everybody just kind of ignores it. They know that Matthew's here and that he's always gonna be around; but, they just don't ask questions about the nature of anything, and I don't divulge."

"Whereas with me," Matthew says, "it's a little bit different, because I'm an only child; so I'm the last of my namesake. And my parents want grandkids. It's come out before, but it's never really been disclosed. I sleep together with Bob whenever they're here, but, you know, it's always kind of awkward. It's the elephant in the room."

Coming out can be especially difficult in a small town, when families believe they must project a degree of "normality" in order to fit into their communities and churches. Some family members asked narrators to not let anyone else know that they are gay. Other family members with children withdrew, seemingly concerned that the couples' relationship could somehow negatively influence their children. Overall, and similar to the couples' recounting of both positive and negative experiences living in their communities, the couples described mixed reactions from their families regarding their relationships. Some couples described intolerance in which family members were abusive or frequently expressed their disapproval. A few couples described amazing support and acceptance by their families. Most described families that *tolerated* them as a same-sex couple, never or rarely talking about the nature of their relationships, like Howard's (1999) social compact of silence that I applied in previous chapters to today's communities: *We [the family] will tolerate you [gay people] if you don't act too queer and if you don't ask us to talk about it.* For their part, these couples stayed silent to avoid rocking the boat and to not make their family members uncomfortable.

SOCIAL COMPACT OF SILENCE

The older couples were the most likely to describe the "social compact" in which family members knew that they were in a same-sex relationship, but never discussed beyond cursory statements. This is not surprising when one considers that their parents grew up, themselves, during a time when homosexuality was considered by society to be a mental disorder and not a gay identity. If they did come out, as Sam did to his mother, it was never discussed again, at least not directly. Most of these couples described family members who supported them quietly and included their partners into the families.

Marty and Sam

Marty and Sam (introduced in Chapter Two), the couple who have been together over thirty years and live "in the middle of nowhere," describe how their families knew but preferred not to talk about it.

"Obviously my parents knew after we'd been together so many years and moved from house to house," Marty says. "You'd have to be an idiot not to know. I didn't feel the need to make it an issue or sit down and talk to them about 'this is what we're doing in the bedroom' and all that. My father was a Marine sergeant, and he was like, 'Are you happy?' I go, 'I think so.' And he goes, 'That's all I need to know.' And so it was that 'don't tell me anything else; I don't want to know anything else.'"

I turn to Sam and ask him about his parents.

"When we first moved back down here we were renting a house. It was so cold that we had to move out to my parents' house and we stayed out there for about what? A year?"

"Uh-huh."

"When did you come out to your parents, Sam?" I ask.

"It was actually before Marty and I had gotten together. It was kind of a funny story. I was living in Jackson, and I was around twenty-two. I had come home to meet my best friend that was from here. She was a lesbian and she worked in Jackson. She was coming home that day, and she was supposed to bring a birthday cake I had promised to some people. I don't know what happened, but I kept calling her and couldn't get her. I called friends in Jackson, and they couldn't find her. I had been out with my straight friends drinking, and I was mad so I went home and started packing my clothes. And this was like two o'clock in the morning. My mother got up [out of bed] and said, 'What's wrong?' Where are you going?'

"I said, 'Can you make a pot of coffee? I got to go back to Jackson and pick up the damn cake I had promised these people.'"

I nod my head, encouraging him to continue.

"So when she made the coffee she says, 'Are you okay?' And I say, as the coffee's brewing, 'Oh, I got something to tell you. I'm gay. The only thing she said was, 'Oh no!' And I said, 'Oh yes!'"

The three of us laugh at his response to his mother.

"Did you ever talk about it again?" I ask.

"No, that was just it. Before I met Marty, I used to bring boyfriends home. Because we lived on a river, we'd go canoeing, and she accepted them and was nice to them all. When Marty and I got together, we stayed out there. They counted on him to do stuff for them."

"Did you ever say that to your dad too?" I ask.

"No, I never really said anything to him. She probably did, but he never . . . never said a word. Well, actually what I think helped is that they had a gay friend back in the forties. They knew he was gay, and they were all friends and partied with him. So I think that gave them a little heads up that they knew someone."

I nod and think out loud, "If you know somebody you're less likely to be prejudiced about it."

Mary and Nancy

Mary and Nancy (introduced in Chapter Two), the retired grade school teachers, recount amazing support from their families over the years.

"We were very blessed," Mary says. "My Mom and Dad and her Mom and Dad were good friends. They didn't know each other until we got together. But because I did a lot of family things with her, and she did a lot of family things . . . my mom and dad had a pool in the backyard, and we'd all cook out and the kids and all would come over. And my mom and her mom were just like this," Mary says using her hands to indicate they were very close. "They would come together wherever we were camping, and my Dad, you know, loved her Dad. I mean, we had a very unique and very unusual circumstance, I would say."

"Yeah, we felt accepted, and we were accepted in both families; as if we were family of both families. Like when my mom died, Mary was listed as one of the daughters. It was important to my dad. It was his decision to put that in there, not mine. It was his. And that's how he wanted it put in there, as one of the daughters. They're very loving families."

"When did you both come out to your families? Or did you?" I ask.

"Actually, Mary, you did," Nancy says.

"Yeah, [to] my mom. I don't know that I ever actually said, 'Mom, I'm gay.' But my mom said: 'Ellen's [DeGeneres] pretty cool, isn't she Mary? I kind of like her. I like that she likes a girl. I don't see anything wrong with that.'

"You know, she would say stuff like that."

"She was trying to tell you it was okay," I observe.

"Yeah, she was trying to tell me it was okay. And my father—he and I went on a ride in the truck one day. I had someone [another woman] hit me a pretty good bit in a relationship before. . . . Mary pauses to catch her breath as she becomes emotional.

"I rode with him somewhere, and he said to me: 'Mary, you know, the situation you had with . . . before?'

"I said, 'Yes sir.'

"He said, 'Is everything okay?'

"And I said, 'Oh, Dad, it's wonderful! It's wonderful!'

"And he said, 'Well, I'm gonna tell you, as long as you're happy I'm happy for you.'" Mary pauses again to catch her breath. "And he loved Nancy. He took her hunting. He said she could run faster than a dang beaver," Mary finishes by laughing now.

"That's hilarious!" I say as the three of us laugh.

"Yeah, he did. He did. That's all he ever said. But that was some major support. And you know, my baby sister's always known. And my oldest sister, bless her heart, I mean, I had gotten to the point where I was so worried about it as a teacher in the school system that I got engaged [to a man]. We were gonna get married and all this stuff. I was in my twenties probably, and my oldest sister called me down to her house and she says:

"'Mary, you and I need to talk. I know that you're getting married because, you know, everybody is supposed to get married. This is what your mom and dad expect you to do, and you're doing it. Mary, that's not what you want. I know you, you know. You need to be happy. You need to go on and go for your life.'

"And she was very honest and I was so happy that she did stop me."

"That's a good sister. She must have really loved you," I say.

"Oh, yeah. She did," Mary says smiling.

"When did you come out to your parents? Or did you come out?" I ask Nancy.

"I did not. Now, my mother married my stepdad when I was twelve. He had all three boys that he had custody of, and I had a brother and a sister that had already moved out. So in early childhood there was abuse within my family unit. And it was very hard on all of us. And mother always blamed herself for that. So for me, it was like, 'I'm not gonna give her one more thing for her to have to deal with and hurt.' So, there was never an *I'm-gay*. But, you know, everything she did and everything I did, we were very open about our relationship. At that time, when we first got together, we didn't even have air conditioning in our place in town; so, in the summer we'd move out to my mom and dad's and live with them in the summer, because they had air, you know."

"And were they okay with you being in the same room together?" I ask.

"Yeah, we were in the same room. And my younger brother is closest to me in age, eleven months younger than I. He moved out, he went to Atlanta and contracted AIDS. And, he died within eleven months of the diagnosis."

"I'm so sorry," I sympathize.

"So, watching them and the dealing with that—the pain—but then it also was liberating in the fact that I didn't have to say a word because it seemed to be that everything they said during that time, it was all . . ."

"Nonjudgmental," Mary finishes.

Nancy nods. "Nonjudgmental. It was like, you don't have to say anything to know they love you. But like for my dad—my dad was just a country boy—and I call him *Dad*; he's my stepdad, but he was my dad. And when my little brother went to the hospital in the very last stages, and we walked in . . . we were there . . . we couldn't go in the room because at that point you had to wear all that stuff. All that stuff. And, so we were in like the ICU room where all families are. We were there, and the young man that he was with at the time happened to come in and the young man stopped and said, 'I'm sorry. I didn't know you were here.' And started to leave and my Dad—this country boy that he was—he jumped up and said, 'No, don't leave.' He said, 'I don't understand this, but I know that you love my son, and you're welcome here.'"

"That's amazing," I say.

"Yes, it really is. And then to watch my parents with that—losing a son and then to come back within the Baptist Church; and the church did the best they could but it was not . . . the way they said it's okay is they didn't say anything. So there was not a *I'm-sorry-your-son-died*. There was not any recognition of the death. It was just pretend like it didn't happen. So to watch that pain . . . and so I guess I say all that to say, it was my way of protecting them."

"When her mom got sick," Mary says, "right before she passed away, we were up in her room with her; sitting with her. She had pneumonia, and she was kind of asleep and awake, asleep and awake. And she turned around to me, and she said, 'I see y'all. Y'all are rocking in a love . . .'"

"Love seat," Nancy finishes. "That was one of the last things that we heard her say."

"It sure was."

COMING OUT TO MIXED REACTIONS

Other couples who did come out to family members received mixed reactions, including acceptance, tolerance, disapproval, or disbelief, depending on the family members. Even after coming out, silence was again a theme for many narrators. Some, like Drew, were encouraged by the person to whom they came out to keep their sexual orientation a secret from other family members. Others, like Neal, chose to keep their sexual orientation a secret from some family members to avoid rejection or withdrawal by them.

The dilemma that many of the couples expressed is being true to themselves in the face of unspoken messages from their communities and families that they should not "rock the boat." Coming out to oneself and to others, though, is a developmental process important to the identity development of lesbians and gay men. Research by marriage and family therapists has indicated that hiding one's sexual orientation is related to psychological distress such as anxiety, depression, and substance abuse. "Increased outness" has also been shown to be related to increased relationship satisfaction (Knoble & Linville, 2012). This makes sense, because the more a couple is out, the more likely they are to have support for their relationship, itself. On the flip side, being more open about one's relationship risks facing prejudice and discrimination, either overt or subtle.

Psychology researchers have also found that support from family and friends for both same-gender and heterosexual couples is related to higher levels of overall well-being and less psychological distress (Graham & Barnow, 2013). On the other hand, as with any minority group, gays and lesbians must deal regularly with minority stress, "the excess stress to which individuals from stigmatized social categories are exposed as a result of their social, often a minority, position." (Meyer, 2013, p. 4). Couples have reported experiencing minority stress not only in their communities and places of employment but also as a result of interactions with their families (Rostosky, Riggle, Gray, & Hatton, 2007). Not surprisingly, minority stress is related to higher levels of psychological distress (e.g., depression, anxiety, substance abuse) (e.g., Cochran & Mays, 2009; Lewis, Derlega, Griffin & Krowinski, 2003).

In another study, gay and lesbian couples reported that they coped with the minority stress they experienced by "reframing negative experiences, concealing their relationship, creating social support, and affirming self and partnership" (Rostosky, Riggle, Gray, & Hatton, 2007, p. 392). In a study of fifteen gay and lesbian couples, Knoble and Linville (2012) reported that a couple's level of outness depended on the situation and that being out was a "constant decision making process" that was often affected by the fear of physical harm or losing one's job (p. 333). As with the many of my couples, the couples interviewed by Knobe and Linville said that being in a relationship "increased visibility as a sexual minority" and is a "catalyst for coming out" (p. 334). Being out was a mixed bag, though, leading to increased relationship satisfaction and social support but also increased stress from interactions with their families.

Drew and Neal

Drew and Neal (introduced in Chapter Two), the couple who live in a gated community in Jackson, had mixed reactions from family members when they came out to them. When I interviewed them, Drew's mother had recently called him to ask about his relationship with Neal. They both have close family members they have chosen not come out to, because they are not sure how they would react and because they do not want to make them uncomfortable.

"So are you able to be yourselves with your families?" I ask.

"How topical . . ." Neal says laughing.

"How topical," Drew repeats. "I've more or less been out with my friends and with people at work since college, but never with my family. And that's a real thorn in my side right now. For years, you know, I grew up in a very Baptist family, a very churchgoing family. And for years it was like, there was no reason to bring this up; it'll just be a point of contention that we don't need. And then I would think, 'Well, they know, they just don't want to talk about it.' And what I really meant was that I didn't want to deal with the conflict. And only recently, you know, my mom called me up one day, and out of the blue she just said, 'What is your relationship with Neal?' And I said, 'Well, it's what you think it is. He's my life partner.' And, uh, . . . we talked a little bit and she, because of her religious beliefs she . . ."

"She followed her convictions," Neal finishes.

"Yeah, she said, 'Well, I just don't think that that's right.'"

"And we'd had a warm relationship with my in-laws," Neal says. "Regular Sunday lunch visitor into their family."

"We never spent a lot of time, but lots of that kind of stuff; just going home for lunch on Sunday afternoons or something. I really always thought in my mind that I'd have this conversation with my parents one day, and it would be kind of, 'Well, we were just waiting on you to tell us.' And then we'd all have a good laugh about it."

"I always assumed that they were much more progressive in their acceptance," Neal says. "Even though their church lives might have taught them different, I thought that they were more accepting, because they've always been extremely kind and warm and compassionate towards me."

"You felt very welcome when you were there?" I ask Neal.

"Absolutely. Yeah."

"Yeah," Drew agrees, "and I think they are that way. My mom, to my knowledge, has not talked to my father about this, and I've kind of backed off of the idea of doing that. I think that I still need to do it. I'm certain that my brother and my sister and their spouses know that I'm gay. I have cousins who are gay, and we are kind of out to each other. I have other cousins and relations that I've talked with about this, but, you know, my sister is married to a Presbyterian minister [who is] very conservative. I would imagine that he would have a little bit of a problem with this. It's one of those things where, you know, you keep meaning to do something, and thirty years pass and you haven't done it yet. I don't know why I've never done this; other than, I'm by nature a person who really doesn't believe in conflict of any kind. I'd rather not have unpleasant conversations, because I have to do that at work a lot and so, I don't need that in my personal life. And I regret it now. I regret that all this time has passed and that I've never done this. I think that probably my whole family knows that I'm gay, but they're not going to bring it up if I don't bring it up. And I'm not bringing it up because I don't want. . . . I would feel awful if my sister found herself in a position where her husband was saying, 'I don't want our kids around him,' because I know that would be very hurtful for her. I don't necessarily think that he would do that, but I think that it would make things uncomfortable for everybody."

"I know Joey less well than you, and I think he would do that," Neal says with conviction.

"You think he would?" Drew responds.

"Yeah, because he has two boys. I think it would be like, 'Stay away from Uncle Drew.' I think he would do that."

"Because Uncle Drew would rub off on them somehow?" I ask.

"Or even worse, it wouldn't even be Uncle Drew's fault. Maybe, somehow genetically, there's this 'gay thing' going on within the family. If Joey knew that there were some cousins that were gay too, he would freak out that there's something that came to those boys through their mother. I think that would just internally kill that man. It would be hard for him. I wouldn't want him to have to feel that. Because I feel like he would; because he wouldn't want to blame Drew for anything. He would blame something that he had no control over."

"So all these years, you would go over to the house for, you know, lunches and . . ."

"It's always been, 'This is Drew's friend Neal' or 'Drew's room-mate Neal,'" Drew says anticipating my question. "It's amazing what people can . . ."

"The delusion," Neal adds.

"The denial. The delusion people can live with when they want to," Drew finishes.

"Don't ask, don't tell," I say.

"That's what it was," Drew agrees.

"How about you?" I ask, turning to Neal.

"I came out to my dad at sixteen and a half."

"What happened that you came out at that point?"

"Uh . . . I'd gotten my driver's license. I'd started spending a *great* deal of time out. I used to go to a neighboring town, Biloxi. There's an Air Force Base there, and I used to pick up men or be picked up by men; generally, the airmen who were essentially high school seniors. I mean, they'd just gotten out of high school, and they en-listed. They were a year or two older than me. Somebody who looked more or less like me would slip me his ID card, and we'd get to go out drinking and stuff. My dad was concerned with my drinking and coming home wasted and sometimes not coming home at all; just calling and saying like, 'I've had too much to drink. I'm gonna stay here.' And you know, this is a sixteen-year-old boy saying these things, so he said something like, 'You're gonna talk to me. What's going on here?' I told him. I said, 'I have a driver's license, and I know where to go to have fun.' And he just was patient with that but told me, 'If you're going to drink, I don't want you to drive. And if you don't come home, you just call me and tell me where you are and that you're okay.' And that level of understanding and that level of leniency allowed me to feel comfortable to tell him where I was."

"That's amazing. How did he react when you told him?"

"He said, 'Well, I know people who are like this and if you have a problem with it, if you want to have counseling, I'll help you find it. But, if this is the way things are then take care of yourself.' We agreed that we were not going to tell my mom, because of her Baptist background. He said, 'This would do her no good at all. Sleep on this as a news issue, because sometimes people experiment, and sometimes they change their mind. There's no sense owning that; there's no sense making that as a statement when it might not be the way that you stay.' So, I think it was a good idea not to be candid with my mom."

Jerry and Karl

Jerry and Karl (introduced in Chapter One), the couple who were married in Vermont, have also had mixed reactions from family members, receiving both support and concern that they not be too open. When Karl told his mother that he was gay, he and Jerry had already been together as a couple for five years.

"I remember when I told my mother, and you're going to laugh at this. I told her the Saturday before we started the Episcopal Church, and of course she knew. We even had the second bedroom set up to be Jerry's room [so people would think they were just roommates]. Even though she knew, her response was: 'Well just don't let any-body else know.' And I thought, 'Darlin' you're the last person that knows that.' And it was so funny because she's telling me, 'Don't tell this one, and don't tell that one.' And I'm like, 'Mom, actually they already know.'

"And you know she loves me. And Jerry will tell you. We [Jerry and Karl] got in a HUGE argument at Thanksgiving. It was about a year ago, and I don't even remember what it was over. But we got into this knockdown drag-out; I'm talking about, 'It's over!' And my mom came over here and literally took Jerry's side to the degree of saying, 'If you ever leave Jerry, your family's through with you.' And it's like, it was worth getting in the fight to hear my mother say that."

"That's very interesting," I say.

"Yeah, she's gone to a Pentecostal church. She's come a long way. I asked her the other day, 'How did you finally become okay with where we are?' And she said, 'Because I just think if you're wrong, God will correct it.' And that this is her opinion, I can respect it.

Which, I don't think we're wrong but, you know, she's come a long way.

"And before we met, Karl was kind of lonely, and his mother was praying for somebody to come into Karl's life. And here I came!"

We all laugh again. I find that they mix in the laughter with the stories about serious topics.

I switch gears and ask about their fathers.

"My parents are divorced," Jerry says. "I love my dad. My dad loves me. He's supportive or whatever. He treats me more like a friend. And he lives out west, so obviously there's not much of a relationship. My parents divorced when I was five. But I've got a wonderful stepdad."

"Vermont was very much paid for by his stepfather. I think Jerry's mom did a lot, but obviously when you're married your money is pooled together. I think there was a lot of things that we got to enjoy in Vermont because of him. And my father, I think without a doubt, knows. It's never been a discussion that we've sat down and had, but I think he knows. One of the things that gave me a clue is that my mom said a few months ago they were talking about having their will made out, and my dad said that he wanted to make sure it's done right; where Jerry and me and my brother all get an equal share. In a way I've always wanted to ask but it's kind of like, don't rock the boat."

"So your mother hasn't told him?" I ask.

"I think he totally knows that we're a couple, but he doesn't know anything about the marriage. Now my brother's a totally different story."

"His sister-in-law is wonderful."

"Yeah, my sister-in-law is wonderful, but my brother called me up four hours before the wedding. He goes to the Jerry Falwell, Bible-beating, bacon-eating, Baptist church."

"So you're in Vermont, and he calls you on the phone?" I ask.

They both nod.

"I just knew it was gonna be canceled," Jerry says sarcastically.

"And I said, 'I can't do this. I totally respect your beliefs, and we'll talk about this when I get back. And I'm the same person that you've always known. I think what people don't get is the gay lifestyle is not just Pensacola and New Orleans and LA and having a parade with guys in their thongs," Karl continues. "We live a normal life. We don't have sex swinging from the chandeliers like people think."

"And we're not gonna look down on anybody, however they want to be. We've got friends who cross dress every weekend or whatever. I mean, we're just tolerable and that's how we want to be treated."

Noah and Terrance

Noah and Terrance (introduced in Chapter One) are the young couple engaged to be married. They both had negative responses from their families when they were coming out, including Terrance being abused by his stepfather, who told him he needed to have his gayness beaten out of him. Noah describes being kicked out of the house when he came out to his family.

"I came out at twenty," Noah says. "I told my grandmother, and she didn't believe me. She thought I was lying." While Terrance and I laugh, Noah mimics his grandmother:

"*You ain't gay, boy.*' That's how she talked. And then she told *everyone.* So for the next like two, three weeks, it seemed like every couple of days I'd get a phone call from an auntie or uncle. My parents never did call me. My dad sent me a message talking about I should at least come see my mom and my sister, because I was basically kicked out of the house."

"When they found out you were gay?" I ask.

"No, I came out two weeks after I moved out. My dad told me, 'Don't be gay and live in this house.' Because the guy I was dating previous to Terrance would come over to the house, and he was 'my friend.' They just knew, you know. But I just kept denying it, kept denying it, kept denying it; and then they told me if I felt that way I should be gone, and so I left. And then I told my grandma like two weeks later, you know, when she was like, 'Why aren't you at the house anymore?'"

"I was like, 'Well, I'm gay, and dad told me this, and I left.'

"[And she said,] 'You can't be, because you're not. We don't have any gays in this family.'"

"Did you tell your grandmother knowing that she would tell everyone else?" I ask.

"Part of me knew she would, but part of me thought that she would do it in defense of me. She did it to try to get somebody to talk to me to take me back to Christianity and to my 'straightness.'"

"Do you two hang out with any family members from either side?" I ask.

"Yeah," Noah replies. "Terrance's sister. We just visited her for her birthday in Texas. Actually we did get a chance to see his mom there, because she wanted him and her to go to church, but I wasn't invited. Like we've hung out with his mom before, but now she has a new husband who doesn't like homosexuals."

∾

Silence was a theme that permeated through most of the couples' stories in a variety of ways. The older couples, like Mary/Nancy and Marty/Sam were the most likely to describe the "social compact" of silence in their relationships with their families. Neither the couples nor families ever directly acknowledged that they were in gay relationship. Nevertheless, as Howard (1999) noted, silence does not necessarily equate to lack of support. Their families' silences were occasionally broken by subtle acknowledgements of their same-sex relationships. Within the silence, itself, these couples felt support from their families.

Marty related how his father wanted to know if he was happy, hinting that he was talking about Marty's relationship with Sam. Similarly, Mary and Nancy, who describe touching support from their parents, knew that their parents recognized them a couple without the words "gay or lesbian" ever being said, although they commented in subtle ways such as Mary's mother telling her that it was okay that Ellen DeGeneres "likes a girl."

Another way that silence was used was as a means to protect children, whether for noble reasons or homophobic reactions. As a child, Terrance had to be silent about his sexual orientation and attempt to hide his mannerisms that others interpreted as gay to protect himself from his stepfather's abuse. Alicia and Rae ordered Rae's mother to be silent about her disapproval of their relationship to protect their children. On other hand, in some cases family members believed they needed to "protect" children from exposure to gay couples, often because of an irrational fear such as that the children could be seduced into becoming gay themselves. Rae's sister told her that she and Alicia could not stay in her house because she was concerned it would put "the wrong impression in her [four-year-old] son's mind." Drew has chosen to be silent about his relationship with Neal, because he believes his sister's husband would not allow them near their children.

A third way that silence was used was to protect adult family members, usually parents. Some family members asked narrators to keep their sexual orientation a secret from other family members. Neal's father asked him not to tell his mother, because of her "Baptist background." Karl's mother asked him not to let anyone else know that he was in a relationship with Jerry. In other cases, narrators made the decision to use silence about their sexual orientation to protect the family member or their relationship with them. Jerry assumed his father knew that he is gay, but said, "In a way I've always wanted to ask [if he knows that I'm gay] but it's kind of like, don't rock the boat." Nancy wanted to protect her mother, who had a difficult childhood, from news that would be upsetting to her: "I'm not gonna give her one more thing for her to have to deal with and hurt. So, there was never an *I'm-gay.*"

The question is from what are lesbians and gay men protecting their families? Is it simply to protect the receiver from "distressing news"? Many have written about a southern culture that is accepting of eccentricities as long as they do not threaten the social order (e.g., Howard, 1999; Johnson, 2008). Are same-sex couples tolerated if they are viewed as "friends"? Would openly acknowledging that they are romantically and sexually involved threaten the belief that "normal" families in society should comprise heterosexual couples and their children?

Ruiz (2012), a professor of American studies, wrote that lesbians and gay are socialized not to talk about sex: "Homophobia has meant, of course, that queer sex is both policed and silenced. As such, we are compelled to politely talk about our identities as if they can be easily separated from our erotic desires and practices" (p. 121). Many couples have stated that they want to avoid making others uncomfortable. In the case of many of the couples, like Bob and Matthew, it's enough for their families to know that they are "friends" with another man; knowing more than that might cross an imaginary line into uncomfortableness or awkwardness. Marty recalled when his father asked him if he is happy, subtly referring to his relationship with Sam. When Marty replied affirmatively, his father said, "that's all I want to know." Marty for his part explained that "I didn't feel the need to make it an issue or sit down and talk to them about 'this is what we're doing in the bedroom.'" I think Karl speaks to the pressure felt by many gay people in the South to project a normality in order to fit into their families and communities: "I think what people don't get is the gay lifestyle is not just Pensacola and New Orleans and LA and having a parade with guys in their thongs. We live a normal life. We don't have sex swinging from the chandeliers like people think. And we're not gonna look down on anybody, however they want to be. We've got friends who cross dress every weekend or whatever. I mean, we're just tolerable and that's how we want to be treated."

The social compact of silence and tolerance go hand in hand: We will tolerate you if don't act too *queer* and if you don't ask us to talk about *it*. Crossing the line for some couples is acknowledging to family members that they are gay or talking about their relationship as romantic or intimate. For others, who are openly gay, crossing the line is not being "tolerable," as Karl said. In other words, we don't want to know about or imagine that same-sex couples are romantically or sexually intimate. Larry and I have both had the experience

John and Larry's wedding picture outside Monhegan Community Church.

of noting people, even people who treat us as a married couple, become uncomfortable if we demonstrate any public displays of affection like holding hands. Part of silence, then, is also monitoring one's nonverbal behaviors that might indicate that a couple is more than "friends."

From one perspective, the use of silence to not cross a line could be viewed as internalized homophobia, a desire to be viewed as the "normal" defined by a heterosexist society. However, as Howard (1999) noted, silence can also be a strategy to protect oneself. For the couples, any overt displays of affection in public in their small towns might lead to verbal or physical assault, discrimination, or rejection. Consequently, as I discuss in the next chapter, gay people find ways to create "queer space" within a culture than expects them to be tolerable.

~

Prior to our wedding in Maine, I had found myself becoming more and more angry when I attended Larry's family events. I watched how other in-laws fit in, and I felt that I had never been welcomed as they had. *They never asked about our lives and spent most of the time talking about theirs. When other family members became engaged, there was great excitement and joy. We often listened to their stories of how they met, what the plans were for the wedding, and joined in their excitement. We attended the weddings and gave generous gifts. But, as we prepared to get married, I felt like an outsider and wondered if I should keep going with Larry to his family events. But it's important to Larry, I told myself, and that's all that matters. More than anything, though, I saw how it hurt Larry to not experience the excitement and support over our marriage as we did from my family and from many of our friends.*

A few weeks after returning, two of our close friends threw a party for us at their home on the river. Family and friends who had not been able to travel to Maine came, including Larry's brother and family from Florida, and his father and stepmother. This meant a lot to Larry, who had not had any of his family come to the wedding. Our experience in Maine and the Mississippi party overshadowed any negative feelings. We felt supported and "sent off" into our lives together by most of the people we love. The question that remained for me, however, was "Do we have a future in Mississippi as a married, gay couple?"

REFERENCES

Cochran, S. D., & Mays, V. M. (2009). Burden of psychiatric morbidity among lesbian, gay, and bisexual individuals in the California Quality of Life Survey. *Journal of Abnormal Psychology, 118,* 647–58. doi:0.1037/a0016501

Gates, G. J. (2014). Same-sex couples in Mississippi: A demographic summary. Retrieved from the Williams Institute website: https://williamsinstitute.law.ucla .edu/demographics/mississippi-ss-couples-demo-dec-2014/

Graham, J. M., & Barnow, Z. B. (2013). Stress and social support in gay, lesbian, and heterosexual couples: Direct effects and buffering models. *Journal of Family Psychology, 4,* 569–78. doi:10.1037/a0033420

Howard, J. (1999). *Men like that: A southern queer history.* Chicago, IL: University of Chicago Press.

Johnson, E. P. (2008). *Sweet tea: Black gay men of the south.* Chapel Hill, NC: University of North Carolina Press.

Knoble, N. B., & Linville, D. (2012). Outness and relationship satisfaction in same-gender couples. *Journal of Marital and Family Therapy, 38,* 330–39.

Lewis, R. J., Derlega, V. J., Griffin, J. L., & Krowinski, A. C. (2003). Stressors for gay men and lesbians: Life stress, gay-related stress, stigma consciousness, and depressive symptoms. *Journal of Social and Clinical Psychology, 22,* 716–29. doi:10.1521/jscp.22.6.716.22932

Meyer, I. H. (2013). Prejudice, social stress, and mental health in lesbian, gay, and bisexual populations: Conceptual issues and research evidence. *Psychology of Sexual Orientation and Gender Diversity, 1,* 3–26. doi:10.1037/2329-0382.1.S.3

Oswald, R. F. (2002). Resilience within family networks of lesbian and gay men: Intentionality and redefinition. *Journal of Marriage and Family, 64,* 374–83. doi:10.1111/j.1741-3737.2002.00374.x

Rivers, D. (2012). Queer family stories: Learning from oral histories with lesbian mothers and gay fathers from the pre-Stonewall era. In N. A. Boyd & H. N. R. Ramírez (Eds.), *Bodies of evidence: The practice of queer oral history* (pp. 57–72). New York, NY: Oxford University Press.

Rostosky, S. S., Riggle, E. D. B., Gray, B. E., & Hatton, R. L. (2007). Minority stress experiences in committed same-sex couple relationships. *Professional Psychology: Research and Practice, 38,* 392–400. doi:10.1037/0735-7028.38.4.392

Ruiz, J. (2012). Private lives and public history: On excavating the sexual past in queer oral history practice. In N. A. Boyd & H. N. R. Ramírez (Eds.), *Bodies of evidence: The practice of queer oral history* (pp. 113–29). New York, NY: Oxford University Press.

Part Two

CHAPTER FOUR

Meeting

After I bought my house in Columbus, I wondered how I would meet potential boyfriends. There were some gay faculty that I knew at my graduate school alma mater, Mississippi State University, some twenty minutes away, but it seemed like all of them were either already in a relationship, closeted, or we just didn't click. One of my gay friends described Columbus and the surrounding area as a "doughnut" for single gay middle-aged men: there are the young gay college students at the nearby universities and then there are the gay men who are in relationships or are closeted. Left in the empty space are the few single men. The ones in the middle come and go; in fact, of the gay men I know who grew up in the area or went to the university, most have moved on to a big city in the south such as Atlanta, Birmingham, Dallas, New Orleans, or Memphis. Even Tennessee Williams, the gay playwright who was born in Columbus, only came back to visit.

Every week the Columbus gay happy hour group met. I had been going regularly but had not met anyone to whom I felt drawn or attracted. Going to the happy hour groups was like riding a roller-coaster. Some evenings there would be a large group of men from the surrounding area, a mix of young and old, professional and nonprofessional, closeted and out of the closet. I would leave the happy hour feeling connected to a community and feeling positive about staying in Mississippi. Other evenings, only a few people would show up, and they would be people with whom I had little in common. For example, there was the occasional older married man who was closeted, but

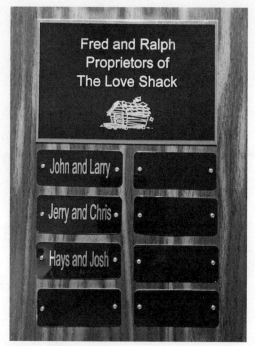

Plaque provided to Fred and Ralph from three couples.

wanted to, as he told his wife, "hang out with the boys." There was the Air Force officer who looked around the room several times when he came into the bar to make sure he did not know anyone.

Often, I found the only thing we all had in common was that we were gay. Although the group met on a Tuesday evening, it met in the back room off the bar of a Mexican restaurant. Tuesday's were slow at the restaurant, but some locals would still come into the bar. Word spread that the "gays" were meeting there on Tuesdays. It often felt like being in a fishbowl, with the locals curiously peering into the room as they walked by. Not surprisingly, people seemed less on guard and were more likely to join the group when people hosted the happy hour at their homes.

Fred and Ralph, the first gay couple I met in Columbus, held their annual Christmas party for the happy hour group at their house. That evening I saw Larry. I was instantly drawn to him both emotionally *and physically. Wearing a Tommy Hilfiger shirt and Levi's, he was leaning against the kitchen counter. He had dark black hair with sprinkles of grey on the sides and a five o'clock shadow on his face. His brown eyes were kind and genuine. I began to approach him and then I paused.*

I recognized him. My heart skipped a beat. I had met him over fifteen years ago when I was a graduate student at Mississippi State University. I had just started dating Michael with whom I ended up spending the next twelve years. We met Larry and his boyfriend at a party. I remembered being attracted to him and wanting to know him. Experiencing guilt that I would be drawn to another man when I was on a date with Michael, I suppressed my feelings.

Now here he was again after all this time; after my spending twelve years with Michael; after my finishing graduate school and moving away; after evacuating back to Mississippi and buying a house; after all this time. Here he was. We immediately clicked. Several months later, he moved into my house. As time went on, it became our house, both legally and emotionally. We sold his house across the border in Alabama and used the money to do extensive renovations.

Larry and I were not the only couple who met at one of Fred and Ralph's parties. Two other couples who live in the area met at their home. Fred and Ralph have been together almost fifty years. After Fred and Ralph were legally married, the three of us couples took them out to dinner and gave them a plaque for them to hang in their home entitled "The Love Shack."

$\sim$

When a single, heterosexual person moves to a rural area in the South, it is not uncommon for community members to introduce them to potential opposite-sex dating mates, especially through their churches. It would be a rare occurrence in small-town and rural Mississippi for community members to ask a newcomer about their gender dating preferences before introducing them to people. We are still years away from a society, at least in the rural South, in which gay people feel safe to be fully out in their communities and in which community members seek to assist them in meeting potential friends and partners.

Although same-sex marriage is legal in the Unites States, we continue to live in a heterosexist society in which people often assume that others are heterosexual, and if they are not, they should be. The extent to which gay people face heterosexism, prejudice, discrimination, and even violence differs based on one's environment. It is obviously more pronounced in a state like Mississippi that had to be forced by the Supreme Court to recognize same-sex marriage and that has no protections for people who are not heterosexual. According to an analysis of polling data, the Williams Institute (2019) estimated that only 3.5 percent of the population in Mississippi identifies as LGBT, including those who identify as transgender. Mississippi ranks forty-second in percentage among all states and the District of Columbia (DC) between a high of 9.8 percent in DC and a low of 2.7 percent in North Dakota. Consequently, the normal struggles people encounter when they enter the dating pool are compounded for gay people. In addition to entering a much smaller dating pool than heterosexuals, they must figure out who is in the pool in the first place and navigate the risks that come from being gay in our society.

When I lived in Wilton Manors, known as the "gayborhood" of South Florida, I could walk from my house to the gay bars, coffee shops, community center, and gym to meet other gay people. In fact, most of my neighbors and many of my coworkers were openly gay. In other words, it did not take much effort to meet other gays and lesbians. I could practically run into a gay person walking down the street! At the time, I was in a relationship; however, if I had wanted to go on a first date with someone, I could have chosen many restaurants where it would be stranger to see a heterosexual couple than a gay couple.

Meeting other gay people for friendships, relationships, and/or sex requires a resourcefulness and courage that is different for most heterosexuals in rural areas and for those gay people living openly in a place such as Wilton Manors. It requires finding or constructing places to meet others like you and acknowledging, at least to them, that you are gay. The more open people are about their same-sex desires, at least to other gay people and allies, the more likely they are to be introduced to others like them. However, being "out" carries risks. In Mississippi and many other rural areas of the country, people can be denied housing and fired from a job simply for identifying as nonheterosexual.

In describing the experiences of "LGBT-identifying youth" in rural America, Gray (2009) wrote that they must balance "the logistical needs to fit in and conform to the familiarity that structures rural life" (p. 168) with a need to be visible and experience LGBT culture. Similarly, my narrators described a push and pull between fitting into their rural and small-town communities, while expressing their sexual orientation identities through connection with other gay people. Connecting with others requires accessing or constructing "queer spaces," in other words, spaces created when two or more gay people meet (Howard, 1997a; Schweignofer, 2016). Queer spaces are constructed to provide safe spaces for gay people to be themselves and support each other, away from the heterosexism and homophobia that many face in their daily lives (Lewin, 2018). Whereas, a queer space may be an institution such as a gay bar or bookstore in an urban area, it can also be something that is created in the moment. In can be an impromptu meeting between two friends, an unexpected meeting between two people at work, or a planned gathering such as a party.

Accessing queer space in rural areas often means having to travel in and out of one's home community (Howard, 1997b). The queer space, itself, can be either public or private, as rural gay people construct their own gay communities out of previously nonqueer space (Schweignofer, 2016). For example, several years ago a single gay man and his single lesbian friend rented a public boat house on the Tombigbee River between West Point and Columbus. They invited all the gay people they knew to a "boat house party" and encouraged others to spread the word. Their goal was to bring as many gay people as possible together to expand their potential dating pools and meet new friends. Over a hundred people showed up from across north Mississippi and Alabama, creating a private party on public land, a gay community for the evening.

GAY PARTIES

There is a "well-documented" history dating back to the 1920s of the importance of parties for gays and lesbians seeking to meet each other and to develop a community when few or no other social institutions for lesbians and gays existed (Bérubé, 1990; Howard, 1997b; Watkins, 2018). These "gay parties" were hosted by other lesbians and gays, usually white men, because it was difficult for single women and African Americans, even those with the financial resources, to own homes, due to segregation and discrimination (Watkins, 2018, p. 87). Gay parties afforded gays and lesbians a place to congregate outside of the public eye during a time when police actively sought to inhibit the efforts of gay people from congregating. In his history of lesbian and gay life in the mid-1900 Florida Panhandle, Watkins wrote that "the mixing that occurred because of the gay parties was between the local and the nonlocal. Through the gay parties, people forged friendships and made connections that spanned the South" (p. 89). In addition Watkins noted that in areas with no gay bars, parties were often gender mixed and sometimes racially mixed.

Gay parties were not entirely safe, especially if they were large, more public parties or if they caught the attention of neighbors. Being arrested risked having one's identity as lesbian or gay exposed to family and employers (Howard, 1997b). In his interview with Howard, Barry Kline, a white, gay man who lived in Birmingham, Alabama, after he returned home from serving in World War II, described his arrest in 1962 during a police raid of a house party. The arrest led to his name and address being published in the local paper.

One way that Mississippi gay parties of today are similar to the gay parties in the past as described by Watkins (2018) and Howard (1997b) is that people still commute to the larger parties from outside their local areas. A LGBT professional group for Starkville and Mississippi State University has regular potluck gatherings at the homes of members willing to host with people regularly bringing friends from outside the area. Occasionally, a gay person with a large enough home will host a party for a holiday or special event such as a birthday, and people from out of the area will spend the weekend at the home or with other friends in the area. Recently, two couples, one gay and one lesbian, hosted a party in the combination gym/assembly hall of an old school building, often used for weddings and other special events, in the countryside outside of a small town in north central Mississippi. The party featured a staffed bar, food, dancing, and a drag show on the stage. People came to the party from Tupelo, Columbus, Starkville, Oxford, and as far north as Corinth.

All of the examples I've described included both lesbians and gay men, and sometimes included bisexuals and transgender people. I believe that having a small community of LGBT people along with no bars or other social institutions means that people are less likely to segregate by gender here, as I have encountered at gay parties in urban areas. Nevertheless, there is still segregation based on socioeconomic class and race. Although the large parties I have attended in north Mississippi are racially mixed, the majority of the attendees are white. I imagine part of this has to do with the hosts generally being white and middle class to upper class, along with the social segregation based on socioeconomic status and race that seems to be common in the South. Alicia and Rae told me that a few young, black gay men in north Mississippi will throw dance parties at an old fairground with African American gay people attending from near and far.

Of course, I am only describing the large gay parties in which hosts encourage their friends to bring other friends, sending an invitation through a Facebook group or email list. There are obviously many other dinner parties and gatherings that are limited to smaller groups of friends, which means they are less likely to be gender and racially mixed. In addition, when someone is not throwing a party, many of the towns that anchor a micropolitan area have weekly happy hours or dinner groups. At the Columbus happy hour, for example, several regulars drive an hour or more from their rural areas to attend. Without a major metropolitan area in a 120-mile radius, the micropolitan becomes the hub for people to meet.

Sophie and Faith

Sophie and Faith (introduced in Chapter One) are the couple who invited me to lunch at their farm. Before they officially became a couple, they were acquaintances from the many gatherings and gay parties that had occurred among the lesbians in their area of south Mississippi. A common friend encouraged them to meet for a date. They had their first date in a public, planned space and solidified their relationship at a gay party hosted by Sophie. In turn, at the parties they have hosted together over the years, they introduced at least one other lesbian couple, as Fred and Ralph did for Larry and me in Columbus.

"How did you meet?" I ask.

"Well we've known each other for a long time," Sophie replies. "[Our friend] Tammy pretty much was kind of putting us together. Tammy is a matchmaker."

"Yeah," Faith nods her head. "Tammy pretty much did it. She called me one night, and I was folding clothes. I remember, she said, 'Are you in? I want to ask you something.' And I said, 'What?' And she said, 'Would you be interested in dating somebody?' And I said, 'Why?'"

"See, Faith wasn't with anybody."

"And she said," Faith continues, "'Well, you know, I think Sophie's ready to start dating.' So that went on for about a month, and then finally Sophie called me wanting to know if I wanted to go to the show."

"Oh that's right," Sophie replies, "I asked if you wanted to go out to the movies with me."

"Movies. Mm-hm. So then we went to the movies."

"We went to see Big Momma."

"Big Momma," Faith repeats laughing.

I remember that they are referring to the comedy, Big Momma's House, in which actor Martin Lawrence portrays an FBI agent who works undercover in disguise as a large, southern grandmother known to her family as Big Momma.

"Yeah, I love comedy. So, I go to the bathroom. She's gonna get some popcorn and a Coke ..."

"Coke ...," Faith repeats.

"I gotta tell this," Sophie says, sounding amused as Faith nods her head smiling. "So she's gonna get some popcorn and Coke. Now, I don't know her that well, you know. So I go to the restroom; I come out and she has spilled this gallon of Coke all ..." Sophie's voice trails off into laughter.

" ... on the floor, "Faith finishes.

"And I thought, 'Oh my God. What am I getting myself into?'"

The three of us laugh in unison.

"I mean it's everywhere!" Faith exclaims.

"She said, 'I don't know what happened.' I was just like, 'Well just go into the movie wet.' You know she did. Bless her heart."

"I did. So, we started seeing each other."

"I should have known then you were the spiller."

"Yep. And I haven't stopped."

"She hasn't!"

"And we love Big Momma. We've seen it a hundred times."

"So you sat there and laughed together on your first date," I say.

"Yeah!" they say in unison.

Shortly after, Sophie threw a party at her farm, and they kissed for the first time. Today, they mark that day as their anniversary.

Faith says, "We got a picture of that on our dresser, that first party that we're actually together."

"It was an outside party," Sophie adds. "We probably had fifty people here."

"We did. We started 'em, because people just kind of drifted away."

"We started 'em because, you know, I was taking care of Daddy, and she was taking care of her mother, and we couldn't see anybody; we couldn't go anywhere."

"Or do anything."

"Or do anything, and I said, 'Look, we just bring 'em out here to the house.'"

"So we started having parties, so we could see people."

'We were having cook-outs, but then we starting having house parties," Sophie explains.

"Yeah," Faith agrees. "And we couldn't travel or go nowhere so the parties was our vacations, more or less."

"We just brought everybody to see us," Sophie says chuckling.

"Mm-hm. A lot of these people would not have seen each other if it hadn't been for us having the parties."

"Have any other people met out here at the parties that are in relationships now?" I ask.

"Well, there's Pam and Cindy," Sophie replies. We've had some potentials that didn't pan out."

"You could be new matchmakers," I say humorously.

"Oh yeah," Faith says laughing.

"But see now we've reached the age where everybody we know is with somebody," Sophie says more seriously.

"Partnered up, yeah. I would say everybody's pretty much either never gonna be with nobody or . . ."

"Or they're happy in their relationship." Sophie finishes.

MEETING IN A BAR

Since at least World War II, gay bars have been a place for gays and lesbians to meet each other for friendship, sexual encounters, and/or romantic connections out of the public eye (Bérubé, 1990; D'Emilio, 1998). Like house parties, they offered a place for people to let their guards down and to connect with a community. Nevertheless, it could be risky to go to bar, because homosexuality was illegal and police frequently raided gay bars unless owned by organized crime that paid off the police. Consequently, according to Escoffier (1997) gay bars were a part of a "closet economy," usually "black market operations" and "located in neighborhoods that were segregated from everyday business and residential activities—industrial areas, red light districts, among bars catering to sailors, or on an isolated road in rural areas" (p. 128). It was not until the period after the New York City Stonewall Bar riots in 1969 that bars became part of what Escoffier terms a "liberation economy" in which gays and lesbians owned bars and other business in the open.

In Mississippi, Howard (1999) noted that gay bars were located in downtown Jackson in the 1940s and 1950s until police raids led them to become "clandestine operations situated on the city periphery" into the 1970s. In the 1980s, Howard reported that Jackson usually had one to two bars open at the same, including bars catering exclusively to African Americans. Not until the late 1980s did other areas of the state such as Hattiesburg, Meridian, and the Gulf Coast have exclusively gay bars, although Howard noted that queer people would congregate at bars "sympathetic" to them (p. 97).

In 2019, Jackson had one of the few and largest official gay bars in the state. Wonderlust is open only three days a week and features drag shows and live DJ dance parties (Garner, 2018; Wonderlust, 2019). Biloxi also had Just Us Lounge (2019), advertised as the oldest gay bar still open in Mississippi, with weekly karaoke and drag shows. People also continue to travel to the bars in cities of neighboring states, especially, Memphis, New Orleans, and Birmingham. In other areas like Tupelo and Starkville, local bars will occasionally allow gay groups to host "drag shows" on their slow nights. The drag shows feature "drag queens" (i.e., gay female impersonators) from large cities such as Memphis who dance and lip sync to music. There have also been bars that have come and gone in the state, such as the bars outside Tupelo, Meridian, and Columbus over the years, including two where the next two couples met.

I remember going to the bar outside the Air Force base in Columbus when I was in graduate school in the early 1990s. The bar was not open for more than a year and was housed in a dilapidated building. The bar did not have a liquor license but sold sodas and beer. There was no running water, and the urinals were filled with ice. A bouncer carefully screened people at the door for IDs and to ensure they were not there to harass the customers. The sheriff and his deputies would frequently show up to ID people and to ensure there was no liquor on site. The bouncer would alert the bartender when the sheriff's car pulled into the dirt parking lot. The bartender would announce to the crowd that they needed to hide any liquor they brought into the bar. As a young graduate student, I felt extremely nervous as the sheriff and his deputies walked through the small bar and eyed us.

Keith and Mark

Keith and Mark (introduced in Chapter One), the couple who said that they live in the "gay house," met at *Rumors*, a gay bar that sat at the crossroads of Old US Highway 45 and County Road 300 in Shannon. *Rumors* was featured in the 2006 documentary *Small Town Gay Bar* (Smith & Ingram, 2006). Shannon is a town of less than two thousand people; however, when the bar was in full swing, a typical Friday or Saturday evening might include people from Tupelo, Columbus, the surrounding area, and the nearby universities. It is no longer open, although it made news in 2013 when a lesbian woman filed a federal lawsuit against the town of Shannon for refusing to grant her a license to reopen the bar (Ward, 2013). The case was later settled outside of court, according to the Southern Poverty Law Center (Clark, 2014).

Rumors was a small wood-framed, ranch-style house on a concrete slab. It made a perfect rectangle, although at the front the v-shaped roof dipped down over a four-foot concrete slab porch that ran the length of the house and was held up by five wooden posts. You could almost imagine a cowboy riding up and tying his horse to one of the posts. The front door was in the middle of the house. It did not have a swinging door but a frame of bars similar to the entrance to a jail cell or what you would see at a business in a hard area of New Orleans. The house was painted white, although it had faded and badly needed a paint job; unmanaged plants grew along the left side of the house behind the electric box. Through the windows, security bars could be seen behind the glass ensuring that nobody could go in or out. A mixture of grass, weeds, and dirt led from the road up to the front porch. In the evening, it was somewhat dark on the porch with only two small lights on either side of the front door.

If the house had ever been divided into rooms, the walls were long gone; several black metal poles ran down the center of the bar, replacing what must have been a load-bearing wall. The entire inside of the building was visible when you walked through the front door. However, there was a bathroom and a dressing room for drag queens who regularly performed in the evenings. Metal flashing served as wainscoting on the walls, below the wood-topped bar, the little cashier/identification check station to the left of the front door, and the dj booth. Rainbow flags covered various windows and the front door, and a few pictures of divas could be spotted on the painted white-paneled walls. One corner had been designated as the dance floor/drag stage with a disco ball, a spinning red emergency light, and a mirrored wall. A few small tables and plastic chairs were scattered off the dance floor.

Keith was at *Rumors* with some friends one Saturday evening on the eve of a Superbowl when Mark walked into the bar. He was not hard to notice.

"He was wearing a pink leather, fringe motorcycle jacket. He says it's red but under the lights it looked pink," Keith remembers. "I said to myself, 'Any man that's man enough to wear a jacket like that up in here is the man for me.'"

Keith walked over to Mark and introduced himself. They were the only two people in the bar who knew who was playing in the

Superbowl. They struck up a conversation and never left each other's side for the rest of the evening. The next day, Mark called Keith on the phone. Although they both planned to watch the Superbowl, they talked right through it.

"There was no doubt that we would be a couple," Keith says. "It was truly like that. I mean, I know that's very rare but it was truly like that."

Keith continues, "I think we both had matured as gay men and as men and as people. Mark had been in a bad relationship, and I had been in one that had turned bad. We weren't just looking for anybody. We were looking for the right person to make the right fit for us, and once we met, we were the right fit for each other. Mark had just made the change from moving to New Orleans and coming up here. He'd been here about a year, and I had been back here about two years."

Keith tends to be the communicator for the relationship, but Mark jumps in and recalls his memory of that night.

"I found out that there was a bar there, and I went and found it. I walked in, and I looked around this whole room, and it was a complete . . ."

Mark pauses for a moment and looks off in the distance.

" . . . Coming back here was a complete cultural shock for me after having lived in the French Quarter for so long."

"I saw that there was only one person in the bar that I wanted to meet," Mark continues, "and it was Keith. And the next thing I know I found him standing next to me. I hadn't been there but a few minutes."

Keith jumps back in.

"Part of the charm of the bar is that the regulars knew where to get so you could see everybody as they came in. All the single guys stood in the place that you could watch and see as they came in."

"There's only one little entrance," Mark interjects.

"Mark had to take his coat off and give it to the bartender and do all that kind of stuff, and by the time he got turned around, I already spotted him," Keith says.

"So," Mark says, "we struck up a conversation and it was just a fluid, ongoing process that was just . . ."

He pauses to find the right words.

"You know, I may have the ability to walk into the bar with a pink jacket on, but I'm not the most social of conversationalists at times. And it just was easy, just complete. And then we started talking and we never shut up."

When they first met, Keith and Mark were both living with their parents. They were only able to see each other on the weekends. In fact, for two years they lived together only on weekends, in hotels or a friend's home, and lived with their parents during the week.

"We stayed in every motel in northern Mississippi," Keith recalls.

"I'd pick him up every Friday," Mark says.

" . . . and stay 'til Sunday," Keith adds.

Mark continues, "And Sunday I'd drop him off and come home. It just wasn't how I'd been and how life was supposed to be. It wasn't gonna stay that way. It was gonna change. Keith was in with his parents twenty miles that way. I was with my parents twenty miles south, and Keith, at the time, didn't drive, and I would pick him up every Friday, and we would live together every weekend, and that went on for two years. And this house came up for sale, which was halfway between the parents, and I saw it for sale . . . and it was . . . I just was tired of living only together on weekends."

When Mark next saw Keith, he said, "Guess what? I bought a house."

"He went and got his stuff, and I picked him up, and we moved in with the mattress on the floor," Mark says.

I jump in a little surprised. "And you didn't even know what the house looked like until you got there?"

"Before he actually signed the papers—yes, he brought me to see it," Keith responds.

"He wasn't real happy," Mark exclaims.

They begin to laugh and look at each other.

"We're kind of exaggerating—just a little bit," Mark says mischievously.

"But he basically told me," Keith says more seriously. "'I bought a house,' and I said, 'Okay . . . Where? What does it look like?'"

Jerry and Karl

Jerry and Karl (introduced at Chapter One), the young couple who showed me pictures from their wedding, met at a bar named Crossroads after first seeing each other at Karl's work. Crossroads, which is no longer there, was located in the woods outside Meridian. I remember going there once with friends when I was in graduate school. We had to look for a dirt road once we took the Savoy exit off Interstate 59. It was known for the goat that was tied up outside one of the trailers that was the bar. If the goat was there, the bar was open. If the goat was not there, the bar was closed. Like the bar in Shannon near Tupelo, this bar was featured in the documentary *Small Town Gay Bar* (Smith & Ingram, 2006).

Before they met, Jerry was dating another man in north Mississippi, driving back and forth on holidays and weekends. He said that when he met Karl, he immediately called and broke up with the other man. At the time, Karl was a receptionist at a hair salon. Jerry came into the salon one day to talk to the owner.

Jerry begins to laugh and says, "Karl was beyond the counter. I always tease him because everybody has these great songs in their relationships. Our song is *Devil in the Blue Dress* because when I walked up to the counter he was singing *Devil in a Blue Dress* and doing his dance."

I can't help but laugh along with them at this image.

"But I had just went to the Miss Mississippi Pageant Saturday night and their theme was *Devil in a Blue Dress*. I think I was technically showing somebody one of the moves when he walked in. I asked Jerry later how he knew I was gay, and he said, 'That was a pretty good sign!' Well, if it wasn't a clue with the dancing, I *was* a receptionist at a hair salon, so that was clue number two."

We all continue to laugh boisterously. It's obvious they both have good senses of humor and enjoy telling a story. Their laughter is infectious.

"I can remember I told Jerry when he was leaving, 'Well, you can come back and see me anytime.' You know, he actually didn't! Didn't you call me?"

"I called! And I was gonna ask if you wanted to go get some lunch or something and the girl who answers said, 'He's gone out with one of his friends to a club in Meridian tonight.' Jerry knew where to find him, because there was only one gay bar in Meridian or the surrounding area for that matter.

After that first date, they never looked back. Today, they have two anniversaries to celebrate: the day they met and the day of their wedding.

Meeting Online

The internet has provided a new queer space for people to find each other. People meet on internet sites such as Gay.com, Craigslist, Grindr, Zoosk, and Facebook, depending on how out they are to others. Sites like Grindr, that are frequented both by those who openly identify as gay and by those with same-sex desires who do not necessarily identity as gay, are similar to the "tearooms" of the past: places such as rest stops, bathrooms of public buildings, and movie theatres, and described by historian Brock Thompson (2010) as "a place forged by reputation and facilitated by gay men seeking anonymous sexual encounters without further involvement emotionally" (p. 121). Tearooms became "queer spaces" that offered men not only sex but a community to meet friends and partners (Howard, 1997a, 1999, 2009). Facebook and other social media sites that promote discussion of political issues are similar to the feminist groups and lesbian separatist communities through which some lesbians connected in the 1970s (Thompson, 2010).

Sociologist Amin Ghaziani (2014), in his book *There Goes the Gayborhood?*, pointed to the internet as one factor, along with increased acceptance of gay people in society, that has led to the decline of gay bars and other institutions in the traditional "gayborhoods" of large cities. Gay bookstores used to be a place I would immediately visit when I went to New Orleans, Atlanta, or Birmingham, but they have disappeared like many other bookstores across the country as people have turned to the internet to order their books. I wonder if the same is true of gay bars in rural areas?

On the other hand, the internet can also be viewed as what Mason (2015) described as a "queer information highway" for those people who would otherwise be isolated (p.1). It provides opportunities for gay people in rural areas to connect, whether it is for sexual encounters, political activism, building communities, or for meeting others to date. For example, I regularly receive emails from an organizer of the weekly happy hour in Columbus. A Facebook group for LBGTQ people notifies me about upcoming parties, political events, and local news in the Golden Triangle, a three-county area including the cities of Columbus, Starkville, and West Point.

Bob and Matthew

Bob and Matthew (introduced in Chapter One) first met online at Gay.com, a popular dating website for gay men. Matthew was a student at Mississippi State University in Starkville, and Bob was a student at Ole Miss in Oxford. They went on their first date in Tupelo, sixty-seven miles north of Starkville and forty-seven miles east of Oxford. Although it's a city of just over 35,000 people, it's a hub for the surrounding area because it's the location of the North Mississippi Medical Center, one of the largest nonmetropolitan hospitals in the United States, and it's the location of the most retail chains and restaurants in northeast Mississippi. For people living in rural areas or smaller towns, going to Tupelo feels like going to the *big city*.

"We had a funny first date," Bob tells me. "We messaged for about two weeks on the internet, and then I finally said, 'This is just taking up too much time. Why don't you just give me your number so we can talk on the phone?' It was around nine o'clock at night when I called him, and we were on the phone until almost two in the morning before I said, 'Okay, we need to go on a date and meet in person.'"

The date began at Vanelli's, a well-known restaurant in the area, having been around since the mid-1970s. It advertised itself as a Greek and Italian restaurant with prices and fare not unlike an *Olive Garden* chain restaurant. It was always packed on the weekends before being ravaged by the tornado that swept through Tupelo in April 2014.

"Our first date was the day after Valentine's Day, so it was really nice timing 'cause everything was half price," Matthew says as I nod.

Matthew turns to Bob and says, "And so . . . what was it? You gave me roses?"

"I gave you roses," he responds flatly.

"I walk up to him, and I have a potted mum in my hand," Matthew says, as Bob and I laugh. "Bob looked at them and said, 'That's really romantic there.'"

"Well I'm sure you meant well," I say to Matthew. I turn to Bob, playing along with the banter, and ask half seriously, "Did you really say that after he brought you flowers?"

"Well . . . no . . . I don't think I . . . I just said, 'Thank you.'"

"Thank you," Matthew repeats mockingly.

"To preface this though, we had had the discussion on the phone of both loving flowers, and how I love having houseplants around. So there was a justification behind it. I just thought it was a very odd first date gift," Bob laughs.

"There's not much at Wal-Mart in Tupelo in February, but there were still mums. Don't ask me how." Matthew says.

"I still to this day don't know how they had mums in February," Bob responds. "It was an interesting first date. Then we went back to Oxford, and he spent the night. He didn't go home until Sunday! And I don't think from then until now we've been apart for more than three or four days at a time. He would come to Oxford when he got out of class, spend the night, and drive back the next morning. Then a couple days later, I would do the same thing and drive to Starkville."

"We became used to driving," Matthew recalls.

"We just commuted back and forth between each other's apartments," Bob says.

Meeting at Work

The next two couples met unexpectedly at work, creating unplanned, public queer spaces. Meeting another gay person at work would seem to require either being out, not being out but being comfortable if people assume that you are gay, or being able to flirt with someone who you think might be gay. However, being "out" carries risks. As I noted earlier, in Mississippi an employer could fire someone from a job simply for identifying as nonheterosexual. In fact, in Chapter One, narrators provided several examples of workplace discrimination. Alicia recounted how she was fired when her manager learned that she had married another woman. Rae complained that she is continuously passed over for promotions even though she knows she is qualified and has more experience than other workers. Many of the other couples stated that they were not out at work, because it felt too risky.

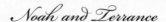

Noah and Terrance

Noah and Terrance (introduced in Chapter One) are the young male couple engaged to be married. I ask them how they first met.

"We were on the same work team," Noah explains. "We had similar interests."

Terrance recalls noticing Noah the first time he saw him come into the office, because he felt drawn to his eye color and lips that reminded him of a Russian man. He assumed that Noah was gay, because Noah showed up to work on Halloween wearing a pink Power Ranger costume based on one of the superhero movies. Noah, on the other hand, was not sure about Terrance's sexual orientation.

"I thought he was African, because of his clothes. I didn't know that Terrance was gay until he hit on me. He knew, because I didn't necessarily flaunt it, but I didn't deny it. And Terrance's personality is to be quiet and just soft spoken, fun. But he was mysterious to me. I didn't know if he was or wasn't. It was Halloween, and we had a costume contest at work. I dressed as a pink Power Ranger." Noah chuckles as he recalls his costume. "Terrance walked by me, said that I had nice legs."

"So, y'all met at work. Where did it go from there?" I ask.

"Well, I had a previous lover at the time," Noah responds as Terrance nods, "and so Terrance and I were just friends at that point. We were great friends. He was a great guy to talk to. I think that the reason a lot of people love us and respect us and look at our relationship as something is because a lot of people did not start off as friends. Our friendship was, you know, him and I having some similarities like we both do drag shows and stuff like that. We both like the same genre of music—he was more of a Britney fan, I'm more of a Beyoncé fan. We both love [Lady] Gaga. He taught me a hip-hop and stuff, right? The first time we went out, we played tennis together. After we did some choreography in the parking lot because he was a dancer; so he taught me [Lady Gaga's] 'Telephone.' We did 'Telephone' together in that Wal-Mart parking lot. We actually did our last [routine] for some of my friends who was here last night. We always dance to stuff together. He always teaches me different dances and stuff. I love to dance. I'm also more of a stage actor, but I love to do stage work and stuff. He's more of a performer in general."

"So y'all were friends for a while before you officially became a couple?" I ask.

"Yes," Noah replies. "About three or four months we were good friends, and I kept talking about him to all my other friends, because he was awesome. And I knew that he was single, and I just started realizing that maybe I should give him a chance; 'cause I realized I started liking him, and I knew he liked me already; so I left [the other guy]!"

Alicia and Rae

When they first met, Alicia was working in a restaurant, and Rae was working for a supply company that had a contract with the restaurant. She was delivering supplies on the day they met in 2011.

Rae says she was unloading the supplies from the truck and "minding my business," before Alicia playfully interrupts her as Rae laughs.

"She was running her mouth like, 'You sure ain't doing no work. You wanna come do my job for me?' I'm like, 'You're so smart. Naw, you have it.' And a year . . . exactly a year later, I was working for another restaurant. And she came into my restaurant, but at that time she was in a relationship, so. . . ." Alicia's voice trails off.

"How did y'all know you were both gay when you saw each other?" I ask.

"I didn't," Alicia replies. "No. I had two children. I was back and forth with my son's father. I had been with him for eight years. But you know, I kinda had a question like, 'You really don't do it for me.' You know what I'm saying? Like, it's something missing between us; like something ain't clicking. And when I met Rae, we started out being friends. We were friends for a little bit over a year and then I was like, 'I think I like her.' And I was like, 'Am I gay? I don't think I'm gay.' [And I said to myself,] 'She's gay, Alicia. You think you're ready for a gay relationship?'"

Rae interrupts her laughing and says, she was like, 'I ain't fooling with you. You fixing to mess my head up,' and I was like, 'Man, I'm good person. Just give me a chance.'"

"But you were so young."

"I wasn't that young. You're crazy!"

They both laugh together before Alicia says, "My momma said, 'I knew you was a little curious.' I said, 'How did you knew that?'" She said, 'Just how you act.' 'Cause I just treated guys like entirely different, you know, it was entirely different. Now it feels right. Now I'm a homebody. I don't go nowhere 'cause now I am complete."

"Like you feel settled." I remark.

"Exactly. Exactly. You know, I just had to find out what I was looking for. When I did date guys, I'd just date one guy and I would just stay there. Lord knows I mistreated them real bad, because I wasn't very sexual and, you know, I didn't want you to touch me. No kissing; no none of that. It's not like it is now."

"Like going through the motions or something," I say.

"Exactly. I was doing what society say you're supposed to do. You just kind of roll with the motions, rolling with the motions, yeah. Following along what everybody thinks you're supposed to. And so I talked to my kids. I made sure that this is actually what I was about to do."

"How old are your kids?" I ask.

"My little girl is about to be fifteen, and my little boy is eleven."

"So when did you tell them?"

"Me and Rae had talked for a year and I told Rae, 'My little boy, he like everybody. He don't meet a stranger. My little girl, on the other hand, . . . ooooweee,'" Alicia says making a sound to indicate that she knew it would not be easy. "I didn't have any trouble though. When she met Rae—the very first time she met Rae—Rae fit in like a glove," she says clapping her hands for emphasis. "Like she had been there all the time. And my little girl don't like nobody."

"You must be good with kids," I say to Rae.

"I love kids. I love kids. I met her for a birthday party. I came to the house."

"Yep, she came to the birthday party."

"The second time I met her she said, 'I wanna see your house.' And so she came in and she looked around and was like, 'You stay in a big house by yourself?' I like, 'Yeah.' She was like, 'I want that room,' out of nowhere.

"And I was like, 'Now I need to pick out a room!'" Rae says, leading them both to laugh heartily.

"And [before this happened] I'm thinking 'Lord, please don't let this little girl go in here and say the wrong thing, because it's new. It's new to me and it's new to her.' But when I tell you, Rae just fit like a glove; She just fit like a glove."

The Mississippi couples created queer spaces within an environment that encourages and even, at times, demands their silence through lack of protections afforded to heterosexuals. A few of the couples even met at work, creating a public queer space that eventually led to one of the women losing her job. Unlike most of the other couples I have interviewed, both of the couples who met at work were in nonprofessional jobs at the times of the interviews. On the other hand, most of the narrators who were in professional jobs stated that they were not out at work, because they were not sure how it would affect their job security or the way their coworkers treated them at work. In addition, all of the narrators in professional jobs identified as white. Consequently, I wonder if being openly gay might risk losing the privilege afforded to white Mississippians who do not "rock the boat" by not being visible as lesbian or gay.

In the case of the two couples who met at work, both Noah and Rae told me that they do not care what others think about them. Rae describes herself as being "masculine" and commented to me that she is often mistaken for a "young boy." Noah stated that he doesn't "flaunt it" but also does not hide aspects of his personality that others might assume indicated that he is gay. For example, he wore a pink Power Ranger outfit to work, something I am certain that few southern, heterosexual men would have the courage to do! Although Noah and Rae describe a freedom in being able to be themselves, later in the interview, Rae wondered if she has been passed over for promotions because she is an African American, "butch lesbian." Terrance admired Noah's ability to not care what other people think about him but also worried about him being too flamboyant in public at times. I think Terrance's admiration of Noah but his own reticence of being too "out" reflects the conflict for many of the couples in this book, including my own experience as a gay man living in the rural south: being true to one's self versus protecting oneself from real risks.

Most of the couples met in queer spaces that were not at their places of employment or even in their home communities. For gay people living in rural areas, where the population is less clustered compared to metropolitan areas, commuting may be the only way to access or construct queer spaces to broaden a small dating pool. Although the internet has provided another means for gay people to meet who might not have encountered each other in the past, it also means that they will likely meet other people who do not live nearby. Bob and Matthew met on the internet but each had to drive over an hour to see each other in person. Couples who met at the bars drove from their communities to the remote locations outside micropolitan areas. House parties and local happy hours continue to draw gay people across county and even state lines.

Driving from county to county and even state to state, as I did when Larry owned his house in Alabama, is not unlike what Howard (1999) described about queer Mississippians before the internet. Howard wrote that there was constant "movement" by queer people across the state from house parties to bars in the cities. In particular, he noted that cities were "centripetal, but also centrifugal forces—locations from which emanate any number of forays and journeys, many of which are short term, leading to a variety of opportunities for encounters, meetings, and rendezvous" (p. 14). These movements from small towns and rural areas to the cities, to bars, to house parties and get-togethers in neighboring towns, continue today.

∽

After talking to Larry on the phone regularly and meeting at the weekly happy hours, I decided it was time for us to go on a real date. Larry met me at my house on a Friday evening to go out to dinner at a restaurant on the shores of Columbus Lake and the Tombigbee

Waterway. When he arrived, I had company. I had invited my good friend Heather and her partner, Melissa, to dinner with us, because I was nervous about going out on a date. Larry seemed too good to be true, and I didn't trust myself not to jump into another relationship for the sake of a relationship. I wondered if he was really this kind and real. I needed a second opinion from someone I trusted.

The next day after our double date, Heather told me that she and Melissa had decided that "if you don't keep Larry, you're crazy." I called Larry that afternoon and invited him to meet me at their home. I had told them I would make pizza for their young son, who was having a spend-the-night-party. Larry assisted me in the kitchen as I made the dough and put together the pizzas. After dinner, I talked with Heather in the kitchen, as Larry and Melissa played video games with the boys. He was so easygoing, so warm with the boys. Everyone seemed to gravitate to him.

After our first date, we continued to date for about four months before we considered moving in together. Larry lived across the state line outside of Vernon, Alabama. He had inherited the small, ranch-style house from his great-aunt and had been living there since I first met him back in graduate school. The house was on a two-lane road in the country. We began to spend more nights together than we did apart, yet we still had separate houses. After work, Larry would drive out to Alabama to check on his dog, Sparky, and then head back to Columbus. Sparky was a cute little white terrier whose name described his energy. I wanted to hug him the first time I met him. Like many other dogs in the country, Sparky lived outdoors and would come running out of a nearby field when Larry drove up. He would follow Larry into the house for a dog biscuit and then rush back out the door. Larry said Sparky hadn't wanted to stay in the house since he was a puppy. The first time I met Sparky, he walked around me, easing up to sniff my hand before darting off if I made the slightest move. Eventually, he discovered that I was safe, and we became fast friends.

I began to worry about him being all by himself in the country while Larry stayed with me in Columbus. I'd say, "Larry, maybe you should stay out in Alabama tonight so that Sparky is not alone." And he'd respond, "John, Sparky won't stay in the house anyway." On the weekends, we would stay out in Alabama, and Sparky would follow us around everywhere we went except for inside the house.

I was still nervous about the idea of Larry and me moving in together. I still remembered how trapped I felt at the end of my last relationship and did not want to lose the freedom I had discovered in having my own house. On the other hand, I missed Larry when he was not there. One weekend, I suggested that we stay in Columbus rather than Alabama, because of a party that we'd be going to Friday night. I suggested, though, that we go out to Alabama and bring Sparky back with us. I couldn't stand the thought of him being alone all weekend. If he wouldn't come in the house, he could at least stay in the backyard. Larry was concerned that Sparky would not want to stay in a fenced-in backyard when he had the run of the Alabama countryside, but he agreed to give it a try.

Sparky loved riding in Larry's truck, and hopped right into the cab when we called him. We drove back to Columbus with Sparky in my lap. When we arrived at my house, I whistled to him to follow me into the house. To Larry's amazement, he followed us around the house and then went to sleep by our feet as we watched TV. Sparky had apparently decided that he and Larry were there to stay, that I would not be leaving Mississippi, at least not now. Over the next month, we spent weekends moving Larry's belongings to my house and combining households.

References

Bérubé, A. (1990). *Coming out under fire: The history of gay men and women in World War II*. New York, NY: The Free Press.

Clark, J. B. (2014, May 23). Settlement reached in gay bar lawsuit. *Daily Journal*. Retrieved from http://www.djournal.com/news/settlement-reached-in-gay-bar-lawsuit/article_f4944fc9-f4f6-560f-bd8e-13856dcfa81c.htm

D'Emilio, J. (1998). *Sexual politics, sexual communities: The making of a homosexual minority in the United States, 1940–1970* (2nd ed.). Chicago: University of Chicago Press.

Escoffier, J. The political economy of the closet: Notes toward an economic history of gay and lesbian life before Stonewall. In A. Gluckman & B. Reed (Eds.), *Homo economics: Capitalism, community, and lesbian and gay life* (pp. 123–34). New York: Routledge, 1997.

Garner, G. (2018, Sept.). The queer oasis of Jackson, Mississippi's lone gay bar. *Out*. Retrieved from https://www.out.com/out-exclusives/2018/9/04/gallery -queer-oasis-jackson-mississippis-lone-gay-bar#media-gallery-media-0

Ghaziani, A. (2014). *There goes the gayborhood?* Princeton, NJ: Princeton University Press.

Gray, M. L. (2009). *Out in the country: Youth, media, and queer visibility in rural America.* New York, NY: New York University Press.

Howard, J. (Ed.). (1997a). *Carryin' on in the lesbian and gay south.* New York, NY: New York University Press.

Howard, J. (1997b). Place and movement in gay American history: A case from the post–World War II south. In Brett Beemyn (Ed.), *Creating a place for ourselves: Lesbian, gay, and bisexual community histories* (pp. 211–25). New York, NY: Routledge.

Howard, J. (1999). *Men like that: A southern queer history.* Chicago, IL: University of Chicago Press.

Howard, J. (2009). Southern sodomy; or, What the coppers saw. In Craig Thompson Friend (Ed.), *Southern masculinity: Perspectives on manhood in the south since reconstruction* (pp. 196–218). Athens, GA: University of Georgia Press.

Just Us Lounge. (2019). Mississippi's oldest LGBT+ bar. Retrieved from https://www .facebook.com/JustUsLounge/?rf=474425999246004

Lewin, E. (2018). *Filled with the spirit: Sexuality, gender, and radical inclusivity in a black Pentecostal church coalition.* Chicago, IL: University of Chicago Press.

Mason, C. (2015). *Oklahomo: Lessons in unqueering America.* Albany, NY: State University of New York Press.

Schweighofer, K. (2016). Rethinking the closet: Queer life in rural geographies. In M. L. Gray, C. R. Johnson, & B. J. Gilley (Eds.), *Queering the countryside: New frontiers in rural queer studies* (pp. 223–43). New York, NY: New York University Press.

Smith, K. (Producer), & Ingram, M. (Director). (2006). *Small town gay bar* [Documentary]. United States: View Askew Productions.

Thompson, B. (2010). *The un-natural state: Arkansas and the queer south.* Fayetteville, AR: University of Arkansas Press.

Ward, R. (2013). Mississippi town sued after refusing to license gay bar. *Reuters.* Retrieved from http://www.reuters.com/article/2013/10/01/us-usa-gaybar-lawsuit -idUSBRE99015Y20131001

Watkins, J. T. (2018). *Queering the Redneck Riviera: Sexuality and the rise of Florida tourism.* Gainesville, FL: University Press of Florida.

Williams Institute. (2019). LGBT proportion of the population: Mississippi. Retrieved from https://williamsinstitute.law.ucla.edu/visualization/lgbt-stats/?topic=LGB T&area=28#economic

Wonderlust. (2019). Jackson's newest LGBT dance bar. Retrieved from http://www .wonderlustjackson.com/

CHAPTER FIVE

Marriage

Five years into our relationship, Larry and I felt that we were as committed to each other as any married couple. We owned a house together, had joint finances, and were recognized as "John and Larry" by our neighbors, family, and friends. Still, with all this, something felt missing. We had recently attended Larry's niece's wedding in Florida. Larry said he wanted to know that his brothers supported us the way he had always supported his brothers and their wives. I wanted to experience with Larry what I had witnessed my brothers experiencing with their wives: a ceremony expressing our love and commitment to each other in the presence of our family and friends. Plus, we wanted the security of knowing that, at least in some states, we would be recognized as legally married; where we didn't have to worry about carrying power-of-attorney papers with us in case one of us ended up in the emergency room of a hospital. Prior to the 2015 US Supreme Court ruling (Obergefell v. Hodges) that same-sex couples have a federal right to marry, we obviously could not get married in Mississippi. But where would we go?

When Maine legalized same-sex marriage in November 2012, Larry and I knew that we would be married there. We had visited with my family over the summer and fallen in love with Monhegan, a narrow island twelve nautical miles off the coast of Maine. The only access to Monhegan is a ferry from one of three coastal towns. Dating to the late 1800s, the island has been a destination of artists such as Jamie Wyeth and Rockwell Kent, who capture the amazing beauty of the cliffs hanging over the ocean. Less than a hundred people live on the island year round, but during the summer it becomes a tourist destination for mainlanders who walk the seventeen miles of hiking trails, shop in the little village, and simply relax on a spot overlooking the ocean. The only cars on the island are the old pick-up trucks that haul groceries and cargo from the ferry to the village up the hill from the dock. A sign at the dock warns visitors that there are no doctors on the island. Once the last ferry of the day leaves the island at dusk, the only way back to the mainland is on a lobster boat. Most of the island is undeveloped. We hiked the trails amazed at the beauty of Cathedral Woods on one side and the Headlands on the other. We picked a flat spot on the top of a cliff and sunned ourselves listening to the waves hitting the rocks below. We felt connected to each other and to our surroundings.

In May 2013, Larry and I flew to Portland, Maine, to apply for our marriage licensure in anticipation of our wedding in July. It felt like a solemn occasion, yet we wore blue jeans and sweaters. We'd printed the Intentions of Marriage Form and handed it to a woman behind the counter in the City Clerk's Office. She was friendly and walked us through the process. Why had I anticipated a look of disapproval? She handed us an official-looking document that read State of Maine License and Certificate of Marriage. It had our names on it. It wouldn't be official until after our officiant signed and notarized it in front of two witnesses and sent it back to Portland for certification. But it was still the closest thing to official we had ever had. We drove it to our officiant's house for safekeeping until we returned to Maine in July. We didn't want to let it go.

The next day, we met the baker who would be baking our wedding cake, the hotel management of the Island Inn where the wedding party would be staying, and the chef of the Island Inn restaurant who would be cooking our wedding dinner. Nobody raised an eyebrow. Everyone congratulated us. In fact, everyone was almost nonchalant about it. We had rarely experienced that. In Mississippi, we usually had gotten the "I'm-so-excited-to-know-a-gay-couple-like-on-television" response or

the "I'm-changing-the-subject-so-you-don't-know-that-I-am-shocked"
response. I wondered if it would feel the same when we returned to
Mississippi after our wedding in July?

〜

The history of marriage equality for same-sex couples in the United States is relatively short, spanning just over forty years and culminating in the US Supreme Court ruling (*Obergefell v. Hodges*) in 2015 that same-sex couples have a federal right to marry. The Supreme Court had previously refused to hear an appeal by a Minnesota couple in 1972 (*Baker v. Nelson*), upholding the Minnesota Supreme Court's ruling that local officials in Minnesota could refuse to issue a marriage license to a gay couple.

Although there were four other cases in the 1970s in which state and federal courts denied same-sex couples the right to marry in their states, the fight for marriage equality did not begin in earnest until 1993 when the Hawaii Supreme Court *(Baehr v. Lewin)* ruled that it would overturn the state's ban on same-sex marriage unless Hawaii could provide justification for the ban (Freedom to Marry, 2017). Following this ruling and a subsequent 1996 ruling, in which the Hawaii Supreme Court ruled that the state did not provide sufficient justification for banning same-sex marriage, Hawaii amended its constitution to ban same-sex marriage. Meanwhile, the US Congress passed the Defense of Marriage Act (1996) restricting federal marriage protections and benefits to opposite-sex couples. Over the next fifteen years, some states passed constitutional amendments banning same-sex marriage, while other states passed domestic partnership laws that provided "separate but equal" protection for same-sex couples.

In 2004, Massachusetts became the first state to recognize same-sex marriage, following a ruling by the Massachusetts Supreme Court (*Goodridge v. Department of Health*). By 2010, Connecticut, Iowa, Vermont, New Hampshire, and the District of Columbia joined Massachusetts in recognizing same-sex marriage (Wolf, 2015).

In 2012, voters in Maine, Maryland, and Washington approved same-sex marriage in their states, the first time that marriage equality was affirmed by voters (Wolf, 2015). As more states began recognizing same-sex marriage and as numerous national public opinion pollsters reported that a majority of Americans supported same-sex marriage (e.g., Clement & Somashekhar, 2012), in 2013 the US Supreme Court overturned Section 3 of the Defense of Marriage Act (*Windsor v. United States*) and let stand a lower court ruling that found the ban on gay marriage in California unconstitutional (*Hollingsworth v. Perry*). Over the next two years leading up to the landmark *Obergefell v. Hodges* ruling, state and federal courts across the country declared state bans unconstitutional, meaning that a majority of states recognized same-sex marriage by the time the Supreme Court issued its landmark decision on June 26, 2015 (Wolf, 2015). By June 2017, 547,000 same-sex couples were married in the United States, with 157,000 of these marriages taking place after the *Obergefell v. Hodges* ruling (Romero, 2017).

When an amendment to the Mississippi constitution to ban same-sex marriage came to a vote in 2004, 86 percent of voters supported the amendment (CNN, 2004). The 2015 Supreme Court ruling legalizing same-sex marriage nationwide meant that this amendment could no longer be enforced. Nevertheless, Mississippi has continued to resist same-sex marriage and gay rights. In 2016, Governor Phil Bryant signed into law the Protecting Freedom from Government Discrimination Act (HB 1523), allowing state officials to refuse to perform same-sex marriages and businesses to refuse to serve same-sex couples if they have religious objections to same-sex marriage. Although meaningless in the wake of the Supreme Court decision, the bill also defines marriage as between one man and one woman. This law was overturned by a federal court judge just before the law took effect in July 2016. In June 2017, however, the law took effect when a federal appeals court ruled that the Mississippi Center for Justice and Lamba Legal, who represented the plaintiffs challenging the law, did not have legal standing. The plaintiffs vowed to take their challenge all the way to the Supreme Court, if necessary (Mitchell & Pender, 2017).

Overall, the Mississippi couples I interviewed had several different reactions to the legalization of same-sex marriage and different reasons for choosing whether or not to get married. I interviewed most of the couples after *Obergefell v. Hodges*, but I've also included couples who I interviewed prior to the Supreme Court decision. Couples roughly fell into three main areas: (a) those who I interviewed prior to *Obergefell v. Hodges*; (b) those who planned to marry in the future; (c) those who had been married prior to 2015 in another state that legally recognized same-sex marriage or those who had married after 2015.

Interviews Prior to Obergefell v. Hodges

The older, male couples who had been together over twenty years and who I interviewed prior to *Obergefell v. Hodges* were more likely to view marriage with ambivalence or skepticism. There are several possible reasons for their lack of enthusiasm about same-sex marriage. First, their ambivalence may also have been related to the fact that the Supreme Court had not yet ruled. Second, these couples focused on the financial and legal benefits of marriage rather than the emotional and spiritual commitment that some of the younger couples and older female couples described. This made sense to me, because they had lived through a time when marriage was not ever thought to be a possibility. They had already committed to each other emotionally and spiritually through commitment ceremonies or in other special moments in their lives. Third, a few couples viewed marriage with skepticism, viewing it as a religious institution or viewing the fight for marriage equality as something promoted by activists in the cities that was unrealistic. For some, their views may reflect how they have been shaped by the more conservative views of rural Mississippi and how they were uncomfortable with activism that pushed the envelope too much, something observed by other rural queer studies writers (e.g. Howard, 1999; Fellows, 1998). Others, however, viewed marriage as a heterosexual institution that is antithetical to their views of gay relationships, as D'Emilio (2014) argued, stating that as a member of the "Stonewall generation . . . we experienced being gay or lesbian as a worldview, a political orientation, a form of rebellion against social and cultural norms" such as the expectation to be married and have children (p. 230–31).

Marty and Sam

Marty and Sam (introduced in Chapter One) are the couple who have been together over thirty years and live "in the middle of no-where."

"You've been talking about how things have changed over the years," I say. "Obviously one of the major changes has been some states legalizing gay marriage. What are your thoughts about that?"

"Oh, we differ on that," Marty says.

Sam nods, "Yeah, I could care less. You know, if they want to get— two guys want to get married—that's okay. But, you know, it's kind of like somebody said on TV: That would make all the attorneys really happy for when they decide they want to break up. And what I think is funny about it is that they're fighting about not letting gays marry, but half the heterosexuals are not married anymore. So, it's kind of like marriage in the United States is going away."

"You said that you differ from him on this," I say to Marty.

"Mm-hmm, because I can understand it. It doesn't bother me about dressing up and having it put on TV and all that kind of stuff, you know. If that's what you want and that makes you both happy, great. I'm happy for you. The part I do worry about is there are *so many* laws that most people take for granted. A lot of them don't even know that . . . say your lover dies, it only takes one relative to say *no* . . . and it doesn't matter how long you've been together. You can be thrown out on the street. Everything you've worked for as a couple. Your loved one could be in the hospital dying, and you could be sitting right there—if the family allows you to or not. You can't even make a decision for them, even though you know this is what they want. If another family, say your sister or brother, comes in there and says, 'Well, I want him to be hooked up to everything and be kept living for the next fifteen years,' you have no recourse whatsoever to stop it. So, you know, you've spent your time being a couple and building a life together and possibly going through different adversities and stuff, but yet you're not legally recognized. You can't even leave somebody your money without an attorney going through all this stuff to sort of create a trust and wind it a way around to you, because even a lot of businesses won't let you leave everything to a nonmember family. I mean, there's so many things. Even Rock Hudson, as rich as he was, ran into this. You know, his boyfriend stood by him, took care of him, everything. Rock Hudson had written down that he was taking care of this guy, and the family threw him out. He was thrown out on the street immediately. Penniless . . . everything . . ."

"What kind of protections have you put in place for each other?" I ask.

"Our will," Sam says. "Plus, my family, they know. I just have a brother and a sister now, and they all love Marty. So, it's all split and everybody gets a portion and as far as this house I told them they can do whatever they want to it. I have not left the house to anybody. It's just . . . if they want to give it to the bank, give it to the bank . . . sell it . . . keep it . . . whatever."

"And I keep a house just in case," Marty says referring to one of the houses they have renovated.

"That's right, you have several properties," I say.

"Yeah, there's always worst-case scenarios. I'm too old to get out on the street and work for this again," Marty says sweeping his arm to indicate the house and all of their possessions.

Doug and Harry

Doug and Harry (introduced in Chapter One), the couple who have been together over forty years, live in a small college town.

"I think that my take on it," Harry replies, "is that the state should not be involved in marriage. It should be done by the church only. Civil unions should be a legal document, and it should be open for all the citizens."

"There have always been the gays that have always been protesting and marching and everything for gay marriage," Doug says. "If they just would've gone for the civil unions—delete the word marriage out—it would've been probably nationwide by now. You know you hear those horror stories, like our friends that were together for fifty-plus years down in Louisiana. They had everything kept separate, because that's the way you did it back then."

Harry picks up the story, "The one had moved in with the one that died to help take care of his ninety-two-year-old mother 'til she died, so he could keep her at home; 'cause he had a townhouse in Shreveport. So he ended up staying there, because by then they both were in their mid-seventies. The one that owned the house died, and the nephew, who he left everything to and who the two of them had doted on him—They would come up to visit us and have to go shopping and buy something for him—Anyway, the day after the funeral, he came in and told Bill he had a week to get out of the house, and 'don't take anything that you didn't buy.' Older people just assumed that it's gonna work out; that the goodness of people will prevail. But when money is involved, the goodness just goes out the window so often. If something happened to me, then Doug would inherit what I have. But if something happened to me, and he died two hours later, his nieces would get all of my stuff, because they're the closest of kin to him. So, all of those things get in there, because I think that one of the issues in the gay relationship is so often family is less tied to the coupling. Our relationship has been part of our families, but our couple relationship has not really been in the forefront. So then you start looking at those issues that, you know, really come into that and come into play in places like Mississippi."

After *Obergefell v. Hodges*, Doug and Harry were married outside of Mississippi. I spoke to them both on the phone to ask them what made them decide to get married. They told me once same-sex marriage became legal nationwide, it would have felt "selfish not to take advantage of the right" for which the gay community had fought so hard to acquire. Harry added that he was concerned "in today's political climate we could lose this right in the future." He said that the more gay people that were legally married, the harder it would be for "them to take away our rights." In addition, they said that although they had legal documents to protect their inheritance and medical power of attorney rights, being legally married would provide additional layers of protection. Finally, an old friend who was a minister called them to say that she hoped they would marry, because she wanted to be the person to marry them. They were married near their friend's home at a gay bed and breakfast in Florida. Doug and Harry were taken aback by the excited reaction they received from the bed and breakfast staff, who told them they were the second same-sex couple to marry in their gardens and the first gay male couple.

John and Manuel

John and Manuel, two gay men in their fifties, have been together over twenty-five years, first meeting at a naval air station overseas where they both served in the military in their early twenties. John identifies as European American and Manuel as Latin American. They live in a small town off Interstate 55, the only interstate in Mississippi that runs almost parallel to the Mississippi River, from the state line outside Memphis through Jackson and down into Louisiana. John and Manuel live in a subdivision of modern, ranch-style houses with well-maintained yards, hidden from one of the town's main roads behind a wooded area of pine trees.

I ask them about their thoughts on legalized same-sex marriage.

"I wouldn't want what married couples have," John says emphatically. "I wouldn't want to have what the heterosexuals have, and most the friends of mine that are gay thinks it's a joke."

"What is it about what the heterosexuals have that you wouldn't want to have?" I ask.

"I wouldn't want to have . . ."

"Kids . . . ," Manuel interjects.

"Kids and the legal problems it causes. The two people that are married, if one incurs the debt and passes away the other inherits the debt. And that's in the dying category. And then you get into the marriage side with the distribution of assets and fighting over the kids and all that stuff."

"If there's a divorce?" I ask

"Yeah, and there's not that in the gay community."

"It feels like you have more freedom?" I ask.

"Much more freedom," John replies. "I think sex life also is very different [for gay couples]. I got some [heterosexual] friends of mine at work that are *pretty* open and talkative. Guys talk about sex all the time. It's rare for them to get laid three times in a month . . . four times in a month . . . rare . . . more like six times a year. And I got a lot of friends of mine that cheat with women on the side. There's some things they wouldn't want to ask their wife to do. They don't want to go to church or go out to dinner with a woman who's done that to them. They would *never* want to ask their wife to put that in her mouth or lick him there or whatever it is."

"That's the south," Manuel adds.

"And I think that is a difference," John continues. "I think gay guys are a lot more sexually active than straight guys. That's just me though."

"So you have more sexual freedom?" I ask.

They both nod their heads before John responds: "It's been very nice. I mean, I don't feel any wild constraints. I always call [Manuel] when I'm on the way home from work. One to see if I can pick up anything at the store, and the other is if anybody's here, anybody's coming over. One particular time I was in the very back [of the house] on the computer doing something, and Manuel walked in and he said, 'You better go take a shower. Some guy's followed me home from the gym.' Remember?" he asks Manuel.

"Yeah. This guy just follows me. And like we were looking at each other, and we just say 'hi.' I put on my clothes [in the locker room at the gym]. I got in my car, and he just started following me. I didn't say a word. He just started following me."

"There's some really neat people," John says. "Good guys around the area. Manuel's got friends. I've got friends, and it's okay."

Some of the couples I interviewed prior to *Obergefell v. Hodges* were ambivalent or skeptical of legalized same-sex marriage. Their views mirrored the split among gay activists during the years prior to *Obergefell v. Hodges*. As major national gay organizations such as the Human Rights Campaign Fund pushed for marriage equality, other activists argued that focusing on it was a mistake. Warner (1999), an English professor, in his book *The Trouble with Normal: Sex, Politics, and the Ethics of Queer Life*, and D'Emilio (2014), a historian, in his essay *The Campaign for Marriage Equality: A Dissenting View*, argued that marriage provides privilege and status to select couples, including government benefits and social status, at the expense of nonmarried couples. D'Emilio (2014) also observed that a fight for marriage moves against a trend in which unmarried heterosexuals increasingly cohabitate or marry later in life. Sam, a member of the "Stonewall Generation," echoed D'Emilio when he said, "Half the heterosexuals are not married anymore.... it's kind of like marriage in the United States is going away."

Two of the couples spoke of the rights that married couples received that they did not, especially related to inheritance and the ability to make medical decisions for each other. Sam's partner, Marty, seemed to view same-sex marriage as something important to activists or same-sex couples in cities that he had seen on TV but not important to him. Instead, he focused on the importance of inheritance and medical rights for couples, the privileges of married couples afforded by the state that concerned D'Emilio (2014) and Warner (1999). Harry and Doug, also from the Stonewall generation, had similar views. Harry argued that marriage should be reserved for churches, but all couples should have legal protection through civil unions. Like Marty, Doug viewed marriage as unrealistic and something promoted by activists in the cities, not by those who lived in rural Mississippi. Both of these couples, at various points during their interviews with me, made statements that indicated they were uncomfortable with activism that pushed the envelope too much. This sentiment is similar to what other rural queer studies writers (e.g., Howard, 1999; Fellows, 1998) have observed. These couples have lived in Mississippi most, if not all, of their lives and have lived in Mississippi throughout their long-term relationships. They expressed something that I heard from other couples, both lesbian and gay, who had worked to assimilate into their communities: *we're not like the gay people in the cities that you see on TV.*

John and Manuel were the most skeptical of marriage, viewing it as a heterosexual institution that is not compatible with their experiences of being gay. They believed that the sexual freedom they experience in their open relationship would not be possible if they were married. Their view is similar to Warner's (1999) concern that a focus on marriage abandons "queer thought both before and after Stonewall" that celebrated "the diversity of sexual and intimate relations," fought state-sanctioned attempts to delegitimize consensual sex outside the norm, and pushed for "queer life" to not model itself on "straight culture" (p. 88).

The few sexuality studies of gay male couples have indicated that it is not uncommon for long-term couples of at least five years to have nonmonogamous or "open relationships" (McWhirter & Mattison, 1984) with most research reporting that only about a third of couples are monogamous (Shernoff, 2006). However, the research conducted has not included a representative sample of the overall population of gay couples. For example, Hoff and Beougher (2010) interviewed thirty-nine gay male couples in the San Francisco area. Of these couples, twenty-five reported having open relationships. According to Hoff and Beougher, among the San Francisco couples, most had agreed upon rules determining when sex with others was permissible and with whom it was permissible. The most common rules were having sex with others only when both partners were present (i.e., "three-way") and agreeing to separate the emotional from the physical when having sex with others.

Of the couples I interviewed for this book, only four male couples revealed that they had an open relationship. This discrepancy could be related to the fact that Mississippi couples live in a more conservative area with a smaller gay community, or even more likely that some couples may not have been comfortable sharing whether they were monogamous or not. Since I did not specifically ask if a couple was monogamous, some couples may have felt that it was not pertinent to our discussion. No female couples revealed that they had an open relationship. Ruiz (2012), commenting on his oral history of queer Minnesota, noted that gay men were more likely to broach discussions about sex with him, whereas, women were less likely to talk about sex with him. He attributed this to being a gay male who may have been reluctant to inquire about women's sexual practices but also because he may have unintentionally expressed more enthusiasm in talking about sex with men. Looking back to my own interviews with couples, I imagine the same was true for me.

Making Plans

A second group of couples planned to get married in the future and now had the option to get married in Mississippi. A few couples had had commitment ceremonies before *Obergefell v. Hodges*. Similar to a wedding, commitment ceremonies were a means to ritualize the commitment between two people in front of their families and communities (Lewin, 1998) when churches and the state would not recognize same-sex marriage. Bob and Matthew (introduced in Chapter One) had their commitment ceremony prior to *Obergefell v. Hodges* on the *Creole Queen*, a paddleboat docked on the Mississippi River in New Orleans, where they exchanged rings in front of thirty friends.

Some couples were hesitant to get married in their towns. They worried that others might find out, because they were not openly gay. For example, Sophie and Faith (introduced in Chapter One) spoke of their desire to get married, especially after they witnessed the marriage of two close friends in their community. Since they were nearing retirement age, they worried about losing their jobs if people found out they were married. Although they assumed that coworkers and other people in their community knew that they were a couple, they feared that marriage would make it too public or "in your face." They planned to get married once they retired.

For the next two couples, marriage is not only about their commitments to each other but also about creating a family. Alicia and Rae are waiting until they can find the right place to get married. Noah and Terrance are waiting until after they finish college and feel financially stable.

Alicia and Rae

Alicia and Rae (introduced in Chapter One) had a commitment ceremony in New Orleans prior to 2015 and the legal recognition of same-sex marriage in Louisiana. As they spoke to me, they used the words marriage and commitment interchangeably to describe their ceremony. They have not filed marriage paperwork at their town's circuit clerk office since same-sex marriage became recognized in Mississippi, because they fear both the reaction of the staff in the office and the possibility that it could be publicized. They included

Alicia's children in the ceremony, because they wanted them to know that they would all be a family.

"Did the kids come to the ceremony too?" I ask.

"They were in it!" they both exclaim in unison.

"When she gave me my ring," Alicia says, "she had got a ring for each of them, and she had wrote a poem for them. And when she married me, she married them."

"That is really sweet," I respond. "Were they excited?"

"Oh yes! My baby, she was crying. It was a surprise for them. My little boy has his ring on right now."

"When I called them up there and I was going through everything, her daughter she was like ..." Rae finishes by imitating Alicia's daughter crying. "But I mean, it's like I didn't have any kids, and I always wanted kids. So my family came perfect. I got a boy; I got a girl. And so I'm not just marrying you. I'm not just committing to you. I'm committing to all three of you. So, I married all three of 'em at the same time."

"[She] had the preacher crying," Alicia says.

"Yeah, the preacher was crying; the people who we paid to decorate the hall and the rest [were crying]."

"And we were the very first gay ceremony that they had ever done."

"They was so intrigued by it, [because] it was the first gay ceremony that they did. They was sitting in there with everybody else. And when I got ready to give the kids their rings, and I read what I wrote to 'em, it wasn't a dry eye in the building. They cried. The pastor cried. Everybody in there cried!"

"So had Louisiana already become legal then?" I ask wondering if they got married after the Supreme Court decision.

"No," Alicia says shaking her head. "When we first got married, we just did the ring with a pastor in a ceremony. He's like some older white guy with fuzz on his head. And he did it. He drew us up a paper, and he signed us up and then we went to the courthouse, and we had drew up an agreement between us, both my kids included;

and we got it notarized and stuff. And now I'm officially able to go and get my marriage license but I'm afraid to here, because I'm scared that somebody might think that I can't do and they won't do it . . . and I'm gonna snap."

Alicia is referring HB 1523, the law that was passed in Mississippi allowing circuit clerks to refuse to issue a marriage license if they had religious objections.

"And now this is our dilemma. We just want to get our official, official marriage license because our paper, it last until 2018, and it says that we're in a domestic partnership, and it's notarized and stuff. I just don't want nobody to say the wrong thing to me."

"Could you go to another state to get married where you feel more comfortable?" I ask.

"Yeah," Alicia replies, "we've been researching and everything to see if we had to be within this state, if we had to live there in order to get it done and stuff like that."

"If I go and the first thing come out of your mouth is something about gay people," Rae says defiantly, "I don't care what's going on. I'm gonna get up, and I'm gonna walk off, and I won't be nice about it. But, you know, I'm the nicest person you will meet."

"For the last two months we been trying to officially get our marriage license," Alicia adds, "and then I thought we might go to Starkville [to the circuit clerk office] and then not too long after that they [the Mississippi legislature] start coming with the bathrooms [law] and the people [can] refuse you because of their beliefs and the woman [circuit clerk in Kentucky] got locked up and I was like, 'Uh-uh.'" Alicia shakes her head and raises her hand to indicate she did not want to deal with a circuit clerk who refused to issue them a marriage license.

"'Cause if I go there," Alicia continues, and they was like 'I don't believe in it,' I would end up in jail after I got through with them. So we was in crisis, because like I'm on her insurance and stuff at work and so we need our official marriage license and the thing that the pastor drew up is our only notarized documentation."

"How did you find the pastor?" I ask

"I found him online," Alicia replies. "I googled him, and found him online."

"We had a commitment ceremony in New Orleans," Rae explains, "because we didn't want to be around here. I said [to our families and friends], 'If you love us enough, you'll drive.'"

"You'll drive," Alicia repeats. "See our guy friend in Starkville, him and his guy they went to Idaho? Iowa?"

"Iowa," Rae says.

"Oh, because Iowa legalized gay marriage before the Supreme Court decision," I say.

"Yeah and that's where they went to. They went to Iowa. I said to Rae, 'Don't you want to go to Iowa?' She's like, 'Well, I can't get off work that long.' You know, 'cause Iowa's a trip," Alicia laughs.

"We was like in New Orleans like two, three days driving back and forth trying to get everything together," Rae says.

"I told Rae, 'I don't know where all that money came from, but our wedding was like $12,000.'"

"I told Alicia I'm like a child in a candy factory when I think about us getting our marriage license, but people ain't right in Mississippi."

Noah and Terrance

Noah and Terrance (introduced in Chapter One) are engaged to be married, but they haven't set a date. Their marriage plans and their families' reactions arose when I came to the end of my interview with them.

"So what haven't I asked you that you think I should? What haven't you told me that you think I should know about?" I ask.

"Kids," Noah replies. "It's a huge issue for Terrance's mom. She believes that it is wrong for us to 'live this lifestyle' and have kids."

Terrance nods as Noah continues to speak for the two of them: 'Whatever. Mom, it's 2016.' But she doesn't get that. She's just super old fashioned. If she doesn't want to be a part of our lives: fine, we don't have to talk about it. But she told him on the phone that she

wasn't sure she could come to our wedding in the spring. And it
broke his heart so much. So I called my mom, because me and mom
are cool; but we're not as close as I would like. I was like, 'Hey, you
and Dad are coming to our wedding, right?' And she was like, 'Yeah.
Why wouldn't I?' And I was like, 'I just want to make sure, because
Terrance's gonna invite his mom.' I told her [about Terrance's mom's
reaction], and she seemed like she was really upset."

D'Emilio (2014) noted that prior to the early 1980s "family and homosexual seemed mutually antagonistic. . . . If straight America
could not imagine queers in the family photo album, neither could
lesbians and gay men imagine themselves within the family's bo-
som" (p. 238). Embracing a gay identity was believed by society to
mean that one was rejecting family, both their families of origin
and a long-term relationship with children (Weston, 1991). Lesbians
and gays have embraced family through families of choice when
they have not received support from their families and when their
relationships have not been recognized socially or legally (Weston,
1991). Families of choice include close friends, partners, husbands,
and wives, and for some, children.

D'Emilio (2014) outlined a number of events in the 1980s that
led the gay community to embrace family, both their own families
of origin and their lesbian and gay families of choice, what Weston
(1998) called "gay kinship ideologies."

First, the "Sharon Kowalski" court case, in which a lesbian partner was denied guardianship of her partner who could not communicate her wishes after a serious accident, spurring a drive for
legal recognition of their relationships in the lesbian community.
Second, the AIDS epidemic "redefining the significance of family for
gay men" as they were often not considered "next of kin" for their
partners in matters such as medical decisions, hospital visitation
rights, funeral arrangements, and inheritance. Third, the AIDS epidemic "disproportionately affected African Americans and Latinos,"
leading them to form organizations to fight the epidemic in their

communities and to turn to their families for help. Fourth, the "baby boom" among lesbians and some gay men, leading to families within the lesbian and gay community. Fifth, generational change as the "Stonewall generation" aged and "settled in long-term relationships" and a younger generation that came out to their families and friends at a younger age than previous generations and expected to receive recognition for their relationships. Finally, a response of "we are family, too" to a "traditional family values" agenda of the Republican Party and evangelical Christians. (D'Emilio, pp. 238–39).

For Alicia/Rae and Noah/Terrance, marriage is not only about their commitments to each other but also about creating a family. Alicia and Rae included Alicia's children in their commitment ceremony to symbolize how they were all becoming a family. Noah and Terrance hope to have children one day. Of the couples included in this book, one other couple, Anna and Delia (introduced in Chapter One) are raising children. However, I did meet other couples who have children. Two lesbian couples are raising children from previous heterosexual marriages. Another lesbian couple recently had a baby together, the male sperm donor being a gay friend of theirs in a same-sex marriage, himself. The local gay community has "adopted" the little girl, throwing a baby shower and inviting her to join her mothers at gatherings.

Gates (2014) of the Williams Institute at UCLA analyzed US Census Bureau data and estimated that 29 percent of same-sex couples are raising children in Mississippi of which 63 percent are their biological children, 15 percent are stepchildren, and 3 percent are adopted (p. 1). Most of the couples with children that I have met either through my research or through social contacts were raising children from a previous heterosexual relationship. Most of these couples have also been female; however, I have met a few male couples raising children from one of the partners' previous heterosexual marriages.

Married

Finally, a third group of couples had either already married in another state where same-sex marriage was legal prior to 2015, married in another state after *Obergefell v. Hodge,* or married in Mississippi after *Obergefell v. Hodges.* In fact Doug and Harry (introduced in this chapter), who had been skeptical of legalized same-sex marriage, later told me that they had been married while on vacation in another state. They said they were relieved that they now had the legal protections and benefits of other married couples, especially inheritance and spousal medication rights. Many other couples, especially female couples and younger male couples focused on the importance of marriage to sanctify their commitments to each other. While these couples discussed the legal and financial benefits of marriage, they focused on the emotional and spiritual commitment that marriage represented for them. When I spoke to these couples, I could feel their love and joy filling the room, as they told me about their wedding ceremonies.

Mary and Nancy

Mary is sixty-seven, and Nancy is fifty-seven (introduced in Chapter One). They have been a couple since 1979. They were married last year in their town, as Nancy explains:

"It was very important for us to stay here among community, because the community had supported us throughout the years, and they very much wanted to be a part; so it was like a celebration of all of us, not only our lives together, but our lives with them as well. It was all our friends: just a very small group and mostly within the Episcopal church. Each one that came, they were all supporting us."

"So y'all got married at the Episcopal church?" I ask.

"We did not get married at the Episcopal church, because at that particular time, the Episcopal Church was just getting to the point where they were going to bless the couples [rather than marry them]. This was just before the Supreme Court decisions came through; so it was within the last year."

"It's changed now, because a friend of ours got married, and our priest did it," Mary explains.

"The way it is in Mississippi," Nancy explains, "[is that] each individual parish had to have these meetings and then to say, 'This is why we want to allow same-sex blessings within our church.' And there were hoops to go through, even for that. I was tired of going through the hoops. So even when it came to the point that we could get married, within the church, I had just reached that point that they were slow. I felt like they let us down. To me that was a gift for us to give back to the church, and the church to give us, to be married within the church. And so it was like, 'No, I don't want to do that.' And we both love nature, so we wanted to be outside."

"We got married under the blue moon." Mary says. You know, we had talked about it [before], because, you know, we feel like we've been married forever. Anyway, she was up at some friends one night; she came home and said, 'I've decided when we're gonna get married.' And I said, 'Really? When?' She said, 'On the next Blue Moon.' I said, 'When is it?' And she said, 'Eight days.'"

The three of us laugh before Mary continues. "So, we went down [to the circuit clerk's office in the county seat] to get our license and everything. We didn't try to go somewhere else, you know."

"How was that when you went down there?" I ask.

"They were fine," Mary replies. "I mean, we didn't have any trouble. She asked us did we want it publicized, and we said, 'Well, not particularly.' You know, it's our business."

"The funny story that went along with that," Nancy adds, "was that, we made a conscious decision that we were going to get those licenses here. So what is the worst thing that is gonna happen if we do that? Can you live with that? Will it be okay? So for us, the worst thing would be that it would be published. I said, 'Are you okay with that?' And she said, 'Yeah. Yeah, I'm fine with it. I'm fine with it.' And

throughout the years, she's been the one that's been a little 'scareder.'
She's older. She's gone through some things that I have not. And I was
like, 'Okay, that's what we'll do.' A lot of our friends were like, 'You're
nuts. You're nuts. Don't do it.' And I was like, 'What? Why not?' So
we went down—and she'd gone down before and talked with the
[circuit] clerk [and picked up the forms]. And so we were taking
them back that day and sitting there waiting. I'm sitting there on my
iPad reading a book, and all of a sudden I here Mary go. . . ." Nancy
stops talking and makes grunting sounds, imitating Mary trying to
get her attention before continuing. "And I'm like . . . 'What?'"

"What on earth was going on?" I ask.

Nancy laughs before continuing, "She wouldn't say anything. She
was just [making these sounds], so I look where her eyes were following. There was a camera. Somebody from the news was there."

"The TV station," Mary interjects.

" . . . the TV station. If I hadn't been between her and the door,
she would have run."

"How did they know?" I ask.

"They didn't," Mary responds. "They were there for . . ."

"The election," Nancy finishes.

"It happened to be election time. So they were down doing a story
on, you know, something to do with the election."

"So they didn't put the camera on you," I say.

"No!" they say in unison while laughing at the same time.

"No, no they did not," Nancy reiterates. "It was just funny, her
reaction. She was so scared." Nancy begins imitating the noise again
as Mary laughs.

"Were you the first same-sex couple to be legally married in the
county?" I ask.

"We were one of the first," Nancy replies explaining that they got
married soon after the Supreme Court decision legalizing same-sex
marriage throughout the United States.

"And so based on what you said before, when you went in they
didn't even raise an eyebrow?"

"No, they were very friendly," Nancy replies. "Well we've been here so long; I mean, we know them. I mean, I didn't particularly know them. I knew the [circuit] clerk. I knew her, but not everybody in the back. Mary is 'Miss Personality.' She doesn't meet a stranger so, she had already been down there talking to all of them and they were all fine."

"That's wonderful," I say.

"Yep. So, yeah there was not a problem whatsoever. Nobody batted an eye or anything. And actually it was more like they wanted to protect us, I would say. You know [they would say], 'Don't worry, we're gonna make sure that it's okay.'"

Jerry and Karl

Jerry and Karl (introduced in Chapter One) traveled to Vermont to get married in 2011. They had been to friends' commitment ceremonies in Mississippi, but they wanted to be legally married which was not an option in Mississippi then. Before I arrived at their home, they had laid out their wedding picture album. They showed me pictures from their wedding as we talked.

I ask them why they chose Vermont versus another state that had legalized same-sex marriage at the time.

"You know," Karl says, "it's funny because even Jerry's mother asked that. She said, 'Number one, Jerry, Why did you pick Vermont? And number two, why did you pick Vermont in the beginning of winter?'"

We're laughing out loud as Karl continues.

"Yeah, because normally they get snow before Halloween. I looked at Iowa. I looked at Massachusetts. Vermont has that—what Jerry and I like as far as—the small-town feel."

"It was perfect. I mean, it's like a *Mayberry*."

"And, we're both winter freaks, and we wanted it to be snowing outside."

"I know that everybody is supposed to feel this way. It was absolutely a fairytale. The little two-hundred-year-old church with the river running behind it. It was everything. Tiffany windows."

"My mom and my aunt (my mom's sister) came. And we knew that when we chose the location that we wouldn't have many people there but . . ."

Karl jumps in.

"In the very beginning, we wanted it private. How do we even break the news to your mom that we wanted it to be us and the priest. And then the closer you get you think people will want to share in this excitement too. And . . ."

Jerry jumps back in.

"And we ended up having a blast with her there. I mean it was fun! We didn't know anybody there. We drove from Mississippi to Vermont just because we wanted to see that part of the country and everything. When we got there, my mom and aunt were already there, waiting outside the restaurant. It was just perfect from the time we got there. It really was. But I had told Karl originally that I want to be there in time for Mass on Sunday, if we're gonna be using their church and their priest or whatever. So we got there and people were so friendly."

Jerry imitates the people speaking to them at the church:

"Oh, you guys are the couple from Mississippi . . . Remind us of the time so the choir comes tomorrow night . . . Do you mind if any of us show?"

"We got gifts from people we didn't even know. It was wonderful! And there's one lady who still mails stuff. We got a package from her this week; just a how-are-you-doing package. "

⁓

As with other same-sex couples across the country, Mississippi couples were provided with new possibilities by *Obergefell v. Hodges*. They could now be legally married in Mississippi. They could also be married in another state and be considered legally married in Mississisippi. For couples like Larry and me who were married in another state prior to *Obergefell v. Hodges*, Mississippi had to recognize our marriages. This fact was most evident the first time that we filled out our state and federal tax forms and filed jointly.

Same-sex couples who marry now have access to rights and benefits afforded to other married couples, including social security spousal benefits, retirement benefits, and filing federal and state income taxes as a married couple. In addition, marriage brings added respect and comfort to same-sex couples. On the other hand, the right to marry does not mean that all same-sex couples will desire to be married or that same-sex couples living in conservative states like Mississippi will automatically be free from discrimination, prejudice, and violence. In several longitudinal studies conducted prior to *Obergefell v. Hodges*, sexual minorities living in states without employment nondiscrimination and hate crimes laws based on sexual orientation (Hatzenbuehler, Keyes, & Hasin, 2009) and sexual minorities living in states with constitutional amendments banning same-sex marriage (Hatzenbuehler, McLaughlin, Keyes, & Hasin, 2010) reported higher levels of psychological distress. I think these findings would be similar today for couples living in states like Mississippi that have not embraced or have actively resisted same-sex marriage.

Throughout the day of the *Obergefell v. Hodges* decision, word spread on social media throughout the area. One of the coordinators of a local gay Facebook group, reserved a room in a Starkville restaurant. We were on the second floor of the Grill by ourselves, looking down on the other diners. In some ways it felt as if we had all floated up there, because everyone was feeling so euphoric. The tables on the second floor were put together to form a giant rectangle. We were a diverse group of over thirty people, a mix of lesbians and gay men, university faculty and locals, couples and single people, black and white, old and young. It reminded me of a setup at a marriage reception. We raised toasts to a new day in Mississippi. Those of us who had been previously married in a state that recognized same-sex marriage realized that we were now "legal" in Mississippi. I wondered out loud if we needed to file our marriage certificates someplace. What did people do when they moved from one state to another to prove they are married?

With all our jubilation, we later realized that this day did not mean that we would immediately be accepted by families, employers, and communities. Soon after *Obergefell v. Hodges*, Mississippi passed HB 1523, as I described earlier in this chapter. Mississippi continues to have no laws preventing employment and housing discrimination. After *Obergefell v. Hodges*, Starkville made national news when the city council refused to grant a permit for a Pride Parade. Although they eventually acquiesced under threat of a lawsuit, it felt like a punch in the gut after such jubilant celebration on that decision evening. It was a reminder that Mississippi still has a long way to go.

The day before the wedding, early in the morning, Larry and I took the ferry from Port Clyde, Maine, to Monhegan Island with my parents and our good friends, Clyde and Marsha, who would be standing in as Larry's parents at the wedding, and their son, Kyle. As the island came into view across the water, we could see the Island Inn perched on a bluff between a lighthouse and the ocean. It felt like going back in time. The inn was built in 1816 and is in the style of a classic, early 1900s summer resort. We're surprised at the front desk with cards from well-wishers who could not make the voyage to Maine. One of the cards was from colleagues at the university where I taught, who had generously paid for our room on the night of the wedding.

It was a beautiful, sunny day with a few wisps of white clouds floating lazily over the island. We met with the inn staff to plan the evening's rehearsal dinner and wedding celebration. They told us that we were the first gay couple to marry on the island. After strolling through the village, we sunned ourselves in the wooden Adirondack chairs on the bluff overlooking the harbor, watching for the afternoon ferry that would bring in more friends and my brothers' families. That evening, we enjoyed a sunset meal of lobster rolls and white wine on the bluff with our guests.

John's brother ringing cowbell at wedding reception.

We woke up that morning at the Island Inn with the sound of waves hitting the rocks on the shore and the sheer curtains dancing from the breeze blowing through the open window. We headed to the dining room for an extravagant breakfast buffet, including scrambled eggs with lobster, fresh fruit, and fresh pastries. We were greeted by our family and friends who had traveled from Mississippi, Tennessee, Florida, and New Mexico to join us. We spent the day hiking, taking a boat tour around the island, and shopping in the harbor village. Late in the afternoon, we put on our matching suits and walk down the dirt path leading from the harbor, past the inn, to the church. Two of our friends who are photographers ran ahead of us taking pictures as we walked hand-in-hand through the village. People moved to the side as we walked by, and I felt like royalty. Maria, our officiant, was waiting outside the church along with my parents and Marsha and Clyde. I could see my brothers, their families, and our friends sitting in the church waiting for us. The music began and Maria walked down the aisle, followed by our best men: Larry's best friend, Rick, and my brother, Chris. Larry followed in between Marsha and Clyde. Finally,

Wedding cake.

I ended the procession between my parents. We stood at the altar. The ceremony began. When it was over we walked down the aisle as a legally married couple.

My parents hosted a dinner for us in the Island Inn, and we began by having a wine reception on the lawn on top of the bluff in front of the hotel and overlooking the ocean. Chris raised his glass to toast us. He ended his toast by stating that he brought something special to "ring in" our marriage, and he pulled a cowbell out of a bag, held it over the top of his head and began to clang it. (It's tradition for Mississippi State University fans to ring cowbells at football games and special events). People stuck their heads out of the hotel windows and applauded.

We were in a corner of the restaurant at several large tables when it was time to cut the cakes. One had two groom figurines on top and the other had the Mississippi State University football logo on top. As

*we held the knife together in the traditional cake-cutting pose, some-
one started clapping, and the entire dining room filled with lodgers
at the inn and a few villagers stood and applauded. I wondered if I
was dreaming.*

References

Baehr v. Lewin, 74 Haw. 530, 852 P.2d.44 (1993).

Baker v. Nelson, 291 Minn. 310, 191 N.W.2d 185 (1971).

Clement, S., & Somashekhar, S. (2012). After President Obama's announcement, op-
position to gay marriage hits record low. Washington Post. Retrieved from https://
www.washingtonpost.com/politics/after-president-obamas-announcement
-opposition-to-gay-marriage-hits-record-low/2012/05/22/gIQAlAYRjU_story
.html?utm_term=.8489bcc09412

CNN. (2004). Election results: America votes 2004. Retrieved from http://www.cnn
.com/ELECTION/2004/pages/results/ballot.measures/

D'Emilio. J. (2014). *In a new century: Essays on queer history, politics, and community
life.* Madison, WI: University of Wisconsin Press

Defense of Marriage Act, U.S.C. 1 U.S.C. § 7 and 28 U.S.C. § 1738C (1996).

Fellows, W. (1998). *Farm boys: Lives of gay men from the rural Midwest.* Madison,
WI: University of Wisconsin Press

Freedom to Marry. (2017). Winning the freedom to marry nationwide: The inside
story of a transformative campaign. Retrieved from http://www.freedomtomarry
.org/pages/how-it-happened#section-14

Gates, G. (2014). Same-sex couples in Mississippi: A demographic summary. Retrieved
from https://williamsinstitute.law.ucla.edu/wp-content/uploads/MI-same-sex
-couples-demo-dec-2014.pdf

Goodridge v. Department of Public Health, 798 N.E2d 941 (Mass. 2003)

Hatzenbuehler, M. L., Keyes, K. M., & Hasin, D. S. (2009). State-level policies and
psychiatric morbidity in lesbian, gay, and bisexual populations. *American Journal
of Public Health, 99,* 2275–81. Retrieved from http://ajph.aphapublications.org/
loi/ajph

Hatzenbuehler, M. L, McLaughlin, K. A., Keyes, K. M., & Hasin, D. S. (2010). The
impact of institutional discrimination on psychiatric disorders in lesbian, gay,
and bisexual populations: A prospective study. *American Journal of Public Health.
100,* 452–59. doi:10.2105/AJPH.2009.168815

Hollingsworth v. Perry, 570 U.S. (2013).

Hoff, C., & Beougher, S. C. (2010). Sexual agreements among gay male couples.
Archives of Sexual Behavior, 39, 774–87. doi:10.1007/s10508-009-939302

Howard, J. (1999). *Men like that: A southern queer history.* Chicago, IL: University
of Chicago Press.

Lewin, E. (1998). *Recognizing ourselves: Ceremonies of lesbian and gay commitment.* New York, NY: Columbia University Press.

McWhirter, D. P., & Mattison, A. M. (1984). *The male couple: How relationships develop.* Englewood Cliffs, NJ: Prentice Hall.

Mitchell, J., & Pender, G. (2017, June 22). Controversial HB 1523 now Mississippi's law of land. Clarion-Ledger. Retrieved from http://www.clarionledger.com/story/news/2017/06/22/controversial-hb-1523-now-mississippis-law-land/419941001/

Obergefell v. Hodges, 576 U.S. (2015).

Protecting Freedom of Conscience from Government Discrimination Act, Mississippi House Bill 1523 (2016).

Romero, A. P. (2017). 1.1 million LGBT adults are married to someone of the same sex at the two-year anniversary of *Obergefell v. Hodges.* Retrieved from the Williams Institute website: https://williamsinstitute.law.ucla.edu/wp-content/uploads/Obergefell-2-Year-Marriages.pdf

Ruiz, J. (2012). Private lives and public history: On excavating the sexual past in queer oral history practice. In N. A. Boyd & H. N. R. Ramírez (Eds.), *Bodies of evidence: The practice of queer oral history* (pp. 113–29). New York, NY: Oxford University Press.

Shernoff, M. (2006). Negotiated nonmonogamy and male couples. *Family Process, 45,* 407–8. doi:10.111/j.1545-5300

Warner, M. (1999). *The trouble with normal: Sex, politics, and the ethics of queer life.* Cambridge, MA: Harvard University Press.

Weston, K. (1991). *Families we choose: Lesbians, gays, kinship.* New York: Columbia University Press.

Weston, K. (1998). *Long slow burn: Sexuality and social science.* New York, NY: Routledge.

Windsor v. United States, 570 U.S. (2013).

Wolf, R. (2015, June 24). Timeline: Same-sex marriage through the years. *USA Today.* Retrieved from https://www.usatoday.com/story/news/politics/2015/06/24/same-sex-marriage-timeline/29173703/

Why Stay In Mississippi?

Larry and I are having dinner at J. Broussard's, a New Orleans–style restaurant in downtown Columbus. We're reflecting on all that has happened since I was blown into Mississippi by Hurricane Katrina. After I had lived in metropolitan areas with large gay communities, I met Larry again at a Christmas party in Columbus. Later we were married. Since then, Larry and I have renovated an 1860s home and become part of a community. We have settled into life in Mississippi. What now? What is our future in Mississippi?

There are definitely reasons to leave. It often feels like "one step forward and two steps behind" here. In 2015, the Starkville Board of Aldermen rescinded its resolutions from 2014 that had added domestic partnership benefits to city employees and added lesbian, gay, bisexual, and transgender persons to the city's nondiscrimination policy. After the US Supreme Court ruled that same-sex couples had a legal right to marry, the Mississippi legislature passed House Bill 1523, allowing state officials to refuse to perform same-sex marriages and businesses to refuse to serve same-sex couples if they have religious objections to same-sex marriage. Mississippi is the only state to continue to have the Dixie symbol on its state flag.

We've stayed in Mississippi because of our friends, our families, and because this is what we know: our home, our neighborhood, Larry's job, the springs and falls, the countryside, the sporting events at Mississippi State University—football in the fall, basketball in the winter, baseball in the spring. But do we want to stay in a place where there is so much resistance to gay equality? Can we focus on the people who support us such as my parents and our friends? Or are the constant reminders that we are different too much? Would we better off in the long run living in a gay neighborhood in a large city? I tell Larry about the research I've read concerning the psychological distress caused by minority stress, but also the importance of support from family and community. We go around and around. Mississippi is too conservative. But we have people around us who love and support us. We loved Maine, but we don't like cold weather, and besides the Supreme Court will eventually force Mississippi to not permit discrimination based on sexual orientation. Or will it?

Finally we stop. "Look," I say. "Do we have to make a decision now? Your job is here. We have family and friends here. What if we decide to not decide? We can travel during our breaks when we just need to go away—to Maine, Fort Lauderdale, New Orleans, New York City, wherever. We can focus on what we love about this area. We can do what many of the other gay and straight Mississippi couples do: see how it all plays out.

"True," Larry says, "When you think about it, there is no easy or perfect decision."

"Yeah, it's like how so many people—straight and gay—felt when Mississippi voted to keep the state flag with the Confederate, Dixie symbol back in 2001. They wondered if this could ever be a place that moved beyond the past."

"I'm still embarrassed about that. But it's not how everyone feels. Think of all the people we know who love this state but are also are open to change. Think of the universities and the cities refusing to fly the state flag until it is changed. Think about our neighbors sending us wedding gifts and treating us like other couples."

"You're right. Remember the time the tornado passed over Columbus but knocked the power out; when we pooled our food with the neighbors and cooked it on the grill?"

"Or the time the whole block got together at Halloween on our driveway and passed out candy to the kids."

We continue to remember stories: the time it snowed and the river park near our home was full of people sledding down a hill; being with a neighbor in his home when he finally succumbed to cancer and comforting his partner; Larry catching a mouse for a neighbor when her husband was out of town; inviting neighbors to watch a beekeeper move the honey bees that had moved into our garden compost box to a new home; seeing my mother in our guest room under layers and layers of blankets after the Mardi Gras party at our house, when the heater went on the fritz on one of the coldest days of the year; the architect's wife telling the workers renovating our house that the reason they kept having accidents was because they had not told the ghost of one of the original owners of the house—a one-hundred-year-old woman whose picture still hangs in the front hallway—that they were not destroying the house but working to make it better.

The server walks over and hands us our check. We realize that we are the last ones in the restaurant. How long had we been talking about life in Mississippi? It's a nice evening, and we walk back to our house. I put the key in the door and say, "You know, Larry, it's hard to imagine leaving here, but I still haven't decided."

"No, I guess I haven't either," Larry says as I open the door and our dogs greet us enthusiastically. "Let's just see what the future brings."

And so that's what we are doing. We have learned that the answer of whether or not to stay in Mississippi is not as simple as it would seem. For some, the answer is simply because this is where a job is. For others, the answer is more complex: it's family and roots; it's something about the smell of the air in the fall, an earthy mix of pine and damp soil; it's azaleas and hummingbirds in the spring; it's something that is difficult to explain; something that keeps pulling people back like a moth to the flame.

∽

Through the voices of the Mississippi couples in this book, we have heard that although there is progress, couples are still not accepted as equal to heterosexual couples; nor are they valued in the same ways as Mississippians by their elected officials and many of the state's population. The couples' stories help us to see their resilience in developing gay communities and families within their towns and rural communities, continuing to promote understanding and acceptance for their relationships simply by interacting with their neighbors, finding their way as same-sex couples in Mississippi, and for some, becoming legally married.

In the introduction, I explained that I wanted to talk to other lesbian and gay couples in Mississippi to learn more about their experiences such as: How do lesbians and gays meet each other? What is it like for them to live in Mississippi, a state predominantly comprised of small towns and rural communities? What type of reactions have lesbian and gay couples received from their families, communities, and churches? Finally, why do lesbian and gay couples live in a state like Mississippi where only a minority of the people value their relationships? Do they plan to stay? Before I review the answers to the first three questions and answer the last two questions, I want to briefly discuss a couple of unanswered questions.

Silence during the Interviews

Queer studies writers (e.g., Hamilton, 2012; Marshall, 2012) have emphasized the importance of interpreting silence in oral histories, in other words, not only interpreting what is said in oral histories but also what is not said. In reflecting on my interviews with couples and listening to the feedback from reviewers, I realized that silence was evident around two important topics, both because I did not specifically focus on them during the interviews and because they were mentioned by only a few of the narrators.

In Chapter Five, "Marriage," I noted that none of the female couples spoke about their sexual histories or its role in their relationships. A few of the male couples, on the other hand, discussed their open relationships, without my prompting. Upon reflection,

I wonder if many of the couples and I avoided a discussion on sex, because we did not want to put gay couples in a negative light.

Rubin (1984), an anthropologist, presented a "sex hierarchy" of the "charmed circle" and the "outer limits" (p. 153), in which sexual behavior in the "charmed circle" is viewed by society as normal and good, and sexual behavior in the "outer limits" is viewed as abnormal and bad. Sex within a heterosexual marriage is one example of sexual behavior that is placed higher on the hierarchy than homosexual sex. Monogamy is valued over nonmonogamy. When she wrote her essay, Rubin believed that American society was already moving behaviors like unmarried couples living together and monogamous same-sex couples closer to the boundary between "good" and bad," although these behaviors were still viewed as less worthy compared to heterosexual marriage. Warner (1999) argued that the desire to be accepted by society—at least those who are at the top of the hierarchy—led major players in the gay movement to push for focusing less on changing society's views of gay sex and focusing more on normalizing gay identity and relationships; in other words, defining ourselves by who we love rather than with whom we have sex. According to Warner, this push led to a split in the gay movement "with sex radicals at one end and assimilationists at the other" (p. 44).

In previous chapters, I have described the dilemma gay couples face to assimilate into their rural and small-town communities, while creating and accessing queer spaces for connection and support. Antigay religious leaders and politicians frequently argue that gay people are promiscuous and have "unnatural" sex; therefore, gay people do not deserve legal rights. Is part of assimilating presenting oneself as "normal"? Did I unconsciously avoid topics during the interviews that could paint gay couples in a negative light based on rigid standards of normality? Is it part of the social compact to not talk about what might make others uncomfortable? Or is it as simple as sex not being the focus of the interview?

A second topic that was not a focus of my interviews or was only negligibly mentioned by the narrators is AIDS, the disease that was first reported by the US Center for Disease Control (CDC) in 1981 and devastated the gay community nationwide throughout the 1980s and 1990s. Today HIV, the virus that leads to AIDS, disproportionally affects gay and bisexual men, especially Latino and black men (Human Rights Campaign, 2019). Nevertheless, the couples and I did not discuss HIV/AIDS in any depth. This is even more surprising to me in retrospect, because back in the early 1990s, I worked as an HIV/AIDS prevention educator at the gay community center in West Palm Beach, Florida. In addition to providing outreach to the gay community, I led safe-sex workshops and discussions groups, usually for gay men.

Still, several of the narrators mentioned HIV/AIDS, although not the main focus of their stories. In Chapter Three, while discussing her relationship with her parents, Nancy talked about her parents reaction to her brother who "contracted AIDS" in Atlanta, dying "within eleven months of the diagnosis." A few older couples indirectly mentioned AIDS when they said that if they had lived in a large city their lives would have been different like the following exchange:

"Sometimes I wonder how we would have been if we would have been living in like San Francisco or New York," the first man says.

"We'd probably both be dead," the other replies.

One middle-aged gay man, spoke to the "stability" he felt his relationship brought to his life, including preventing him from becoming HIV-positive: "And I'll just be honest with you. I would probably be in New Orleans every weekend with a disease or something because I mean, that was very much the life that I was living before him, you know."

There are many possible reasons why the couples and I did not discuss the impact of HIV/AIDS on their lives during the interviews. I have a few speculations. One possibility is that some of the couples and I bought into the myth that HIV/AIDS only occurs in urban areas. There is some reality to this, especially for the older couples who lived in a small town all of their lives and first heard the reports of the "gay plague" in the early 1980s. Howard (1999) said that he ended his history of same-sex desire in Mississippi in 1985, because that marked the period that "queer lives and queer networks were irrevocably altered" (p. 209) by HIV and more Mississippians returned from the cities or remained in Mississippi. HIV/AIDS is more highly concentrated in urban areas and people who are HIV positive are more likely to travel to urban areas for resources and medical care (Wilson, 2013); however, HIV/AIDS does, of course, affect people in all areas, rural or urban. As of 2015, the CDC identified over 9,585 people in Mississippi with AIDS and over 500 diagnosed as HIV-positive.

The myth that HIV/AIDS only occurs in urban areas may also be related to the rural/urban divide that Herring (2010) argued has shaped queer studies and culture in the United States. Rural areas are portrayed as backward and a place for gay people who have not come out of the closet, while cities are viewed as "urban meccas" (p. 14) where gay people can come out of hiding. On the other hand, Herring also identified an anti-urban bias that is evident when the city becomes connected with temptation and debauchery and rural life with wholesomeness.

A second possible reason why the couples and I did not discuss HIV/AIDS is related to the irrational the belief that "it can't happen to me." This belief can be related to the common defense mechanism of repression, in other words, not thinking about something like death to avoid the natural fear that most of us have. This irrational belief is also common with younger people, who have always been healthy and believe that they are indestructible. It becomes hard to imagine that I or someone I know could be HIV-positive, especially if I have never met someone who was HIV-positive or had AIDS.

A third possible reason could be the fact that most of the couples I interviewed were white and have health insurance. Today HIV, the virus that leads to AIDS, disproportionally affects Latino and black men (HRC, 2019). If most of the narrators are or did become HIV-positive, they would be more likely to afford the antiretroviral drugs that have enabled so many people who are HIV-positive to live with the virus in check. In fact, if any of the narrators were HIV-positive, it's likely I would not know unless they had told me.

Finally, not talking about HIV/AIDS could be related to the assimilation dilemma and the social compact of silence that I have previously discussed. People with HIV/AIDS face real judgment and discrimination in society. A fear of AIDS, or "AIDS-phobia," has frequently been related to homophobia and vice versa in society. In addition to the real fear of becoming HIV positive, I wonder if many of the couples and I avoided a discussion on HIV/AIDS, because we didn't want people to assume that if you are gay than you must be HIV positive. If any of the narrators were HIV positive, did they fear judgment from me or their communities if they revealed their status? As with the topic of sex, did I fall into a trap of not wanting to discuss a topic that could give ammunition to some antigay religious leaders and politicians who have a history of tying HIV/AIDS to the "wrath of God" on gay people? All these possibilities are speculations. There could of course be other possibilities or the simple fact that, like sex, it was not a focus of the interview. I will leave it to future readers to make the final determination.

Gay Life in Mississippi

Back to the first three original questions I had when I first moved back to Mississippi: How do lesbians and gays meet each other? What is it like for them to live in Mississippi, a state predominantly comprising small towns and rural communities? What type of reactions have lesbian and gay couples received from their families, communities, and churches?

The Mississippi couples met at work, through friends, at gay parties, in gay bars, and in online gay meeting sites; however, none of the couples said they met in church. This is not surprising since the majority of the couples do not attend the same church they attended when they came out or they do not attend church at all. Some grew up in churches that had negative views on homosexuality. These couples either do not attend church or have found a gay-supportive church. A few female couples attend churches that are not gay supportive and may even preach things with which they disagree, but they continue to attend because they feel a part of its community.

After the US Supreme Court 2015 ruling (*Obergefell v. Hodges*) that legalized same-sex marriage nationwide, Mississippi could no longer enforce its 2004 constitutional amendment banning same-sex marriage. Nevertheless, the majority of the couples who have married or are planning to marry said they preferred to marry outside the state. Some couples spoke of their fear of the reaction they would receive if they were married in their hometowns.

Overall, the couples described both positive and negative experiences living in their communities. Some couples described outright prejudice and harassment, but the majority described communities that did necessarily accept them as a couple but that *tolerated* them. Couples discussed supportive people in their lives but also frequently described a "don't-ask-don't tell" relationship with many of their neighbors and family members. The social compact of silence described by Howard (1999) in his study of male same-sex desire in Mississippi from 1945 to 1985 still manifests in today's Mississippi, although it has evolved as the country has evolved.

Since Mississippi House Bill 1523, allowing state officials to refuse to perform same-sex marriages and businesses to refuse to serve same-sex couples if they have religious objections to same-sex marriage, was enacted in 2016, Gay Pride Day events and parades have been held across the state in Jackson, Tupelo, the Gulf Coast, and the college towns of Starkville, Oxford, and Hattiesburg. The Human Rights Campaign (HRC) has a presence in Jackson, Mississippi, with HRC Mississippi State Director, Rob Hill, a former United Methodist pastor, frequently quoted in state newspapers whenever gay issues are in the news. Since Howard's (1999) book, there are more couples who are out and are willing to push the envelope to promote change, such as the couple who has started a church in Hattiesburg or the couples who were married in their hometowns.

Drag queens lead parade into downtown Starkville.

Nevertheless, outside some signs of sporadic progress in places like college towns, the state capital, and larger micropolitan areas and cities, the couples' stories reflected a social compact of silence that is: *We [Mississippi communities and families] will tolerate you [gay people] if don't act too queer and if you don't ask us to talk about it.* "Queer" means everything from public displays of affection between a same-sex couple to someone who does not meet the societal gender expression norms (e.g., a masculine woman or a feminine man) to talking too openly about one's relationship as a same-sex couple. This silence manifested itself from both sides, such as, on one hand, families asking gay family members to keep their relationships secret and, on the other hand, gay couples saying they don't "flaunt" their sexualities by "flying a rainbow flag" on their homes or "throw[ing] something in people's face[s]." The silence is also enforced through state law, allowing businesses to refuse service to nonheterosexual or transgender people, and a lack of state laws, which enables work and housing discrimination.

As I indicated in Chapter Three, from one perspective, the use of silence to not break the social compact could be viewed as internalized homophobia, a desire to be viewed as the "normal" defined by a heterosexist society. However, as Howard (1999) noted, silence can also be a strategy to protect oneself. For example, any overt displays of affection in public by the couples in their small towns might lead to verbal or physical assault, discrimination, or rejection. Consequently, as I discussed in Chapter Four, couples created and accessed "queer spaces," spaces created when two or more gay people gather, to first meet each other, connect with other gay people, and be in a space where they can be themselves and support each other, away from the pressure to be silent. The couples' ability to meet each other, to honor their religious/spiritual identities while being true to their sexual orientation identities, and to marry again demonstrates their resilience in living in a place that encourages and even demands their silence.

DECIDING TO STAY OR GO?

Finally, the last two original questions I had when I first moved back to Mississippi: Why do gay couples live in a state like Mississippi where only a minority of the people value their relationships? Do they plan to stay?

When I began to travel across the state and interview couples, I expected to hear nothing but negative stories about couples' experiences. I was surprised when many couples sought to portray both the good and bad in Mississippi. Like me, many of them seemed to have a love/hate relationship with the state, loving aspects of the southern culture in a place they call home but hating the prejudice, discrimination, and resistance to change. Similar to their portrayal of Mississippi, the couples were split on whether or not they wanted to stay in Mississippi.

For gay couples, there are reasons to move, such as HB 1523, no protection from workplace and housing discrimination, and a culture that, overall, is not accepting of nonheterosexual couples. Nevertheless, the couples said that there are also reasons to stay including leaving a legacy to future generations of gay Mississippians, being near family and friends, the low cost of living, and not wanting to leave their land and homes where they have lived for years.

STAYING IN MISSISSIPPI

Mary and Nancy

Mary and Nancy (introduced in Chapter Two) are the retired grade school teachers who started the first Integrity gay community group at their Episcopal church almost thirty years ago. I ask them what has kept them in Mississippi.

"I have to say, I ask myself that question as well," Nancy replies. "And then, I always come back to [that] I believe it's our legacy. I believe that when the Episcopal Church first started, even many years ago, even thinking about, even saying the word 'same-sex blessing'; or we had the state convention and there were all these proposals, you know, that just [were] . . . : 'We don't want them in our church.'"

"That's what some people were saying?" I ask.

"Yeah, I sat there. Mary didn't go, because I didn't want her to go; because I knew it was going to be a lot of conflict."

"It's hard to hear that," I say.

"Yeah, it's hard to hear. So I went and sat in that general meeting. Finally, I just . . . I couldn't stand it anymore, and I went to the mic[rophone], and I said: 'Would y'all all just please stop? Just stop and look at me. Because you are talking about this in this big-grand-gays-lesbians, as if big labels. And each one of you loves somebody just like me. I am the face to the label that you are putting out there. So just stop and think about that. Instead of thinking *they*, think about those that you love that will be affected by this.' So that was one of the steps of why I think I am still here. I believe it is a legacy, and that is part of my legacy."

"Wow, that took a lot of courage," I say as Mary nods.

"One of the reasons why we stayed here to be married," Nancy continues, "is because for a year, I thought, 'Okay, we're gonna do a destination wedding. We're gonna go to Arizona.' You know, I'd get online, and I'd look, and I'd look. It didn't feel right in my heart. So, and I think we both agree, it was to stay *here* among those that love us. And they truly love us. And for the next generation of that Mississippi little girl . . ."

"Or little boy," Mary adds.

" . . . or little boy that it'll be a little bit easier to stay in Mississippi; maybe 'cause I was here, or we were here."

"It brings you a real sense of purpose," I say.

"Yeah, it does."

"She talked about standing up at that [Episcopal] state convention," Mary says, "and I was in Birmingham probably six months later. We'd gone over to hear the bishop speak, and he's very supportive of gays and lesbians. And I was just sitting and talking and sharing and things there; this lady came up to me, and she said, 'I'm not sure, but I think I heard your partner speak in Mississippi at the general convention.' And she said, 'I think it was your partner, I really do.'"

"How did she put that together?" I ask.

"Well just some of the things that I said: 'I'd been with my partner so-and-so, and this and that.' And she's real open and real, you know. And it was really kind of weird that it came back around again."

"That is amazing," I say.

"Yeah," Nancy says. "I would say, going back to your original question [about what has kept them in Mississippi]: our families were here, too. Mary was very much a momma and a daddy's girl, and I was very close to my family as well; so this is where we wanted to be. And then once they passed, again it's our legacy."

Brandiilyne and Susan

Brandiilyne and Susan (introduced in Chapter Five) are the lesbian couple who founded a gay-affirming church in south Mississippi. Like Mary and Nancy, they say that they want to make Mississippi a better place for the next generation of lesbians and gays.

"We thought about it," Susan says referring to moving out of Mississippi after the state legislature passed HB 1523. "We thought about it. And we have these people now that are the leaders in the community, and they're moving in July."

"If we don't do it, it's left up to the next generation, and it's not fair," Brandiilyne says. "Somebody needs to do it. Somebody's gotta spearhead it. We're all kind of pissed about it. I mean things aren't changing, but the thing about change is it usually gets worse right before it gets better. I think that's where we are in progress in Mississippi, as far as LGBT community is concerned. And it's gonna change. Mississippi *cannot* stop it. *It is going to change.* Mississippi is like no other place. Mississippi is charming. Mississippi has these wonderful traditions. People wave at you when they pass you on the street and smile at you. The hospitality is really there. It really is until people find out your sexuality, and then there's hostility. But, you know, it's a different place, and it's home. It's always been home. I mean, I love Mississippi. I love the people here, especially in our LGBT community. I think the LGBT community in Mississippi are some of the strongest people and the bravest people I've ever met in my life, and that is inspiring. And that is the kind of people I want to surround myself with: brave and inspiring people."

~

The couples who were older than fifty years of age were more likely to say that they planned to stay in Mississippi or that they were less likely to leave. The age difference makes sense, because, overall, the older couples have more stability financially and have been together longer as a couple. They are more likely to own property that they have worked for years to acquire and, for some, even pay off. They have persisted as couples for years, promoting change simply by living as a same-sex couple in their communities and churches. Mary and Nancy fought for inclusion and recognition in the Episcopal Church. Brandiilyne and Susan even founded their own church. Consequently, in addition to the family roots and financial stability, they also have years of investment in making Mississippi a better place for future generations of gay people.

In addition to the investments they have in staying, some of the older couples, unlike many of their younger counterparts, indicated that they enjoyed living in a small town or rural area. These couples said they were not drawn to a larger city, with some even reflecting tones of anti-urbanism likely in response to the metronormativity or antirural messages they had heard in gay politics and culture. However, it's also common for couples to become more settled, both in their relationships and in their locations, the longer they are together. For example, when I asked Doug and Harry (introduced in Chapter One) about living in a small town versus a city with a large gay community, they spoke to their feeling that they are more comfortable living in a community that is not predominantly gay:

"My question would be what do you want from being gay?" Harry replies. "Do you want stability, civility, friends, relationships of a community as a whole? Or do you want a trick? You know, the pool is very shallow when it comes to available sex. So what drives your life? Living or sex? And if you really are a sex-driven person, you probably need to go someplace with a bigger population. But if you really are someone who likes sex occasionally—I mean, not every night but in a relationship—there are people that come along. It's not a desert. But first of all, if you really want to have a quality of life here, it's really about what you put into the relationships with the place as a whole. It's not all about sex. It's about quality of life."

PLANNING TO EVENTUALLY LEAVE

Anna and Delia

Anna and Delia (introduced in Chapter One) are the younger couple raising two children together in a small town in the Mississippi Delta. They moved to Mississippi with the assumption that they would leave once they finished their grant project assisting children living in poverty.

"Looking back, what's surprises you about your experience here, if anything?" I ask.

"Every—thing," Anna says, drawing out the word for emphasis.

Delia laughs before saying, "She wants to stay. She would stay."

"I didn't expect to have as positive an experience," Anna explains. "I had modest preconceptions about Mississippi that were very negative. I didn't want to live in a small town."

"I think we both feel very embraced here," Delia says. "I think it's particularly surprising in a place where you expected to have to put on armor; like when you're going into a community that you thought would be resistant to you, and they are embracing you. You feel even more accepted, because you have so many preconceived notions about the South. "It's like on an individual level, most southerners are great. Like most people we've met in the Delta are very giving, very warm. The policy level is not great, but I think on an individual level we've had a lot of opportunities to connect individually with people. So I think on an individual level people are very accepting and very tolerant, because they get to know you as a person rather than as a sexuality. I think that part has been our approach as well. It's like we are here; we are queer; like that's just what it is. The end.

Like you can do what you want to do, and we're gonna do what we want to do; and that's just gonna be the way it is."

"It's like the give and take between you and the community," I observe. "And you two have great personalities, so I'd imagine that's made a huge difference. Tell me about your plans for the future."

"Delia wants to leave. I want to stay. I would stay, not indefinitely, but I would stay for another five years or something like that. I very much enjoy my work here, and I like the community here. The only thing that's kind of hard is the childcare/schooling aspect, because schools are pitiful."

"For me, the reasons I'm leaving, I think, aren't to do with anything about treatment. It's career. I can't do the job I'm doing forever. Career is one. Like there are certain things here that you can deal with for a short time like not having a good dentist, or this town has a lot of crime; so locking your house up before you go to bed. Just little things like that I can deal with for [a little while that] I just can't deal with them for [much] longer. I was also thinking of the position I'm in working in policy. I think the most frustrating thing about Mississippi is people in power's constant need to like cut off their nose to spite their face; to make these short-range decisions that have awful impacts on your populous. And there's no accountability around that. For me, it's just . . . it's frustrating."

"It's too frustrating," Anna repeats.

"It's like when that bill passed—HB 1523—," Delia says, "I'm like, 'Okay there's my out.' I don't really want to live in a state where they can snap their fingers and get a super-fucked-up-discriminatory law with like eyes closed. I don't need to mess with that. I'm lucky enough. I'm lucky enough to leave, and it gives me a lot of like guilt about the families that are like here and have no one to advocate for them."

"I wish more gay people could have the experience that we've had here," Anna says as they continue to dialogue with each other as I listen. "I think part of it is kind of like how you approach it. If you approach it with fear you're gonna get a little bit of a different experience than if you are not ashamed; if you're proud."

"I don't even think it's pride; it's just who we are. Like we're at a place where we just accept who we are, and this is who we are; there's no shame around it. For me being black, it's not shameful. It's not something where I'm like super proud and boasting about black history month. It's just who I am."

"But I think we come from very supportive families, and we don't have anyone in our present or previously that has been negative, you know, so we are also able to come into it with that; whereas, I think some of the folks that live here and have grown up here, it's like this person you meet that's the Pentecostal lady that doesn't believe in gay marriage. Or it might be your mom; it might be your uncle; it might be your grandma. People that actively say that [it is not okay to be gay] to you."

"The one thing I want to say that I always find shocking is that we don't know other gay people here. With as out as we are, explicitly, we haven't met other gay people."

"There was that one time at McDonald's."

"Someone asked me," Delia finishes, "Could you speak to my sister? She's dating a woman." She was asking me some questions about how to tell her child and things like that, but statistically it is impossible that there are *not* other gay people here. I find that just bizarre."

Jerry and Karl

Jerry and Karl (introduced in Chapter One) are the couple who traveled to Vermont to be married in an Episcopal church. One of their long term goals is to eventually move to a more progressive state like Vermont, although Jerry feels torn about leaving his family behind.

"You two have talked about the support you feel from family members and your church; yet, you're seriously considering leaving Mississippi and going to Vermont?" I say inquisitively.

"Karl's a lot more serious about it. I'm serious about it, too, but my hang-up is leaving family. That is my hang-up, because it goes back to where I have the Monday through Friday, nine to five job.

And Karl has the traveling job to where he'll have time to come home, and I won't. So, that's my only negative aspect, because as far as Vermont is . . ."

"We'll get you a frequent flyer plan," Karl interrupts.

"But I won't have time to fly. What are you gonna do? Catch the plane Saturday and fly back Sunday? But I fell in love with Vermont, too, and loved the people, loved the town, and everything else."

"I'm thirty-two, and I told him I'd stay in Mississippi until I'm thirty-five."

"So what would be the major drive for you to move there?" I ask.

"I think the people there have the mentality of what I wish Mississippi had which is if it doesn't affect their day-to-day life, they really don't care what you do. We talked about it earlier. It's a Friday night. Could Jerry and I go to dinner and have drinks in Vermont and hold hands? Absolutely."

"But we could also drive into New York City or drive to Montreal."

"Can you imagine? Even now I would be scared to put a Hillary [Clinton] sticker on my car. In Vermont, that's all you saw."

"He wore an Obama tee shirt to our local fair," Jerry says laughing. "How did that go over?" I inquire.

"Not well," Karl replies.

"Did anyone say anything to you or did you get looks?" I ask.

"Very much looks," Karl responds. "You know, it's like a white boy wearing an Obama tee shirt."

"What does that mean?" I inquire.

"Exactly. And every now and then, when you really just want to tick a Republican off, you'll wear it."

"Karl's even got an 'I love my boyfriend' tee shirt but he's never worn that one here."

"But I could wear it in Vermont, and I know what Jerry said about us moving. Yes, we had a great time there, and I think, 'Are we gonna go back a few more times before making a decision?' Yes. And we've even talked about that we would be satisfied with getting some land and just having a travel trailer or something up there to go to a few times a year. But I'm thirty-two. Do I want to stay here and try to

Jerry and Karl visiting Vermont.

fight the battle? Or do I want to live somewhere where I can be who I am and love who I love? I think what Jerry saw in Vermont is that anything is possible. If you want to love who you love, that's fine. I mean, we literally had people stop us on Main Street in the capital city and say, 'We're so glad you're here.' We still don't know who these people were. And we could stay here and fight the battle and maybe be old men and still never have seen marriage recognized here. And what have you really accomplished? I think we're still a few generations in this state away from being where we wanna be. I reference what Martin Luther King said, 'We're not where we want to be but we're not where we were.'"

Bob and Matthew

Bob and Matthew (introduced in Chapter One) are the couple who had their first date at an Italian restaurant in Tupelo and attend a gay-affirming Methodist church in Jackson. Like Jerry and Karl, they are a younger couple who plan to eventually move to a more progressive area.

"Okay, hypothetical situation," I say. "Somebody calls you on the phone and says that they are a gay couple and they're moving to Mississippi. They want to know what it's like, what your experience has been as a gay couple living here. What would you say?" I ask.

"I would say that ultimately we haven't had problems," Bob says. "I don't think that living in Mississippi would be any different from living in any other southern state. I think as with anything I would recommend . . ."

"A bigger city . . ." Matthew interjects.

" . . . an urban area, rather than a rural area of the state," Bob finishes.

"Such as . . . ?" I ask.

"Jackson or Tupelo or maybe somewhere on the coast."

"Yeah, the coast," Matthew agrees.

"'Cause I just think that there would be more gay people to interact with. There's more of a presence and, therefore, more of an acceptance, because nobody wants to move to some small town and be the token gay."

"It's true," Matthew agrees.

"That would be my only advice, because you just kind of have to be aware of who's around and know that when you're living in Mississippi, you're not living in New Orleans. You're not going to be able to walk down the streets of downtown Jackson holding hands. You're probably not gonna be able to have a church wedding in Jackson, Mississippi."

"You're gonna have the people behind you say that you're a "fag" and want to bash the head in of people, but I mean that's all over the place."

"You feel like people are going to talk about you more?" I ask.

"Yeah, I do," Matthew responds.

"I think that especially in a smaller town there's gonna be a lot more curiosity of an oddity," Bob says.

"You're in the Bible belt. You know being an anonymous person is no longer happening because you're out."

"So if this hypothetical couple asked you why you stayed here then what would you say?" I ask.

"We're actually planning on moving," Matthew replies.

"Well, we're not entirely moving, because it's Mississippi. We are moving to a more urban area, where there'll be more to do, and more cultural things to do, and hopefully more acceptance. Really I think the ultimate tie here is family. His family is here. My family is in Birmingham. We're staying local. If it weren't for family we would be in New Orleans or in . . ."

" . . . Memphis or someplace . . ."

"We would be somewhere else and not in Alabama or Mississippi if it were not for the family ties. But I think that being brought up in the south, you're brought up that family stays together; family doesn't move off. It's unheard of for family members to move away and be gone for years at a time and not see each other."

Noah and Terrance

Noah and Terrance (introduced in Chapter One), the young African American couple who are engaged to be married, had similar sentiments as the other younger couples.

Terrance says he wants to live in a place where they can hold hands in public and feel safe. They have discussed moving West to places such as Austin, Texas, California, and Colorado.

"After college we don't want to stay here," Noah says, "Where, you know, just the way we look could be an issue, especially with this [Mississippi HB 1523] law. It doesn't matter that I do or do not get discriminated against, it's that it could be an issue. I don't want to deal with that. I just don't want to."

∽

The common factor regarding whether or not a couple planned to remain in Mississippi was age. The couples who were less than fifty years of age were more likely to be adamant that they wanted to eventually leave Mississippi. Of course, this is not only true of younger gay people. Mississippi's College Board reported that 40 percent of public university students moved out of the state within five years of graduating (Harris, 2017). For many of these graduates, there are more job opportunities in other southern states with large metropolitan areas. The younger gay couples, though, spoke of a desire to live in a place with a more urban area with a large gay community. Several of these couples spoke about wanting to live in a place where they could hold hands without retaliation or feeling judged. Terrance described needing to put themselves in a "bubble" to protect themselves, by constantly being aware of their surroundings. Bob spoke of wanting to be in a place where they could be more anonymous and not the "token" gays. Jerry says he wants to live in a place where he can "be who I am."

For couples planning to leave, many still experience some conflict about their decision. Even Anna and Delia, who are only living in Mississippi temporarily, say that they are surprised it is not an easy decision. Although Delia is ready to move for better employment options, Anna would like to stay for a little while longer because of the relationships they have made in the community. For other couples, although they may plan to leave, it may not be realistic financially as Alicia and Rae articulate.

"I want to take my kids to the city," Alicia says wistfully.

Rae nods and says, "I haven't got the right opportunity to be honest. I've been trying to leave my job for a while. I got my bachelor's degree. But it's not a lot of opportunities. People don't want to pay me what I make there and to start over somewhere is not even a comparison. And you look at everyone in the family and leaving a house that's paid for [that she inherited from a family member] and to have to start all over and make a little bit of nothing, it's *not even* a halfway even trade."

Most of the couples cited family as the reason they have not yet left. Jerry and Karl plan to leave in the future, but Jerry describes the conflict that he feels: "Karl's a lot more serious about it. I'm serious about it, too, but my hang-up is leaving family." For Bob and Matthew the compromise is eventually moving to an urban area in the South near Mississippi. Bob reveals the conflict of identifying as gay but also as a small-town southerner with family values: "I think that being brought up in the south, you're brought up that family stays together; family doesn't move off. It's unheard of for family members to move away and be gone for years at a time and not see each other."

The term "family values" is often used by Mississippi politicians to describe a traditional view of families that does not include gay families. For example, Mississippi US State Senator Roger Wicker advertises himself on his website as "protecting family values": "I believe my values are shared with most Mississippians. As a Southern Baptist, I am a strong supporter of Christian family values. I do not support gay marriage and believe in the traditional definition of marriage" (Wicker, 2019, para 1). The Mississippi gay couples express a different type of family values that not only embraces their relationships as valid and meaningful, but also shows the value they see in caring for their families of origin. Some value their families enough to remain close by even when they feel isolated as gay couples in their communities. Family values is also expressed by couples like Alicia and Rae in Chapter Five when they described ways that they protected their children from negative, anti-gay messages and included them in their commitment ceremony.

Conflicted
Faith and Sophie

Faith and Sophie (introduced in Chapter One), are the couple who invited me to lunch with two other lesbian couples. They have developed deep roots here that would make it difficult to leave, although they do talk about the possibility of someday moving.

"Do you think that down the road you'll stay here or do you think you'll go someplace else?" I ask.

"We talk about it but . . ." Sophie begins.

"We talk," Faith repeats sighing before Sophie continues.

"This one right here has just always been here, and I doubt seriously I could blast her out."

"Nah. I think you'd have no trouble there."

"Yeah, but see your Daddy's still living, and you're not going anywhere."

"But I'm not as tied to Daddy. I just check on Daddy."

"I know you do, but you're still not gonna move out of state."

"You don't know that."

"When are you going?" Sophie asks laughing.

"I wouldn't mind staying some, you know. We would have our main home here."

"There you go. See? You're still coming back here."

"Well, as far as selling out and leaving, I wouldn't do that. As far as selling my place, I don't think I would do that. You're right about that. As far as like going, like where her nieces—they're moving to the mountains—I guess we're gonna have to learn mountains now. But, you know, we talked about just renting a place there for the whole summer."

"It is really good there. They do accept her," Sophie agrees.

"So Faith," I ask, "besides the tie to your father, what makes you want to make sure you have a place here?"

"I guess because I worked and paid for my home; that's one thing. Second, would be my ties. Just look around," Faith says motioning with her arms to indicate she is referring to the land. You work so hard for it. That would be my main thing. As I get a little older, for some reason, that tie is not quite as strong as it once was."

"Hopefully that's because you're getting ready to retire," Sophie says before turning to me and saying, "We get in this discussion all the time."

"You know, Daddy's eighty-nine."

"She's never been close with her daddy."

"But I check on him. I don't want him to be laid in the house dead and nobody know it."

"She'll tell you, and I'll tell you, he's crazy."

"He is. And, you know, his grandma and momma lived to a hundred or so. He's got a long ways to go, and he's in good health, but still I don't think that would totally hold me back. I know I'm closer now to leaving than I have been in my whole life."

"What's that about, do you think?" I ask.

"I don't know. I don't know if it's closer, like Sophie said, to retirement or that we've traveled more, and I've enjoyed other places. You know, when you don't know nothing about nothing, how do you desire what you don't know or want to be there. The last couple years since Momma died, we've done a lot of traveling and it ain't been worldwide."

"No, by any means. It started with me taking you to California."

"Yeah."

"And then we go to Florida a lot to see my nephew and his wife and children, and they accept her."

"Yeah, and I've always loved New Orleans. And we go to Memphis a lot now, and it's just when you go to these places you see there's so much to do. You ain't looking over your shoulder; somebody's staring at ya."

"But at the same time, I don't want to live in a big city."

"She don't," Faith agrees.

"I'm a country person. I like to go visit and be there for a while but I want to go back home to the country."

John and Manuel

John and Manuel (introduced in Chapter Five) are the couple who met in the military. After being stationed in different areas of the country, John moved back to Mississippi to help with his family's business. Manuel followed him here. I ask them about living as gay couple in Mississippi and if they plan to stay.

"Just keep it on a very, very down low," Manuel says. "Don't put it out there."

"We don't have gay flags out here. It's like in the military," John says.

"If they don't ask, don't tell."

"Under the surface, they don't want to know. If you stand out, you'll end up getting killed. Ostracizing . . . you get passed over, you get vandalism against gay guys and stuff. That stuff still happens around here."

"Still happens around here. . . . yeah," Manuel repeats.

"So you've heard of any negative things happening to people you know here?" I ask.

"Here? No," Manuel says.

"No, it's just not a gay-family-oriented kind of place.

"So, what's made you stay?" I ask.

"What has made us stay?" Manuel repeats. "Because you didn't want to move," he says turning to John.

"Maybe it's family. Right now we have too much to move. Who would take care of our shit? We've got land here. We've got businesses here."

"We've still got furniture in storage," Manuel adds.

"The cost of living is inexpensive. Traffic isn't bad. I like having four seasons in the year. When we lived in California, we lived in a $385,000 condominium that wasn't the size of these two rooms," John says gesturing to the living and dining rooms."

"I like the quiet here,"

"But we do try to leave here about once a month."

"Traveling?" I ask.

"Yeah, we just travel," Manuel says.

"We get the hell out of here," John adds. "Sometimes we really need to. We really need to go get back around some good gay guys in a social setting–type thing. Besides, the guys that are around here are nice but older."

"As far as gay life is concerned, there's nothing here."

Drew and Neal

Drew and Neal (introduced in Chapter One), the couple who live in a gated community outside of Jackson, offer advice to another gay couple moving to Mississippi and contemplate their future.

"Make sure that you find a job that you feel secure in, because we have no protection," Neal says, referring to the fact that there is no law in Mississippi banning employment discrimination based on sexual orientation. "There's no hate crime laws. I don't want to discourage anyone from moving here, but I don't want to encourage someone to come here and lose everything, because they lost their job because their boss found out they had a wife or a husband. They just need to understand. They need to know about Mississippi."

Neal pauses, before continuing. "I contemplate what the next phase of our relationship will be. And when I say 'phase,' I mean the forward. And I do think looking back on it, that we have made concession to or been willing to be happy with the fact that we were Mississippians by birth and by education and by coincidence. I look forward to not feeling bound to Mississippi, and I always have felt that so long as my parents and then dad was alive. . . . Well, it would be untenable to think about moving, because I want to be here for our sense of family. I have projected or at least imagined that Drew felt that way—with his mom and dad and now his brother, sisters, nieces, and nephews—that Mississippi was home because it is this season in our lives. I looked forward to the prospect of deciding that Mississippi is our future or deciding that we have the freedom to move to Chattanooga or to Knoxville or to Santa Fe or wherever the next place would be. It is not out of habit that we will stay in Mississippi; it's out of choice that we will stay or we will move. And I have no urgency. I've only acceptance that it will be here, or that it will be somewhere else, but that it will be fun."

"So the reason you've stayed in Mississippi is because this is where you grew up and this is where your families have been?"

"It's been a combination of that, and this is where work is," Drew says. "His family was nearby, and I didn't feel so tied to my family because my parents are a good bit younger than Neal's. But I've got a brother and sister, you know, who would be closer, and I could attend to them in any kind of emergency. When I was younger, I just always imagined that I would be here for a few years and then I would move with whatever company I was working for. I wanted to live in a larger city, whether that was gonna be Atlanta or wherever; but, we just were here and then we became a couple. There was [also] that particularly with Neal's parents—'cause his mother was in poor health for a while and then now as his dad's gotten older—it just made sense for us to be here."

"What do you like about living here?" I ask.

"It's as great place to start a vacation from." Neal says laughing. "I like the seasons."

"You know," Drew says, "when you ask that question, the next question is: so why haven't you moved? You know, Neal and I are pretty low key, and we stay at home a lot. We're not a lot about going out. He and I used to go to restaurants pretty regularly, and we'd have dinner with friends a lot. I think eventually you get tired of some of that. We just stopped. We made a conscious decision to stop spending so much money on restaurants; then work and those circumstances kind of interfered with some of that. But Mississippi, in general, is a state of small towns, and you have to kind of enjoy that lifestyle. Both of us would be very comfortable living in a more urban setting with an apartment versus a house, so that there's not the responsibility of maintaining the house and the yard and all of that. We both like the idea of being able to walk out of an apartment and be able to walk places rather than having to drive a car. So, honestly, it would make sense for us to look at Memphis, Nashville, Atlanta; some place like that, but there's a much higher cost of living in those places, and we own a house. Our house is paid for, so there's been that incentive to stay here and kind of invest in that."

"You know, the whole idea is bloom where you're planted." Neal says. "Right now there's no determination that this is not going to be enjoyable; that it's not pleasant. I mean, everybody has to live somewhere, and this is known and is comfortable. And without a need to contemplate moving...."

"If you said, 'Go pick some place new to live,'" Drew interjects, "I would probably still want to be in the southeast. I'd like to live in a bigger city for more options in the area of the arts, theater, music, but I'm so dull I don't know that I would participate or be involved in that any more than I do right now. But, it'd be nice to know it was there."

"Every time we travel, I intentionally talk with Drew about: 'feel this place; this is kind of nice; could you consider this?' And, I wouldn't want to live in Chicago, but I'd want to live somewhere near that Chicago would be our New Orleans. We could get to enjoy it."

"We've been to Wisconsin a number of times for an event up there, and we have kind of fallen in love with it; because it's in a beautiful town; and it's very much out in the country—five minutes in any direction—which is kind of like Mississippi."

"I'm not putting my foot down and saying it's not gonna happen, but I don't want to go anywhere that puts salt on the roads in the winter."

～

Although the couples who are planning to leave and even some of those planning to stay expressed some conflict about their decision, other couples, like the couples in this section, expressed conflict that was unsettled. The conflict that some couples express is something that is not only experienced internally but also externally within their relationships as we saw with couples, like Jerry and Karl, who are planning to leave. Sophie, explaining her desire to leave compared to Faith's ties to her roots in Mississippi, says: "This one right here has just always been here, and I doubt seriously I could blast her out." When I ask Manuel and John their reasons for staying in Mississippi, Manuel turns to John and says: "Because you didn't want to move." The conflicting feelings for these last two couples could be related to John and Faith both being born and raised in Mississippi, while Sophie and Manuel were not.

For other couples, their difficult decision is related to the lower cost of living in Mississippi compared to other areas, especially urban areas with large gay communities. Mississippi has one of the lowest cost of living and cost of housing rates in the country. (LeBlanc, 2018). John referred to the cost of living in Mississippi, remembering that their current home of the same cost is double the size of the condominium they owned in California. Neal and Drew like the idea of living in a city but also cite the cost of living in urban areas compared to their owning a house with a paid-off mortgage.

In addition to family, work, owning property, and the cost of living, couples also wondered where they would go. Even if they did leave, they are not sure exactly where they would go, other than Neal insisting that he does not "want to go anywhere that puts salt on the roads in the winter." Faith and Sophie have only recently begun to travel and realized that there is another world outside the South, as Faith explained: "You know, when you don't know nothing about nothing, how do you desire what you don't know or want to be there."

I believe this unsettled conflict that couples expressed is similar to what I felt when I moved back to Mississippi, an underlying push and pull for many Mississippi gay people, a desire to live someplace with more possibilities for gay people but feeling drawn to a place where you were raised and have roots. Even those Mississippians who have left have described these mixed feelings. Howard (1999) wrote that he felt an "ambivalent attraction to my birthplace, Mississippi . . . an expatriate returning again and again, turning page after page, to Mississippi" (p. 124). During an interview with Mississippi Public Broadcasting in 2009, Kevin Sessums (2007), author of *Mississippi Sissy*, an autobiography, had similar sentiments as he described people like himself who grew up in and later left Mississippi: "In a strange way, we had to escape it, but you never can escape your home. Your home lives in your heart."

Jeffrey and Leonard

I'm in the home of Jeffrey and Leonard (introduced in the introduction and Chapter One), described by another gay couple as the "couple that lives in the woods." We've been talking for a couple hours and are nearing the end of the interview. They are explaining to me why they have stayed in Mississippi.

"You know, it's a southern thing," Jeffrey says. "I mean, you know, there have always been eccentric people, and a lot of the gay people, that have lived here all their lives and never left, are just considered eccentric. And I have to say, some really are eccentric, lovely, wonderful people, but you know to me, it's just our southern way. It's in our literature, our art, and I'm always proud of that. When I finished high school, I wanted out of Mississippi so bad, and I never wanted to come back. But I'm here, and there's so much to be proud of. At the same time, I think we've come a *looong* way, as far as acceptance of gay people here, and like I say, though, locally we certainly enjoyed a huge acceptance in this little community for quite a while."

"We're not as social as we were ten, eight, seven years ago," Jeffrey says. "We're much more just at home, and people just come here.

Jeffrey pauses for a moment before continuing, "We have some friends that are very back to earth. They raise most of their own vegetables and everything. It's a male gay couple, and we're kindred spirits. We kind of socialize with them quite a bit. They're really our best friends. And then we have a neighbor across the road who moved in a few years ago. She's a lawyer, and she has a gay son, who she treated terribly when he came out."

"Until she met us," Leonard adds. "We became some of his foster grandparents."

"We had to go and train her."

"She's developed a wonderful relationship with her son now, and he says, 'You've got me calling my mother 'Lucy!'"

They both laugh at that before Jeffrey continues. "He comes to see us when he comes to visit his mother. They all come over together. She's come a long way."

"Some of the couples I've talked to have said that we're all doing a huge form of activism just by living in a small community," I
share. "You're showing people that gay people are not monsters or
something."

"Yeah, it's important. I wish we were involved more. We were
when we first started, but we live pretty quietly. But I think in town,
people see these [gay] people functioning every day, running businesses, keeping their homes, keeping their yards, being involved in
different things. They see good stuff."

The cat jumps on the table and nudges the recorder with her
nose. "It looks like it's time for us to stop," I say laughing as I rub
the cat's head.

"Why don't you stay for some wine and cheese before you head
out," Leonard says.

We move to their front porch and chat about our lives in Mississippi.

∽

*In 2018, students from Mississippi State University approached the
Starkville Board of Alderman to request a permit for the first Gay
Pride Parade in the city's history. The Board voted 4–3 to reject the
permit request, although the majority of citizens attending the board
meeting supported the event. Some of the board members cited religious concerns as their reasons for not supporting the students. Under
the threat of a lawsuit and the fact that the board's actions had made
national news, the Board voted again. One of the Alderman abstained
and the mayor, who had originally supported the students, broke a
3–3 tie.*

*The original rejection by the board and the national news led to
an outpouring of support in the community. A local Baptist minister, Bert Montgomery, called for "acceptance and affirmation." On
March 24, Starkville's first Gay Pride Parade drew a reported 2,500
people, the largest parade in city history. Included in the numbers were
Larry and me, my parents, and hundreds of Starkville's citizens who
wanted to show their support of their gay friends and neighbors. A*

former teacher from elementary school hugged Larry and me before the parade. Neighbors from childhood came to show their support. One young mother told me that she brought her children, because she wanted them to see that everyone deserves respect and love. Parishioners from the Episcopal Church handed out Mardi Gras beads to marchers as the parade passed near their church. People lined Main Street running out to hug marchers, and people stood on balconies cheering and throwing candy.

Larry and I walked in the parade holding hands and overcome by emotion. The parade represented what is possible in Mississippi. As with many other rural states, it's often the college towns that lead the way into the future. Shortly after, we made our decision. We were moving; not out of Mississippi but thirty-one miles west of our home in Columbus to Starkville.

References

Center for Disease Control. (2015). Diagnoses of HIV infection in the United States and dependent areas. Retrieved from https://www.cdc.gov/hiv/pdf/library/reports/surveillance/cdc-hiv-surveillance-report-2015-vol-27.pdf

Hamilton, C. (2012). Sex, "silence," and audiotape. In N. A. Boyd & H. N. R. Ramírez (Eds.), *Bodies of evidence: The practice of queer oral history* (pp. 23–40). New York, NY: Oxford University Press.

Harris, B. (2017, Dec. 4). Mississippi's brain drain: 'We've got to figure out how to keep our students at home.' *Clarion-Ledger*. Retrieved from http://www.clarionledger.com/story/news/politics/2017/12/04/brain-drain-mississippi-higher-education-leader/918913001/

Herring, S. (2010). *Another country: Queer anti-urbanism.* New York, NY: New York University Press.

Howard, J. (1999). *Men like that: A southern queer history.* Chicago, IL: University of Chicago Press.

Human Rights Campaign. (2019). How HIV impacts LGBTQ people. Retrieved from https://www.hrc.org/resources/hrc-issue-brief-hiv-aids-and-the-lgbt-community

LeBlanc, R. (2018). The 10 states with the lowest cost of living. https://www.thebalancesmb.com/states-with-lowest-cost-of-living-4137935

Marshall, D. (2012). Gay teachers and students, oral history, and queer kinship. In N. A. Boyd & H. N. R. Ramírez (Eds.), *Bodies of evidence: The practice of queer oral history* (pp. 167–83). New York, NY: Oxford University Press.

Mississippi Public Broadcasting. (2009). Kevin Sessums. Retrieved from https://www.youtube.com/watch?v=90m51t-4y50

Murphy, H. (2018, June 21). How a pastor and a popcorn shop owner helped save pride in Starkville. *New York Times*. Retrieved from https://www.nytimes.com/2018/06/21/us/pride-starkville-mississippi.html

Protecting Freedom of Conscience from Government Discrimination Act, Mississippi House Bill 1523 (2016).

Rubin. G. (1984). Thinking sex: Notes for a radical theory of the politics of sexuality. Retrieved from http://sites.middlebury.edu/sexandsociety/files/2015/01/Rubin-Thinking-Sex.pdf

Sessums, K. (2007). *Mississippi sissy.* New York, NY: St. Martin's Press.

Warner, M. (1999). *The trouble with normal: Sex, politics, and the ethics of queer life.* Cambridge, MA: Harvard University Press.

Wicker, R. (2019). Family values. Retrieved from https://www.wicker.senate.gov/public/index.cfm/family-values

Wilson, L. E. (2013, Jan. 22). Comparing rural and urban care in HIV. *Physician's Weekly.* Retrieved from https://www.physiciansweekly.com/rural-urban-care-hiv/

About the Author

Photo by Robert Lewis

John F. Marszalek III is clinical faculty of the online clinical mental health counseling program at Southern New Hampshire University. He lives in Mississippi with his husband and their two dogs.